IMAGES
of America

AROUND CONNEAUTVILLE

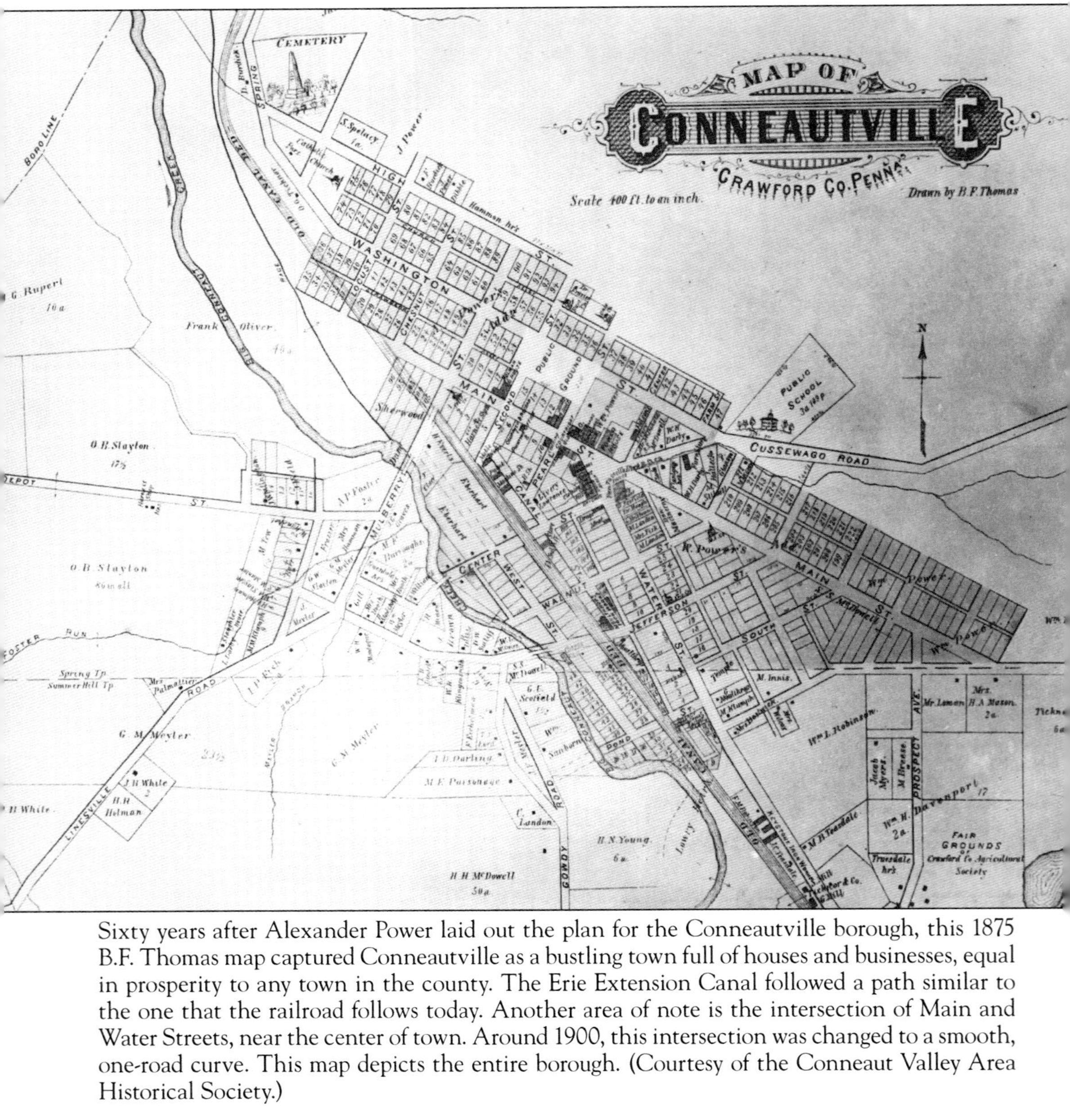

Sixty years after Alexander Power laid out the plan for the Conneautville borough, this 1875 B.F. Thomas map captured Conneautville as a bustling town full of houses and businesses, equal in prosperity to any town in the county. The Erie Extension Canal followed a path similar to the one that the railroad follows today. Another area of note is the intersection of Main and Water Streets, near the center of town. Around 1900, this intersection was changed to a smooth, one-road curve. This map depicts the entire borough. (Courtesy of the Conneaut Valley Area Historical Society.)

On the Cover: The centennial parade of 1914 featured many attractions of the time, including numerous motor vehicles. This particular scene shows a Ford Model T covered in paper flowers. The car is rounding the bend by Center Street on Main Street while parade spectators look on with curiosity. (Courtesy of the Conneaut Valley Area Historical Society.)

IMAGES of America

AROUND CONNEAUTVILLE

Tyler Mattera

ARCADIA PUBLISHING

ISBN 978-0-7385-7517-9

Published by Arcadia Publishing
Charleston, South Carolina

Printed in the United States of America

Library of Congress Control Number: 2010940353

For all general information, please contact Arcadia Publishing:
Telephone 843-853-2070
Fax 843-853-0044
E-mail sales@arcadiapublishing.com
For customer service and orders:
Toll-Free 1-888-313-2665

Visit us on the Internet at www.arcadiapublishing.com

CONTENTS

Acknowledgments

The history of an area is written by the individuals who live it, not just the people who record it. This book is the work of many people who all played a significant role in its creation. To begin, this book would never have been completed without the guidance of my editor, Erin Vosgien. By way of some gentle nudging, she kept me on pace to have this book finished in a timely manner. I would especially like to thank Betty Kovac, whose insight and knowledge led to me discovering many of the images in this book. Thank you for generously donating your time to seeing that the Conneaut Valley Area Historical Society is a beautiful working museum dedicated to keeping Conneautville's history alive. Another very special acknowledgment goes out to Patricia Vedner and Betty Logan for lending many of their extraordinary personal images for use in this project. Again, I would like to thank these ladies for sharing their substantial knowledge of Conneautville history. Also, a very special thanks needs to go out to every member of the historical society for their dedication and interest in local history. It is because of their work that projects like this are possible. Thank you to Arcadia Publishing for allowing me the opportunity to create this book. Lastly, thank you to the past and present citizens of Conneautville, to all those who recorded the history that made this possible, to the members of the sesquicentennial committee who researched and wrote Conneautville's history decades ago, and to the people who shared their own accounts for this project. Without them, this would not have been possible.

Unless otherwise noted, all images are from the archives of the Conneaut Valley Area Historical Society.

Introduction

In the fall of 1794, surveyor Alexander Power and his brother William arrived in Crawford County, where they were to document Pennsylvania's western land on behalf of the state. Filled with giant trees, the dense wilderness made traveling nearly impossible, even on horseback. At best, the journey was slow and tiresome. But pace was not the only thing these pioneers had on their minds, as this was a dangerous place; the Powers faced threats including wolves, wildcats, panthers, and Native Americans.

On August 3, 1795, the US government and a group of Indian tribes signed the Treaty of Greenville, in which the tribes ceded much of the land in the areas now known as Ohio and western Pennsylvania and agreed to put an end to any warfare or threat in said areas. That same year, the Pennsylvania legislature passed an act giving 400 acres of land to any person who would make an actual settlement on it, clear and cultivate 25 acres, build a house, and pay the state $25 for each 100 acres. With the threat of warfare removed and the enticing land offer from the state, a great immigration began. New claims were established so rapidly that by 1800, nearly every tract of land along Conneaut Creek had been bought. Alexander Power was heavily involved with this movement. By 1797, he had possession of three tracts: one at Conneaut Lake, near Harmonsburg, and two near the Conneaut Creek Valley. Power knew that the fertile soil surrounding the creek was an excellent place for agriculture. To make the area more appealing to those looking to make a permanent settlement, he built a gristmill in 1779 on the creek across from the present day Saint Peter Church. For two years, it was the only place around Conneaut where grain could be ground to make bread. Although his focus was on his Conneaut Creek land, Power was living with his wife on Conneaut Lake. In 1804, Power and his wife, Mary, packed their belongings and moved closer to his mill, building a log cabin where Samuels Market now stands. This particular piece of land was appealing because of a cold, deep spring nearby, which meant clean water was always at the ready. In 1805, the area around the Conneaut Valley was still mostly forest with a few acres of cleared land around a few scattered log homes. Another early settler, Power's brother-in-law, James McNamara, had a 400-acre tract of land on the west side of Conneaut Creek, with his house standing near Center Street. A third individual, John Fulwiler, owned the land that joined Power's to the south. Out of these three farms came the land of the present borough.

The rush of immigrants into western Crawford County that started in 1795 began to dwindle by 1800 and had nearly ceased by 1805. For the next 10 years, the population remained practically stationary. Soon, however, all was about to change. As the United States continued to expand westward, tiny settlements like Alexander Power's became much-needed stops for those traveling west. Anticipating that there would be an influx of people following the War of 1812, Power created the plan for Conneautville in 1814. Alongside his house on Main Street, he laid out 10 plots from Mulberry Street to Pearl Street. On the opposite side of the road, he laid out 15 lots that extended from Pearl Street to Chestnut Street. In 1815, Power sold two lots across from his house to William Douglas and Henry Christie for $30 each. Soon after, William Crozier, a millwright and carpenter, bought two lots beside Power and erected the first frame house west of French Creek. By 1821, Conneautville—or Powers Town, as the settlers referred to it—was developing into a respectable place. It had five houses, a general store, a hotel, two mills, a post office, a cooper shop, and several farmhouses.

Always insisting that the village be called Conneautville instead of Power's Town, Power informed the citizens of his desire and the latter was disregarded. The word "conneaut" may have many meanings, but it is generally accepted that it comes from the Seneca language and means "snow" or "place of snow." Conneautville experienced steady growth over the next 20 years and was eventually incorporated as a borough in 1844. An election was held soon after and John Patton was elected to be its first burgess. The first order of business for this newly created town was to build a secondary school. A schoolhouse had been built on the south end of the borough in 1811, but was far too inadequate. Its walls were made of rough logs and its lone window was greased paper. To make matters worse, the clay fireplace barely gave off enough heat and the split log seats were cramped and uncomfortable. In 1827, a newer building that functioned as a home for almost every organization in town was erected across from the present Stone Memorial Library. With competition from dances, meetings, and church services, this space could only be used for classes a few months out of the year. To solve this problem, a vacant building in the cemetery was moved to where Saint Peter Church now stands and used as a schoolhouse. It opened in 1849 and was known as the Academy.

By the middle of the 19th century, with the addition of the schoolhouse and many businesses, there was a new need for travel routes. Conneautville's isolation had meant traveling was slow and tiresome and done on rugged paths that were usually unsuitable for any mode of transportation but horseback. In 1827, Pennsylvania began building an extension of New York's Erie Canal that would run from Erie to Pittsburgh, passing through Conneautville on its 130-mile journey. Jubilation exploded through Conneautville when the *Queen of the West*, loaded with passengers, and the *R.S. Reed*, a coal ship, were the first two boats to pass through town. Everywhere the boats arrived, they were received with excitement, cheering, bonfires, gunfire, and parades. These boats reached Erie on December 5, 1844, bringing with them the possibility of limitless trade. Trees that were only a nuisance to be cut and burned suddenly became valuable for lumber. The lumber trade initiated one of the first economic booms in town. Sawmills were built wherever there was water to run the machinery and their products were shipped as far south as Pittsburgh. Many farmers stopped tilling their land and focused on clearing trees. Conneautville, characterized by its population increase and construction of numerous buildings, soon became the trade center of western Crawford County. Although this era was more than 150 years ago, its influence can still be felt today. Each of the redbrick structures along Main Street was built during the height of canal use. The ability to import stronger materials allowed the townspeople to create structures that stand to this day. By 1850, Conneautville had 750 inhabitants; soon after 1860, the population rose to about 1,200.

The days of the canal made for a colorful period in Conneautville's past that seems almost impossible to imagine now. Sadly, not one known photograph of the canal, or a boat passing through town, remains. What do remain, however, are the stories that offer a unique look into the Conneautville of yesteryear. When boats would meet in the locks, it was not uncommon for one crew to cut the lines of the other boat in hopes of making a quicker journey. It was a usual occurrence for a fight to break out. Cristopher Cram, or Crit, as he was known, was a husky, redheaded Irishman and town resident who became known for being one of the best fighters on the canal. His name alone could prevent even the angriest captain from cutting another ship's towlines and his presence allowed for the safe passage of many ships.

Although the canal was responsible for the development of hundreds of towns, its downfall was inevitable. In 1856, the Erie & Pittsburgh Railroad was chartered and began running trains from Erie to Jamestown by 1859. It was not until 1864 that the first train completed the journey the canal had made decades before. The canal simply could not compete with the railroad and towns that grew from the canal were forgotten. As a result, Conneautville began a slow decline.

The small rural mills that kept Conneautville useful fell victim to larger factories in bigger cities. Empty buildings quickly became the scene around town, and by 1870 Conneautville's population had dropped from 1,200 to 950. The townspeople organized a commission to advocate the widening of the canal (where it still existed) but soon discovered that the railroad owned the property. The canal was finally closed in 1878.

Over the course of its history, Conneautville has experienced more than a few disasters. In 1867, a fire destroyed the greater part of a business section of town. Seven years later, an even larger fire occurred. The fire of 1874 claimed 45 buildings and made 23 families homeless. Luckily, no lives were lost, but a large section of town had been destroyed.

By the late 1800s, cameras were becoming more widespread and people began capturing scenes of daily life—the delivery boy taking bread around town, patriotic children waving flags, the general store owners who supplied the town with goods, the high school faculty, trains making the journey on the old canal bed, and a centennial celebration overflowing with pride and excitement. It is because of these pictures that a clearer understanding of the town's past can be known. Few pictures remain of Conneautville from before 1880. In looking at the ones that do, we can see a developing rural settlement that is not much different from Conneautville today.

One

The Early Years

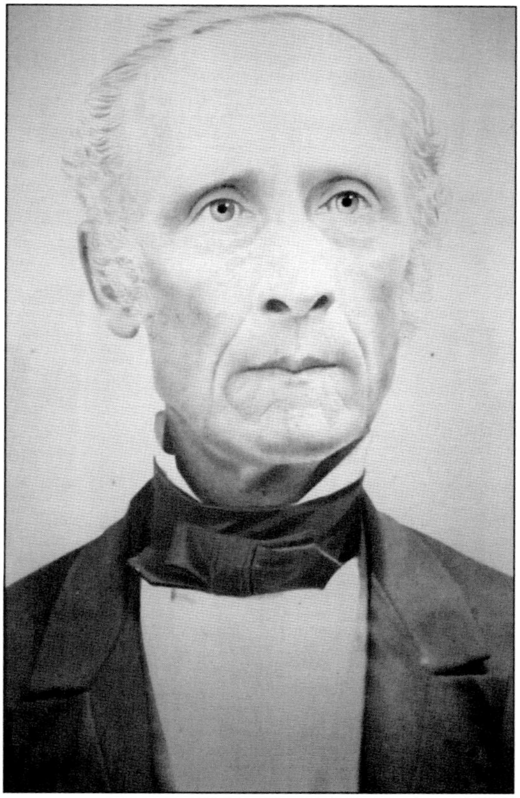

Alexander Power originally surveyed the Conneaut Creek Valley in 1794 and 1795, taking land as payment for his services. After other pioneers began to settle in the area, Power recognized the need for structure and designed a plot that would eventually become the Borough of Conneautville, in 1814. Out of his home (where Samuels Market now stands) he ran an inn, tavern, and general store. A prominent citizen, Power became the county's justice of the peace and Conneautville's first postmaster. Power died on May 13, 1850, and was interred in the Conneautville Cemetery.

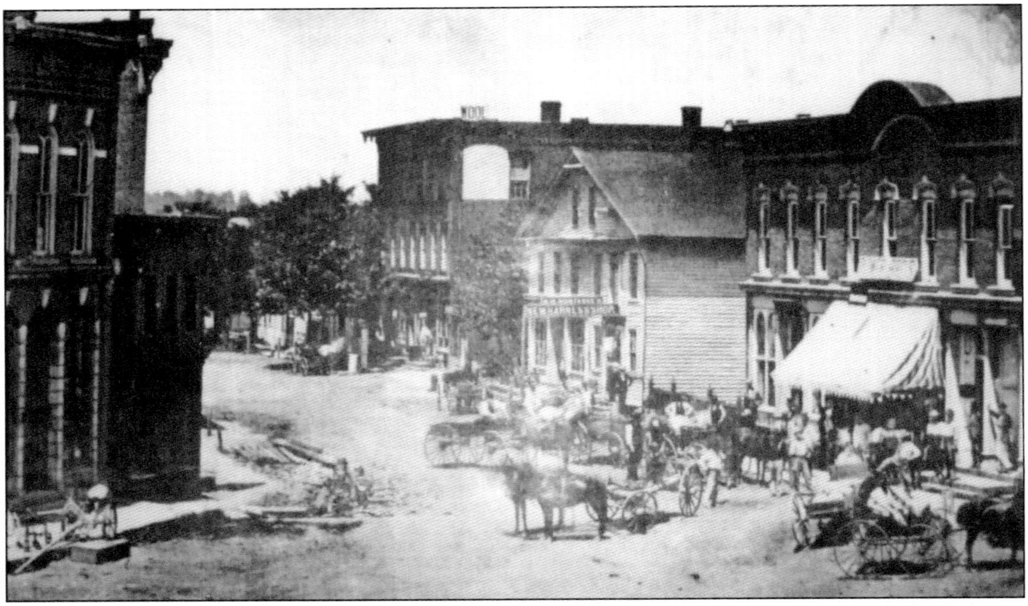

This image of Conneautville from 1868 was taken shortly after the Power Block (right) was completed. William Power financed the structure, which opened in April the same year. The two-story building was first occupied by general stores in the middle and left sections, while the right section contained a bank. All of the buildings in this photograph were constructed during the days of the Erie Extension Canal.

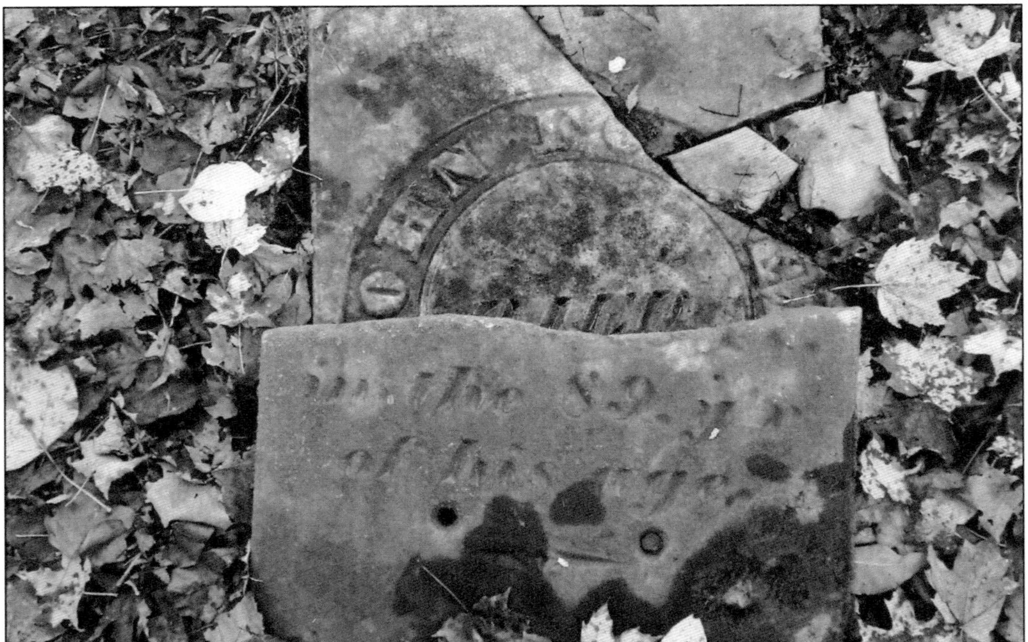

John and Mary Foster settled along Conneaut Creek in 1799, becoming another early family to call this region home. They made the journey from Cumberland County with only one horse and few necessities. It was recorded that in 1805 Native Americans kidnapped their young son while he was fetching his father for dinner. After a search, no trace of the child was found. John Foster's grave is in the family plot in the woods along Smith Road.

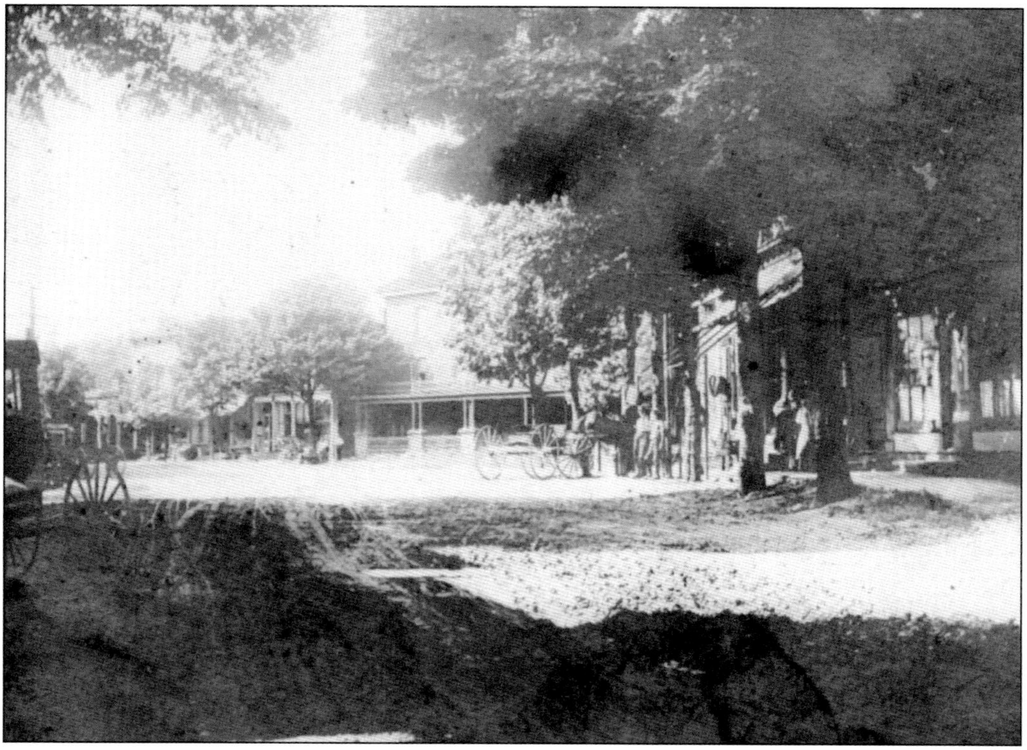

Main Street, seen here around 1903, has always been Conneautville's most traveled route. Cutting through the heart of town, this road was once a rugged dirt path before being transformed by a beautiful brick surface. Looking north (above), the road curves at the Hotel Power and originally ended at Mulberry Street, connecting Conneautville to nearby Linesville. Looking south (below), the street is lined with maple and oak trees. The trees were removed when the road was widened in the early 1950s to accommodate larger motor vehicles.

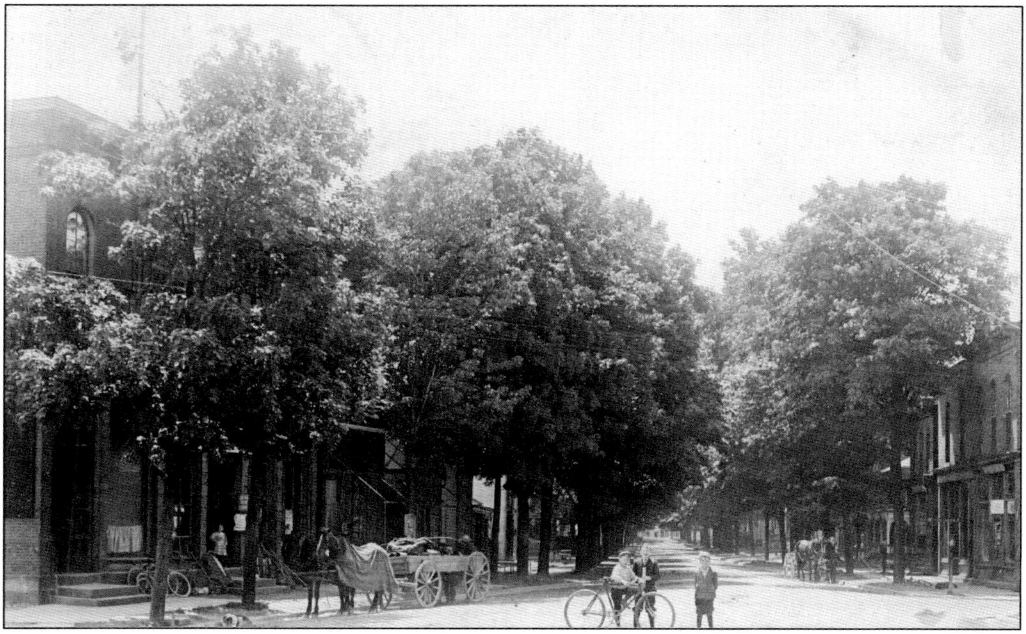

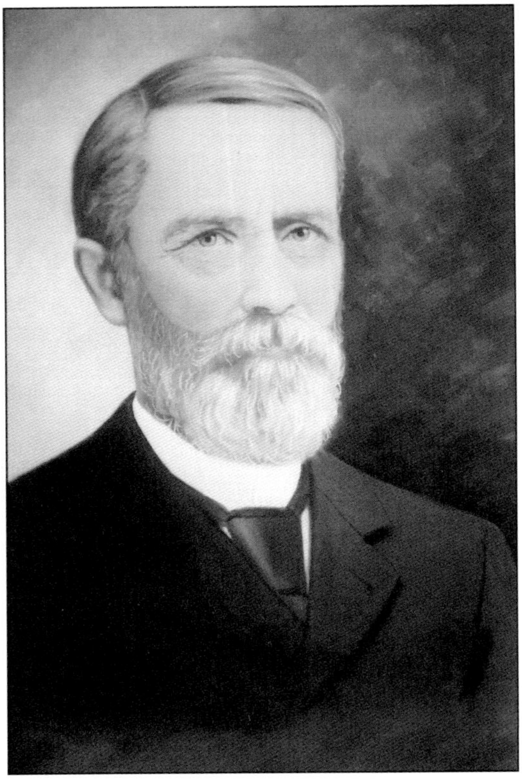

The will of James A. Stone (left) and his wife, Julia Leet Stone, made public in May of 1894, set aside $5,000 to form an association to be known as the "James A. Stone Memorial Library Association of Conneautville." On May 10, 1897, the James A. Stone Memorial Library was formally opened with a reception at the library rooms located in the northwest corner of the Stone/Gleason/Van Tassel Block (pictured below around 1890). On opening day, the library contained 600 volumes, all donated. For over 100 years, this library has served the Conneautville area.

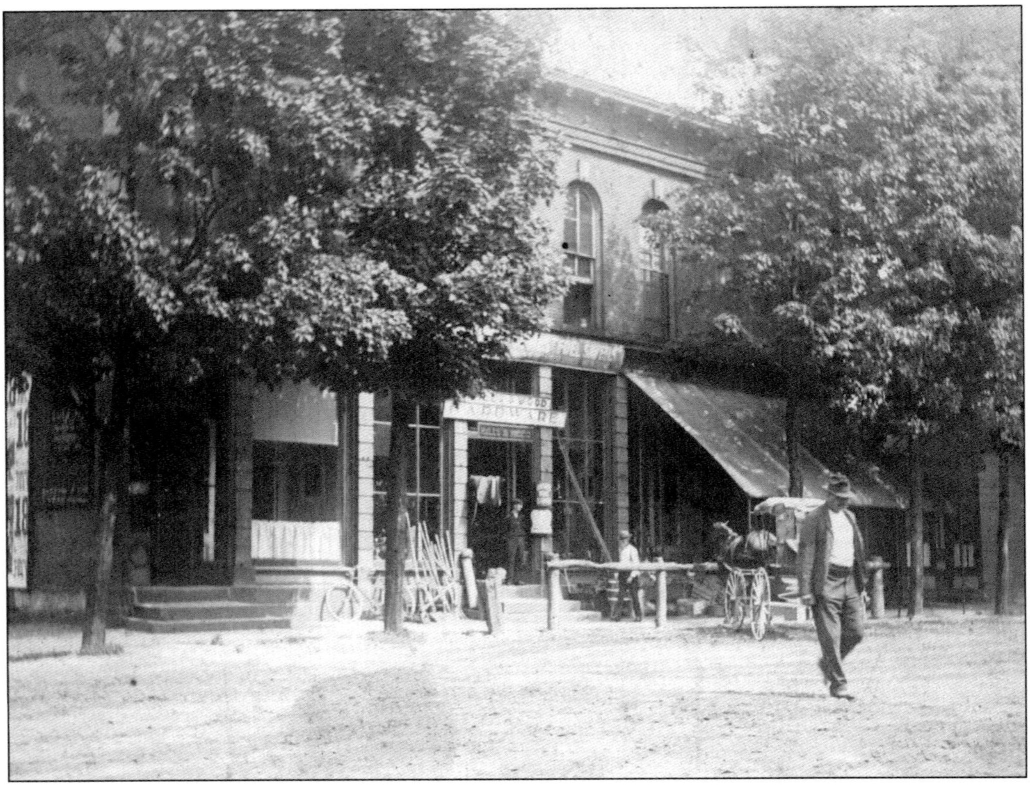

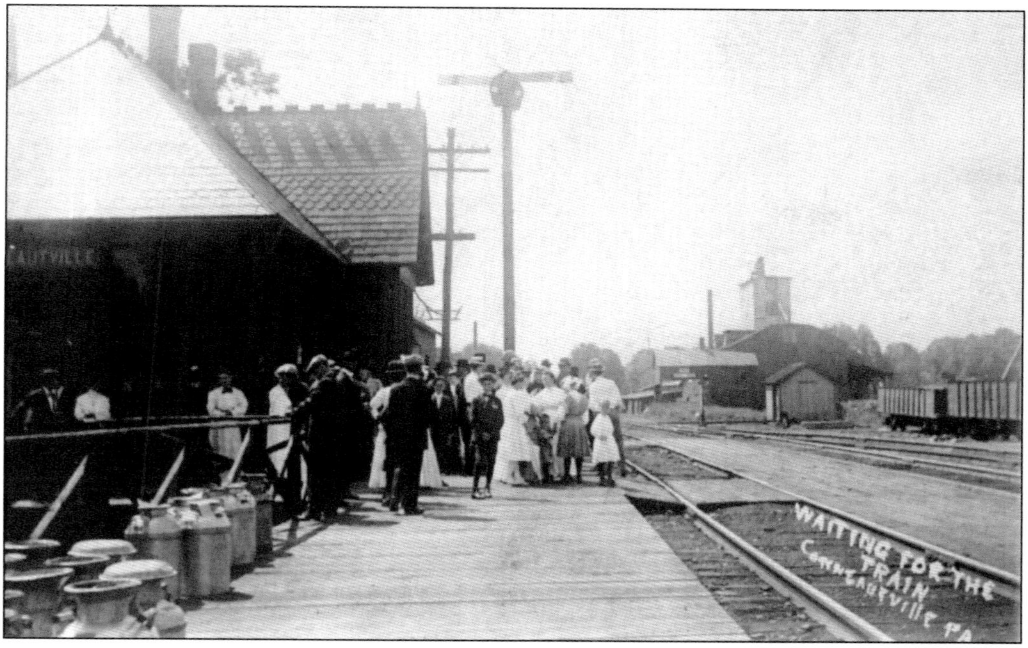

In November 1888, plans were completed to build a rail line—the Pittsburgh, Shenango and Lake Erie Railroad—that would follow along the canal route. Upon hearing this, Conneautville residents raised money and constructed a depot at the northern end of town. In 1906, a second track was added. Due to declining passenger travel, the last train left the depot on March 5, 1955. In this c. 1915 photograph, passengers wait on the rear platform.

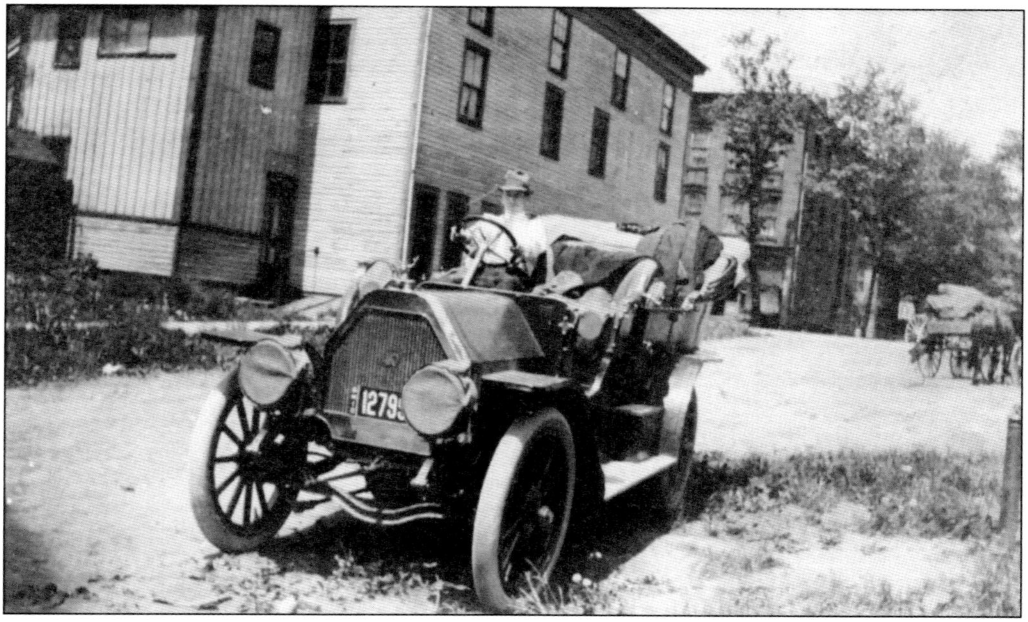

In August 1899, the first automobile passed through town. The driver came from Linesville, entering Conneautville on Mulberry Street, driving across Main and eventually on to Washington Street, where it then proceeded toward Springboro. Two passengers enjoyed this journey and the car reached speeds of about 25 miles per hour. The following month, a vehicle following the same route parked at the *Conneautville Courier* office, making it the first vehicle to stop in town.

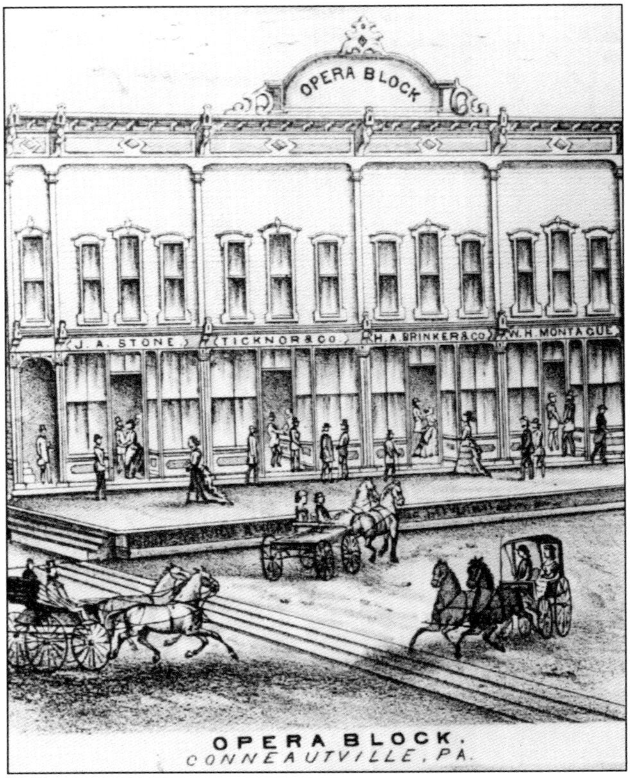

For many years, the Opera Block was the center of life in Conneautville. The building itself had numerous functions for both business and leisure. The first floor and front half held storerooms while the second floor contained a stage and basketball court. The theater could accommodate 500 people and hosted many musicians and theatrical productions. This building was also used for large town meetings, school graduations, Independence Day celebrations, town dances, and for when notable speakers came to town. The depiction of the Opera Block at left was probably done shortly after its construction in the 1840s. The stage (below) is beautifully decorated while not in use.

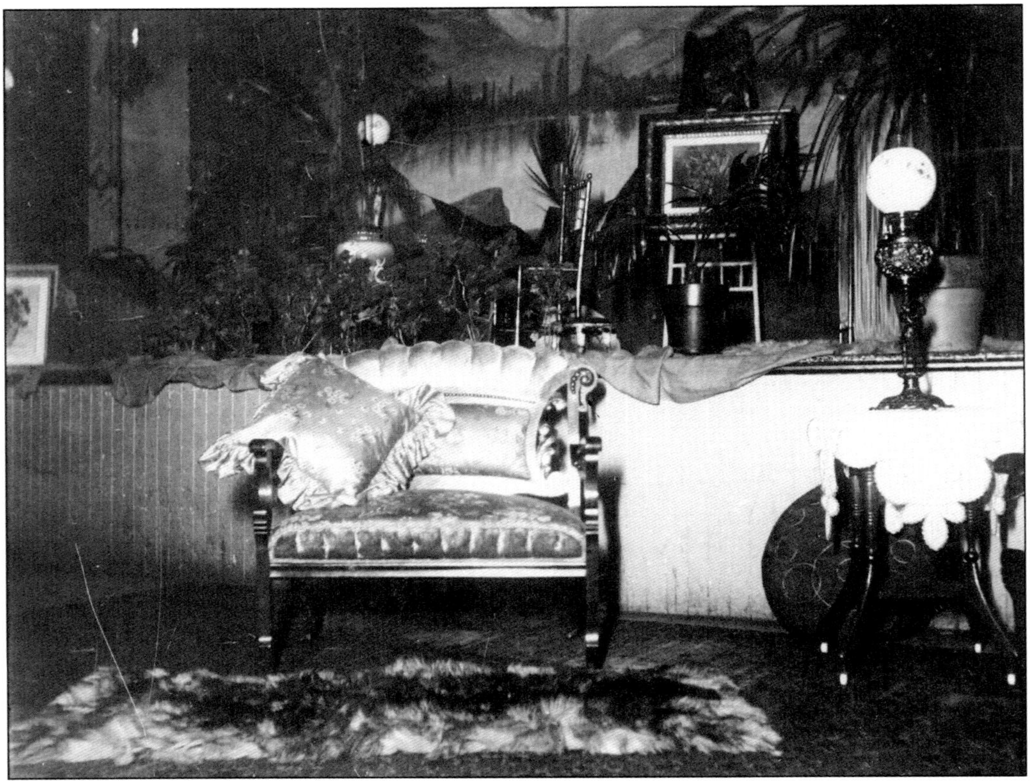

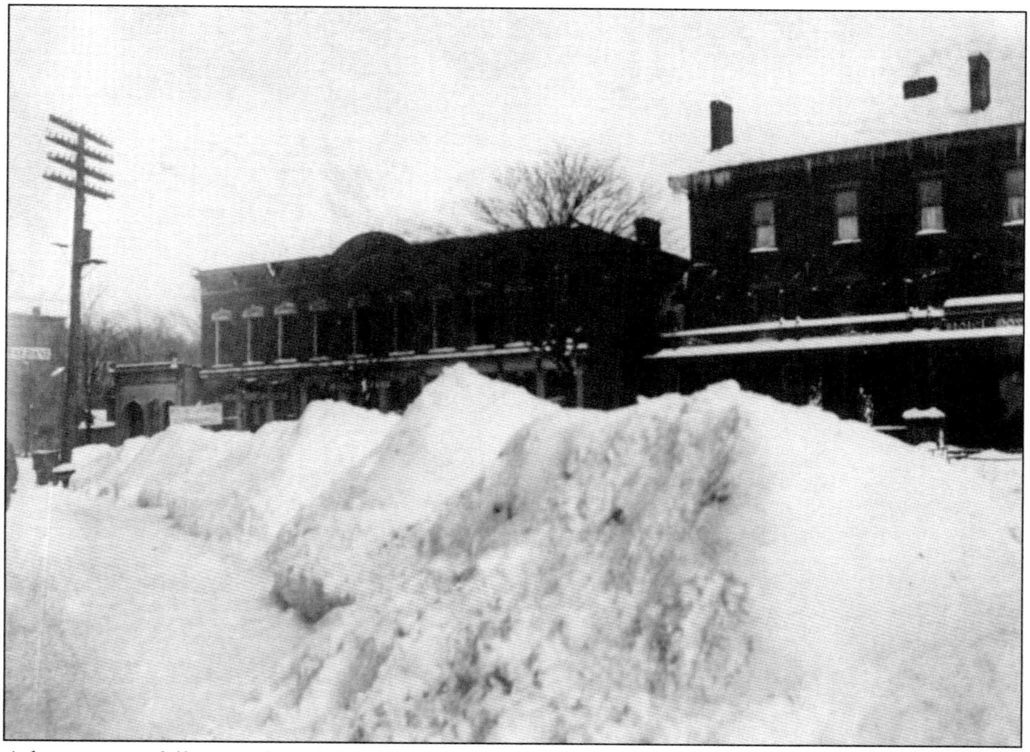

A heavy snowfall around 1910 would surely have halted any motor vehicles in town. Seen here, a large pile of snow lines the roadway after it was cleared from the sidewalks. The Hotel Power (right) and Power Block (left) are pictured in the background.

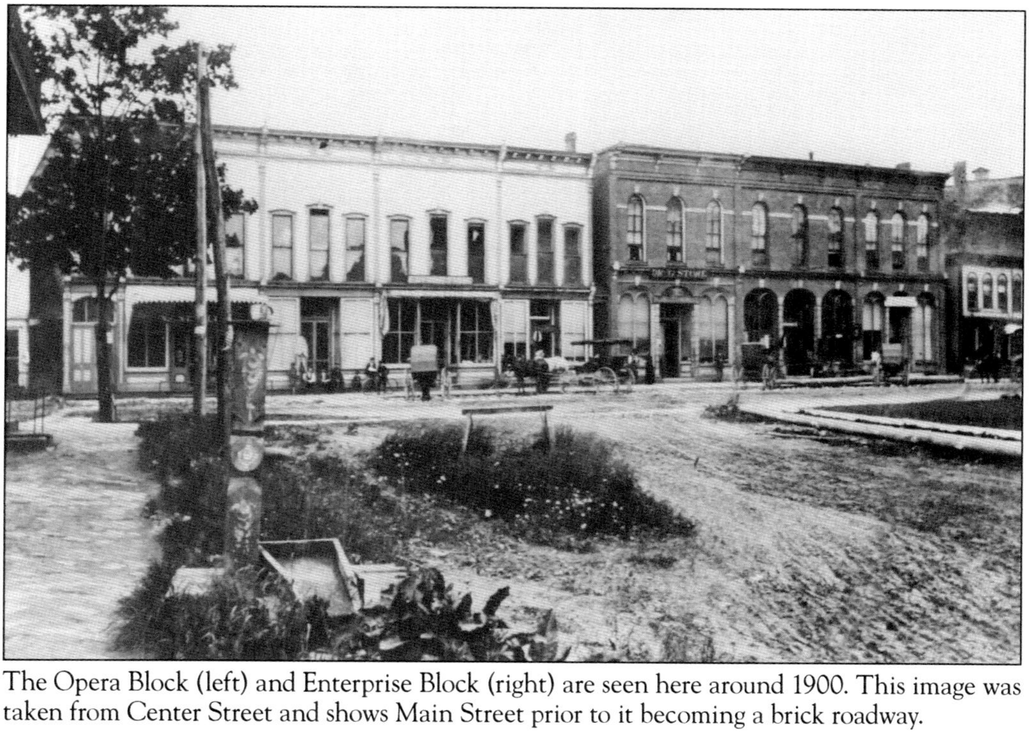

The Opera Block (left) and Enterprise Block (right) are seen here around 1900. This image was taken from Center Street and shows Main Street prior to it becoming a brick roadway.

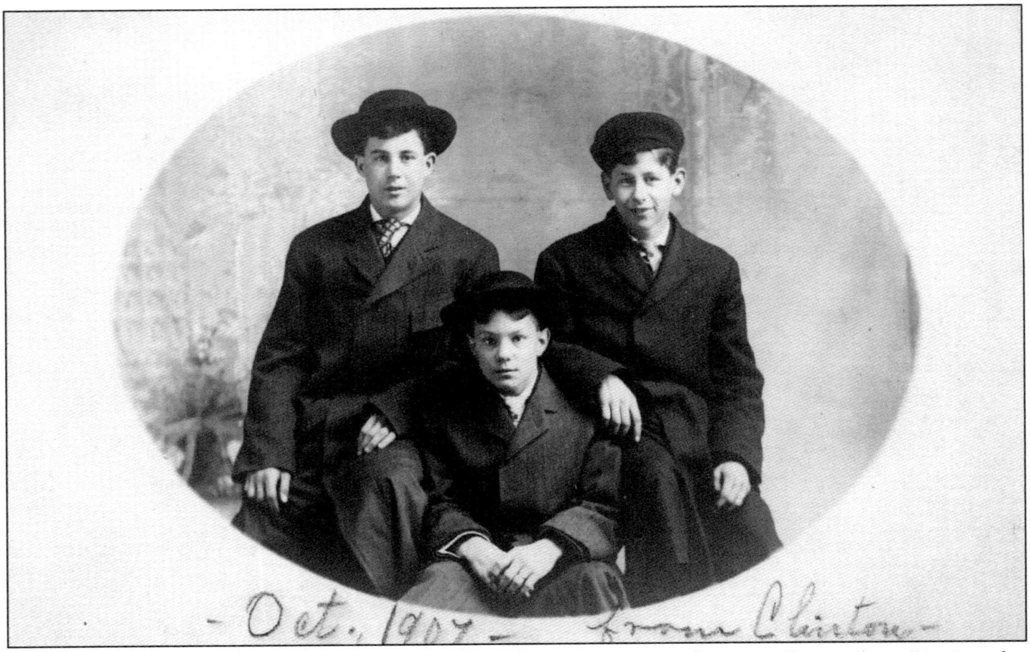

Throughout its history, Conneautville has been home to many photography studios. During the latter half of the 19th century, there were as many as five. Friends Milo Thompson (left), Harry North (center), and Clinton McCarty posed for a picture in October 1907.

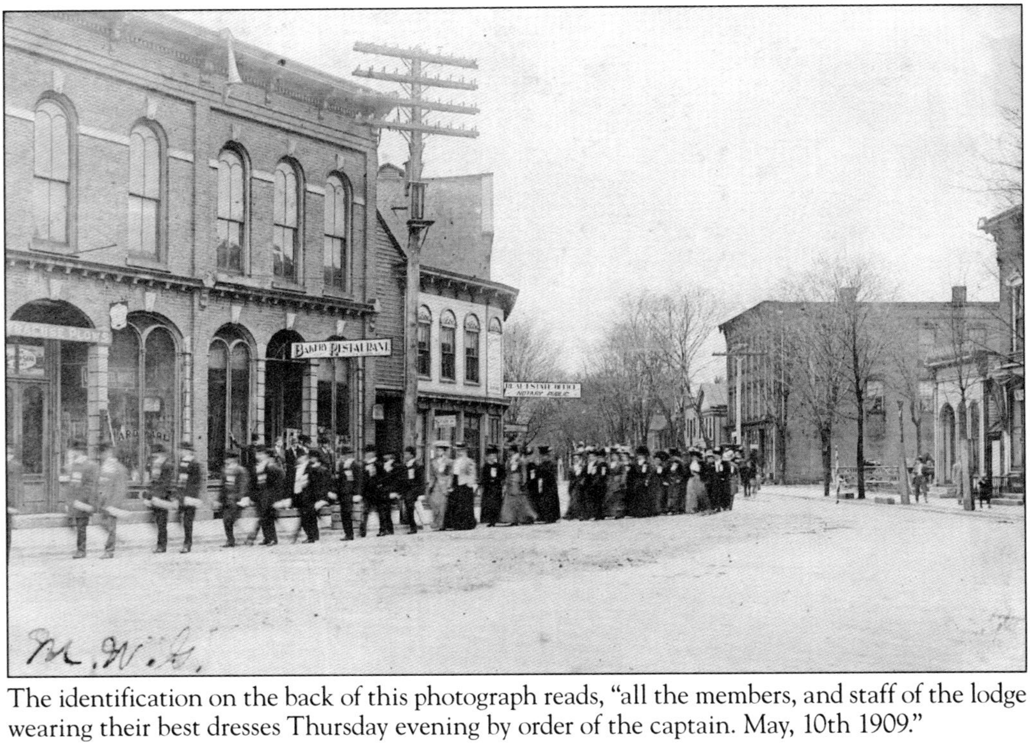

The identification on the back of this photograph reads, "all the members, and staff of the lodge wearing their best dresses Thursday evening by order of the captain. May, 10th 1909."

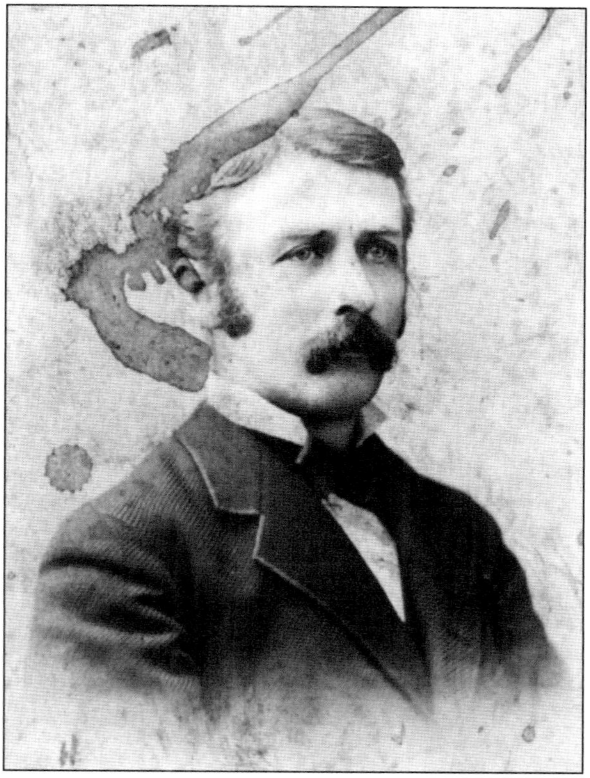

In August 1898, Horace Power, who owned a mineral well in town, purchased the Hotel Power. He remodeled the structure at a cost of $80,000 and installed mineral bath facilities, making the hotel one of the finest in the country. In 1912, he again made a significant change to the property by adding an irrigation system to the grounds. The *Conneautville Courier* wrote that it was "the first in this part of the country." Seen here are Power in 1900 and the Hotel Power as it looked in 1897, prior to renovations.

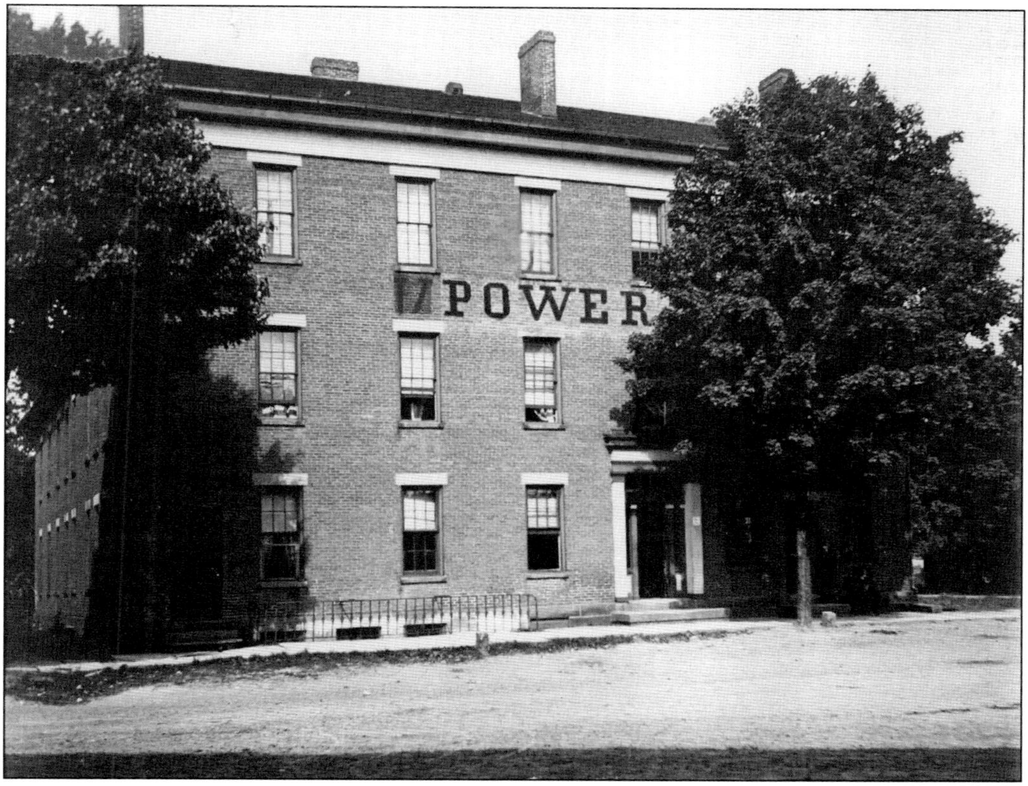

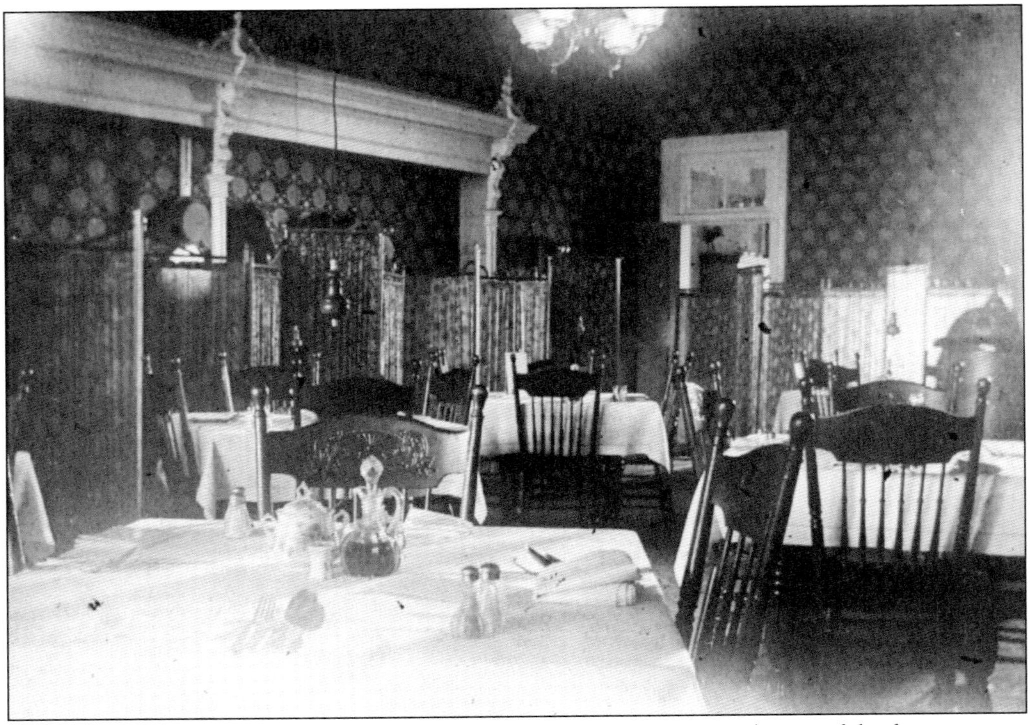

Dining at the Hotel Power meant being treated to an elegant setting and some of the finest cuisine around. Much of the food served here was locally grown and produced. The dining room was open to both hotel guests and those looking to enjoy a night out.

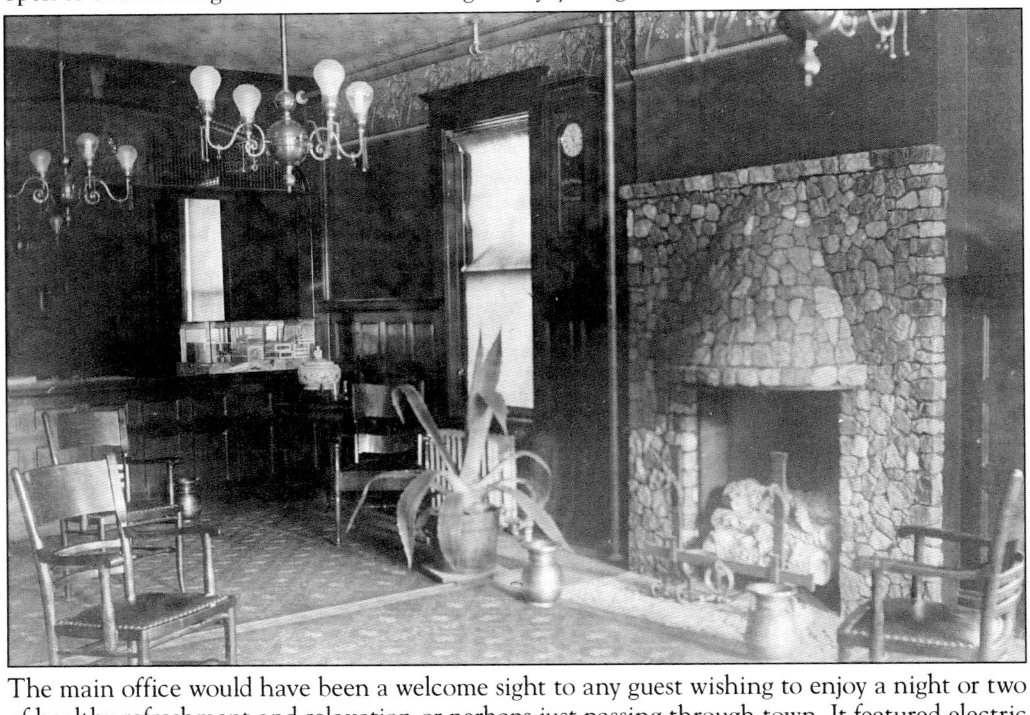

The main office would have been a welcome sight to any guest wishing to enjoy a night or two of healthy refreshment and relaxation or perhaps just passing through town. It featured electric lighting and a beautiful fireplace.

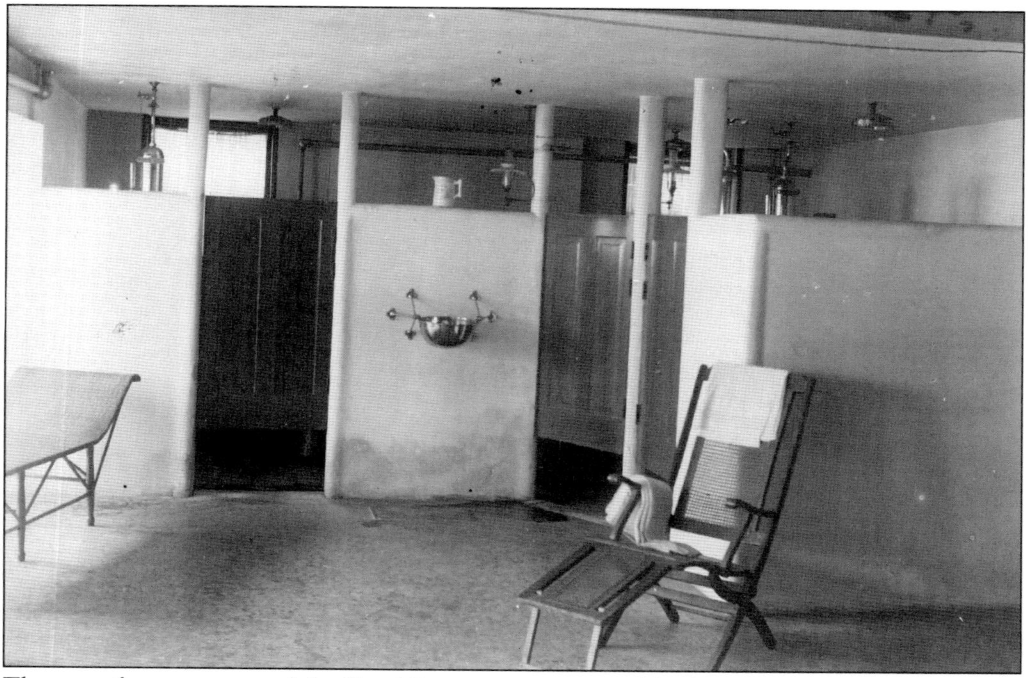

The most famous aspect of the Hotel Power was its mineral baths. The facility brought people from all over the country to enjoy the water's healing properties. Besides being used for bathing, the water was bottled and shipped for an array of uses. This was a thriving business at the turn of the century.

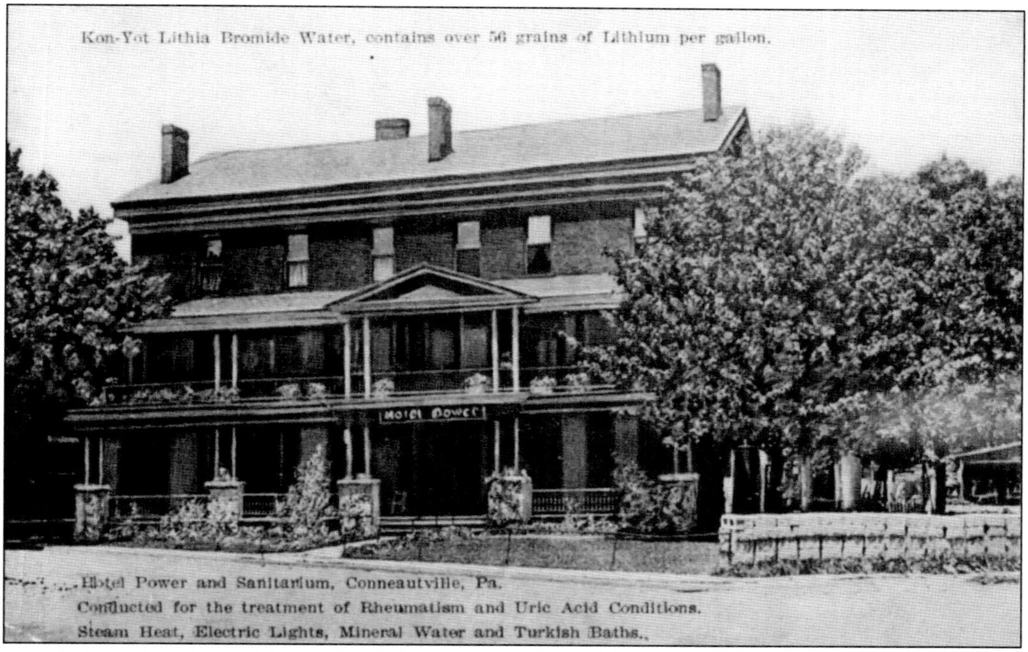

A Bessemer Railroad route map of November 1901 described the Hotel Power as "New and elegantly furnished throughout. Steam heat, natural gas, and Turkish Bath-Rooms in connection with the celebrated Conneautville Mineral Water. If you need a rest or want to recuperate, don't fail to visit the most comfortable and hygienic hotel in western Pennsylvania. Round Trip from Pittsburgh $4.65."

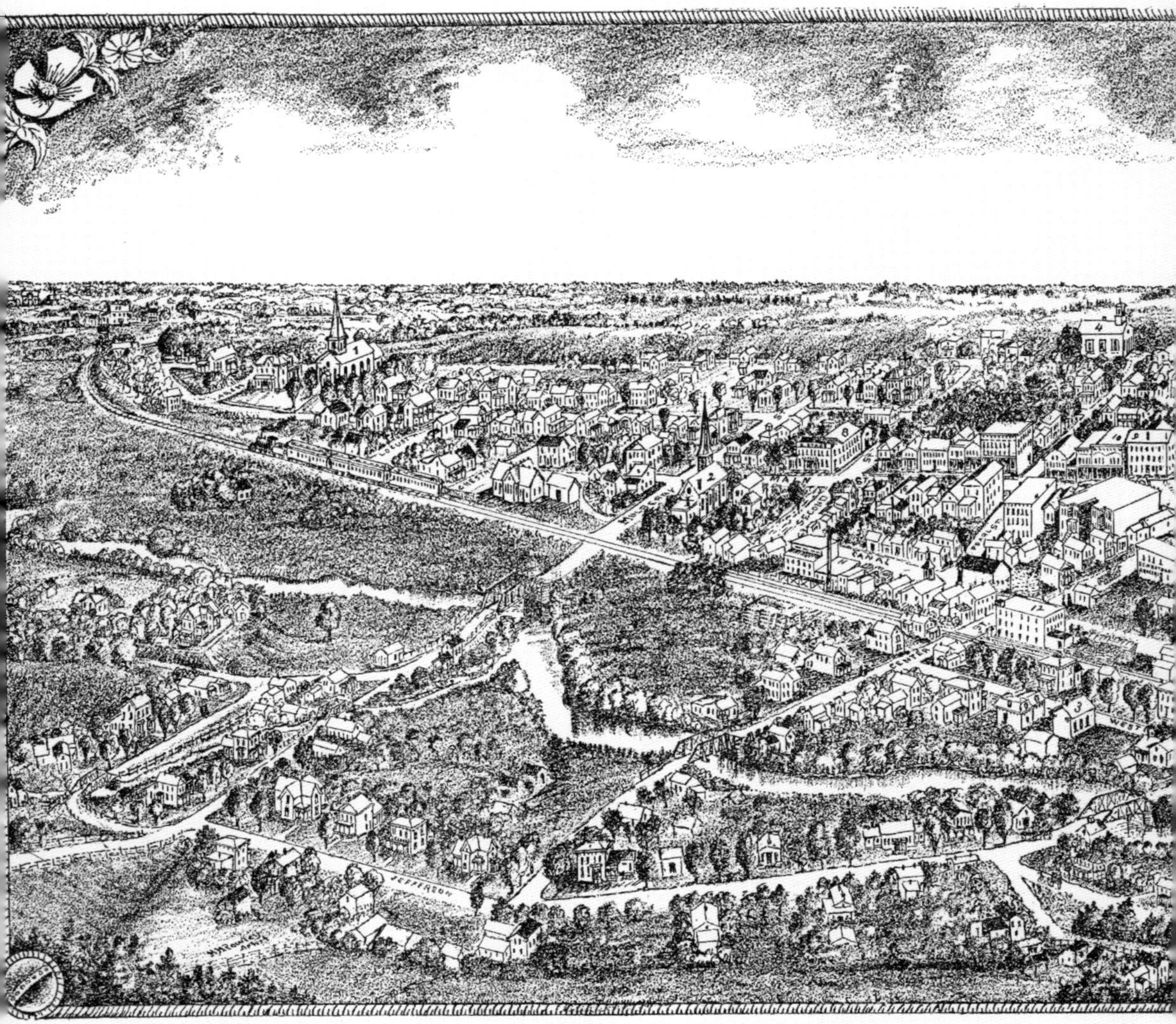

oman Catholic Church. 2—Presbyterian Church. 3–Second Advent Church. 4—Universalist Church. 5—Methodist Church. 6—Episcopal Church. 7—High School. 8—A. Stage's Hotel.

In 1898, artist H.H. Powley sketched this panoramic view of the borough. Powley captured nearly every building in town in this extremely detailed map. The numbered structures on the map are as follows: Roman Catholic Church (1), Presbyterian Church (2), Second Adventist Church (3), Universalist Church (4), Methodist Church (5), Episcopal Church (6), High School (7),

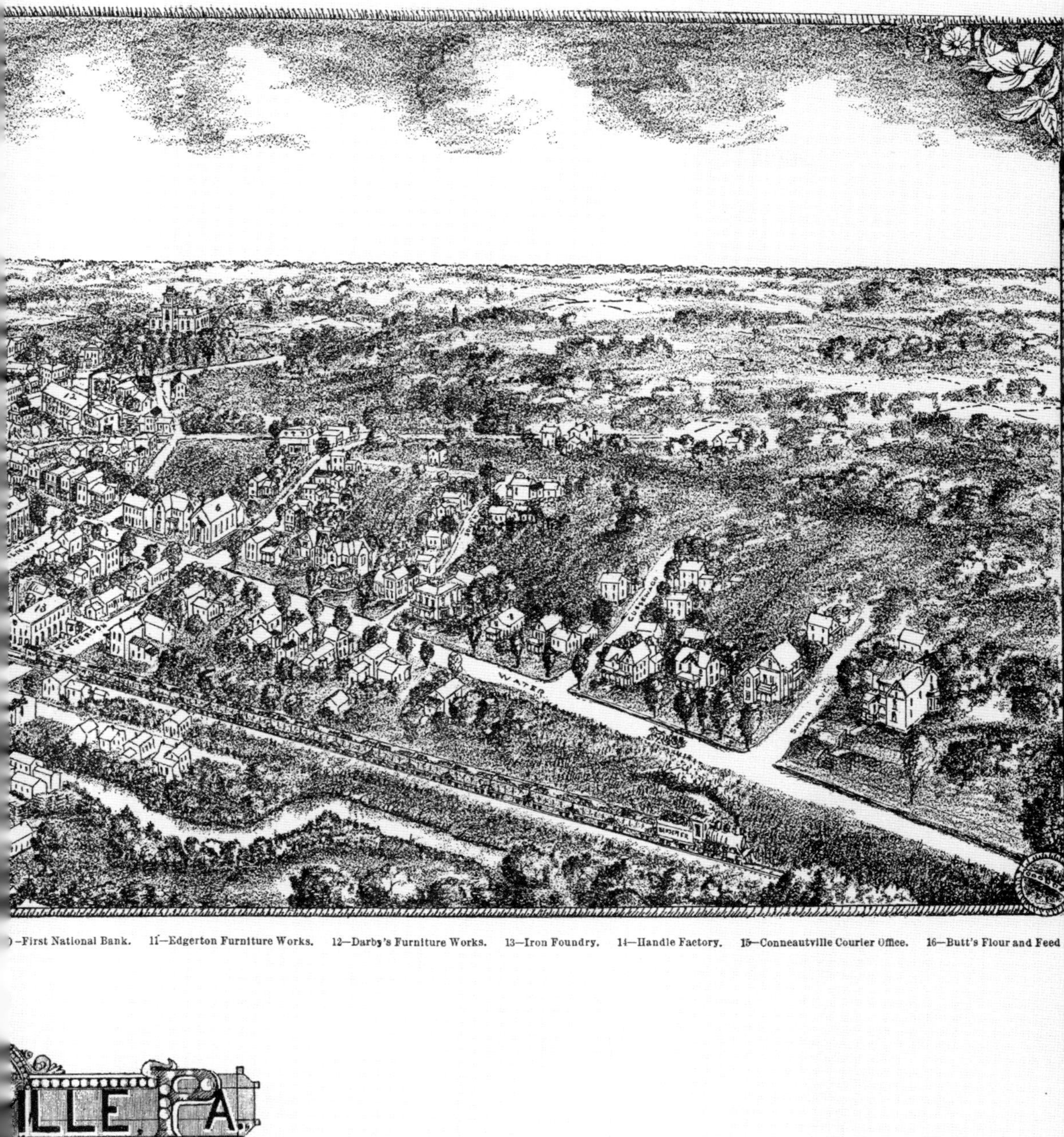

A. Stage's Hotel (8), Power Hotel (9), First National Bank (10), Edgerton Furniture Works (11), Darby's Furniture Works (12), Iron Foundry (13), Handle Factory (14), *Courier* Office (15), Butt's Flour and Feed Mill (16).

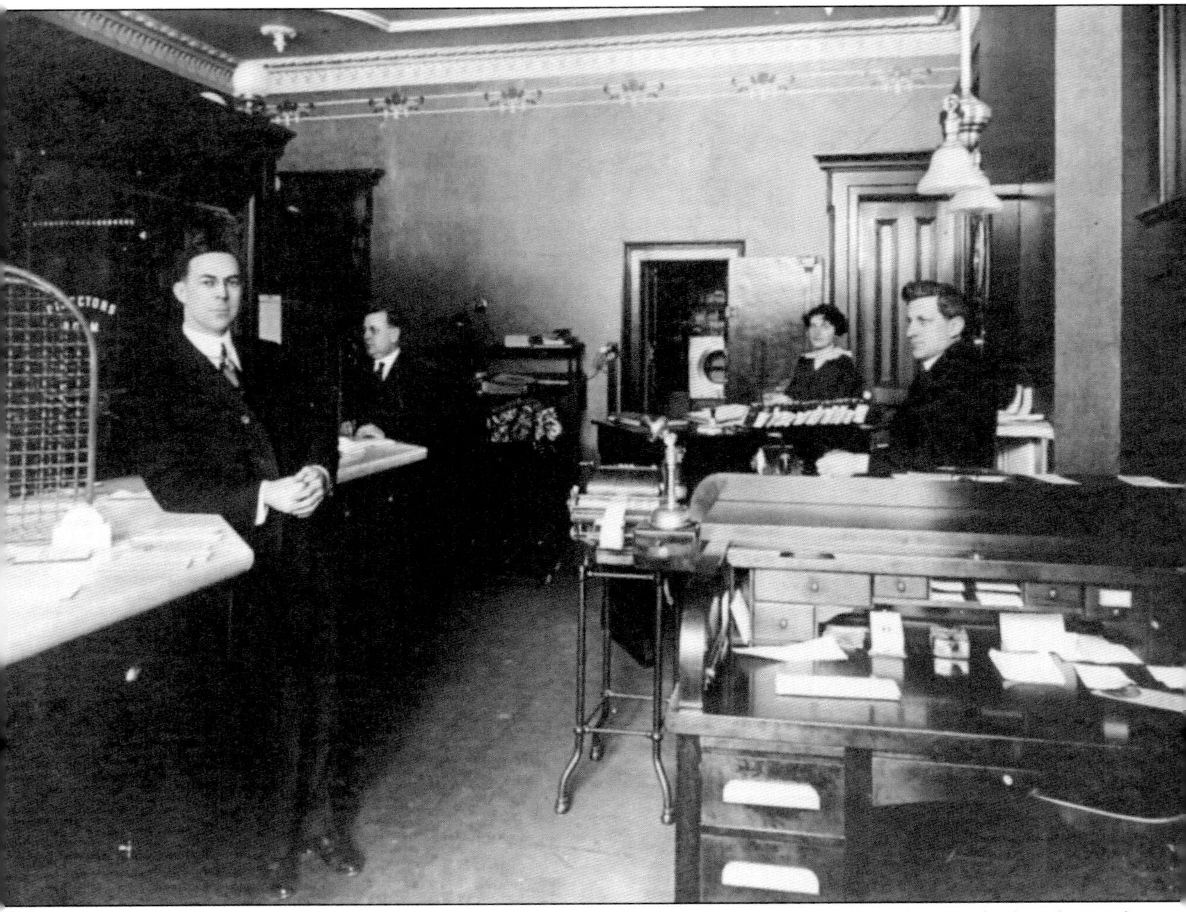

The First National Bank of Conneautville was organized on January 1, 1864, during the heightened economic times of the canal. In February 1874, someone entered the bank late in the evening while cashier D.D. Williams was still at work. He was bound and gagged while the criminal emptied the drawers and took $14,000 in cash and around $30,000 in government bonds. The robber was never caught. This and the following image of the bank were taken while it occupied a portion of the Power Block around 1930.

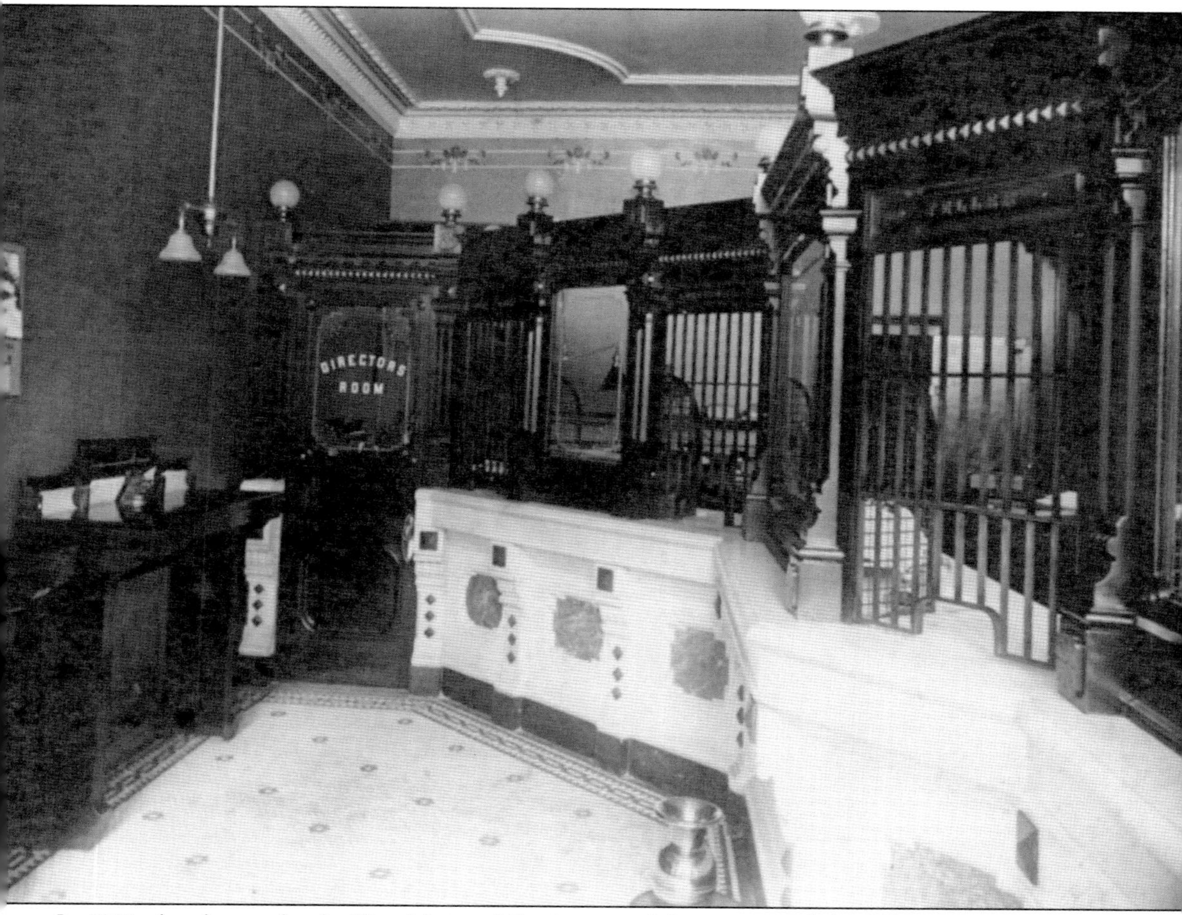

In 1901, the charter for the First National Bank expired. It was opened the following day under the name Bank of Conneautville. In January of 1934, the bank was reorganized again under the name Farmers National Bank of Conneautville.

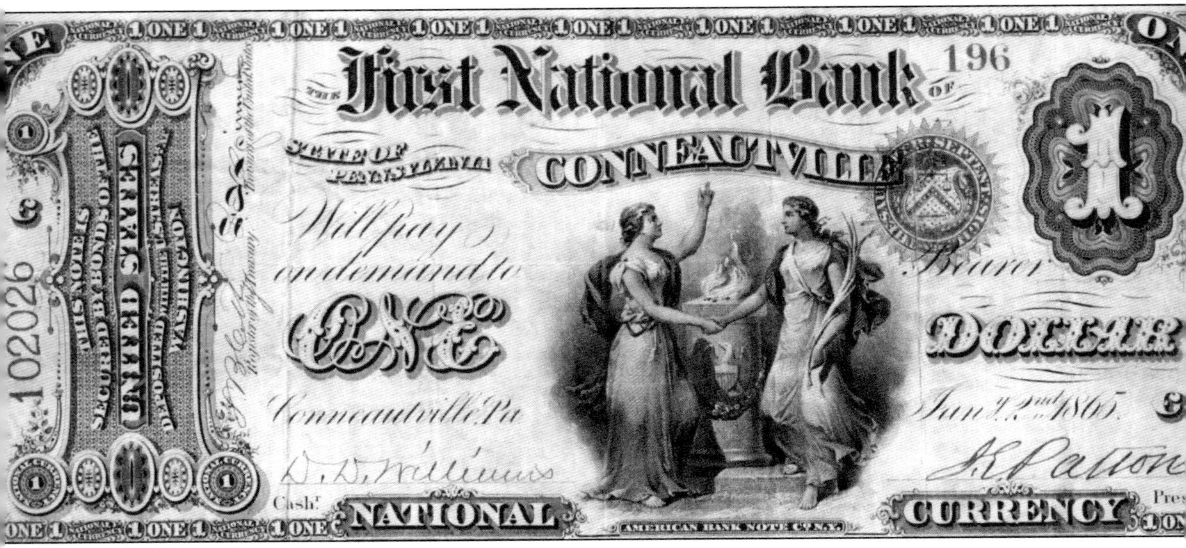

Pictured here is a bank bond.

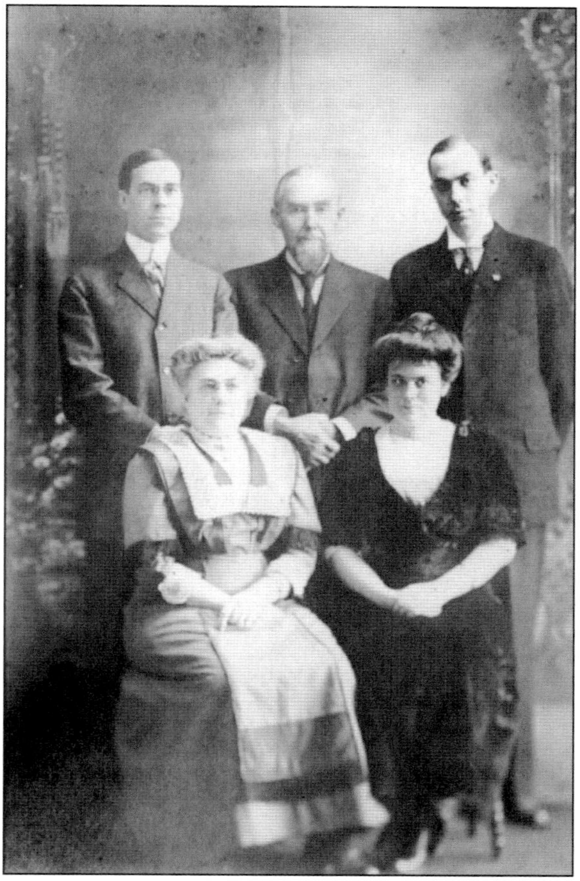

The Honorable John C. Sturtevant (middle) was one of Conneautville's most prominent citizens. Born on February 20, 1835, he taught school for eight years before representing Crawford County in the state legislature in 1865 and 1866. Upon returning to Conneautville, he opened the law firm Krick & Sturtevant before becoming president of the First National Bank in 1878. In 1896, he was elected to the US House of Representatives. While there, he used his power to secure the Civil War cannon that now sits at Lord-Mason Park and to erect the soldiers' monument in Spring Cemetery. He is pictured here with his wife, Sarah (left), and his sons Watkin (left) and Paul (right). The woman on the left is unknown. The cannon, seen below in a photograph from 1914, sat on the lawn of the Hotel Power.

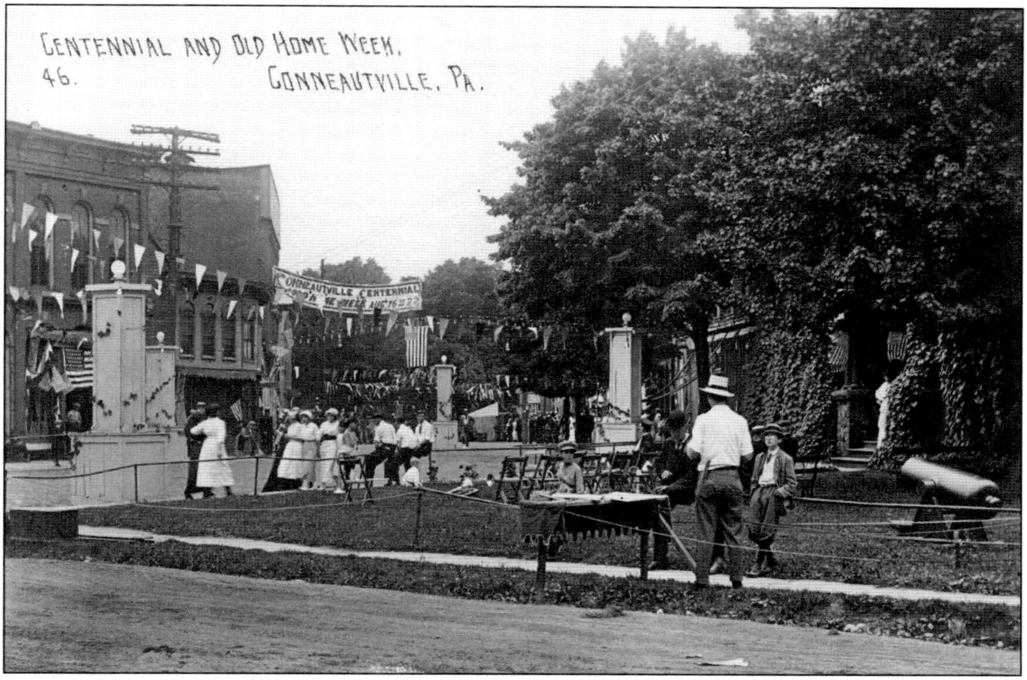

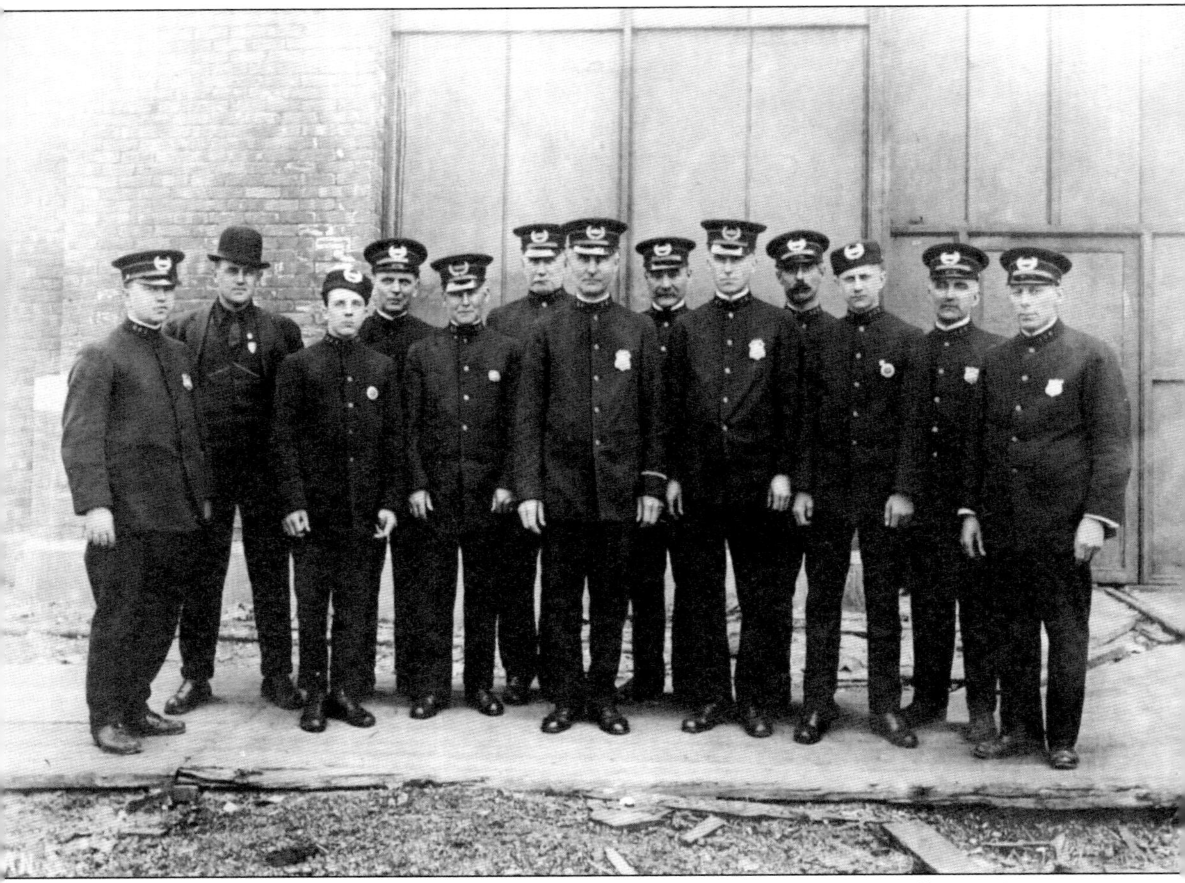

This group is either the Goodwill Fire Company of 1867 or the Conneautville Fire Department of 1875. Either way, these men fought one of the most destructive fires in Conneautville's history. On June 1, 1874, a fire broke out in the Borough Office Building along Canal Street. Ironically, it was also used as the engine house for the Goodwill Fire Department. The fire quickly spread though the dry frame building and soon reached J. Field's Cabinet Manufactory, located just one foot away. With the winds picking up, the fire spread across the street. At the Moulthrop Foundry, four blocks away, the firemen made a stand but the flames were out of control. The fire eventually damaged 15 acres in the center of town, damaging 50 buildings and leaving 23 families homeless. The entire burnt area encompassed Main Street to Canal Street and Center Street to Jefferson Street. The total loss was valued at $150,000.

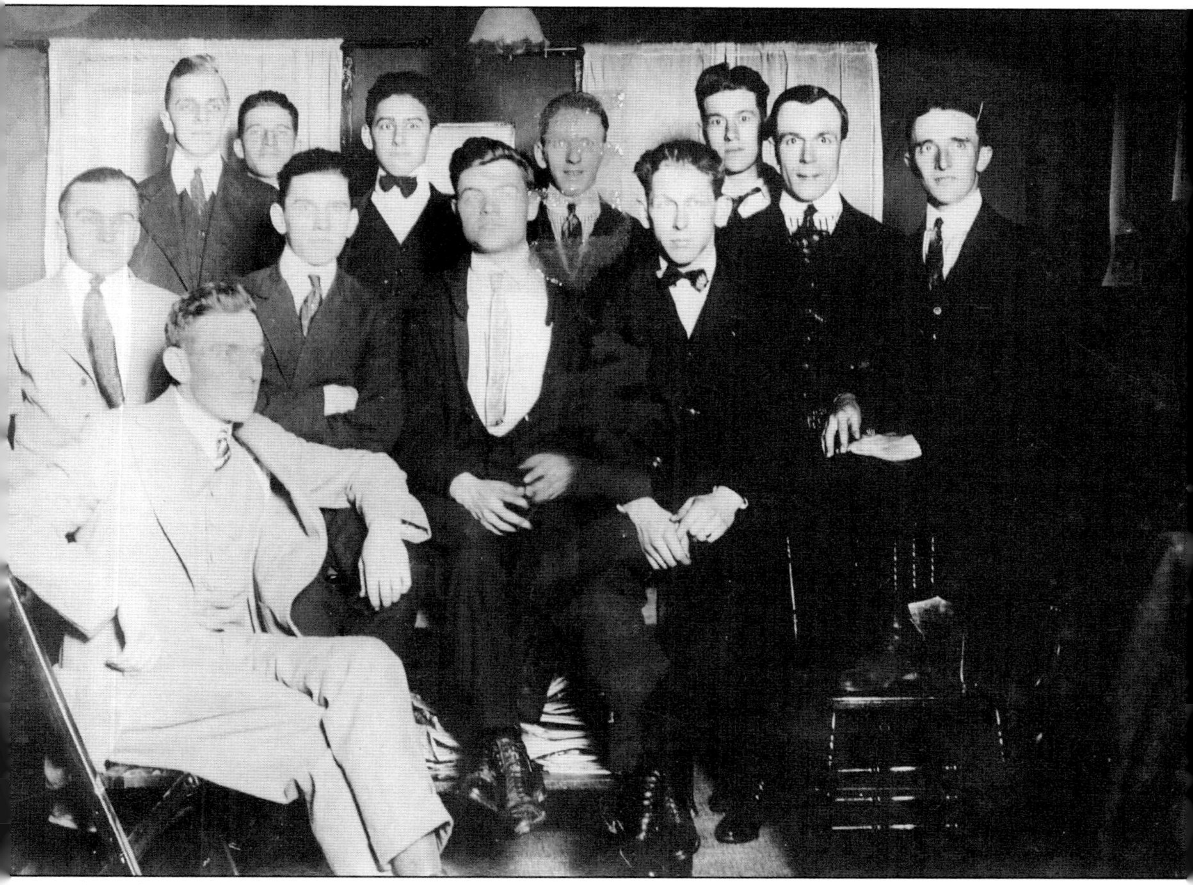

The Fellows Club, where young men met socially once a week, was organized in 1914. Among the early members are, from left to right, (seated in front) Andrew Frazier; (second row) Kenneth Bail, John Flynn, Eugene Zimmerman (president), Clint McCarty, Frank Seeley, and Howard Corey; (third row) Park Lawrence, Homer Bail, Wilson Means, Walter "Scoop" Rager, and Ellison Morell.

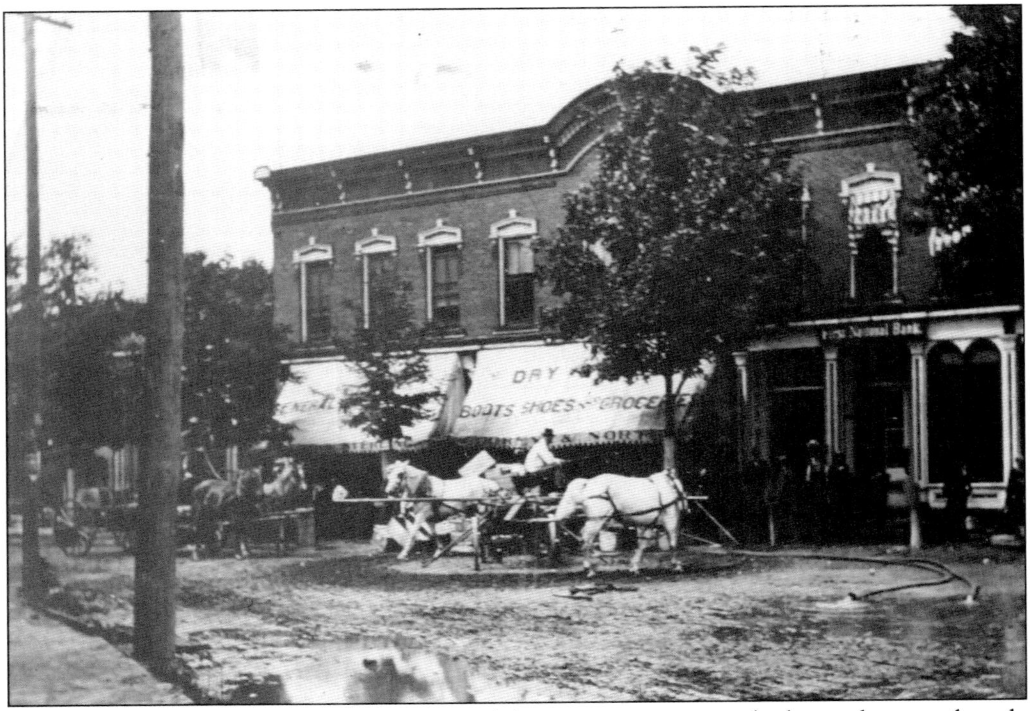

After several disastrous fires, and with a need for newer equipment, the borough council made a special motion at a meeting in August 1882 for the $600 purchase of a fire engine that was on loan to the department. The pistons in the horse-drawn Remington engine were operated either by a team of men or a team of horses walking in circles around the apparatus while turning long poles. Two of these vehicles currently exist in the United States—one in Arizona and this one, which is on loan from the Fellows Club Volunteer Fire Department to the Erie Firefighters Historical Museum. Above, the pump is being used to extract water from the Power Block basement around 1900. Below, Conneautville resident Dave Nichols pulls the Remington engine during the homecoming parade in 2002.

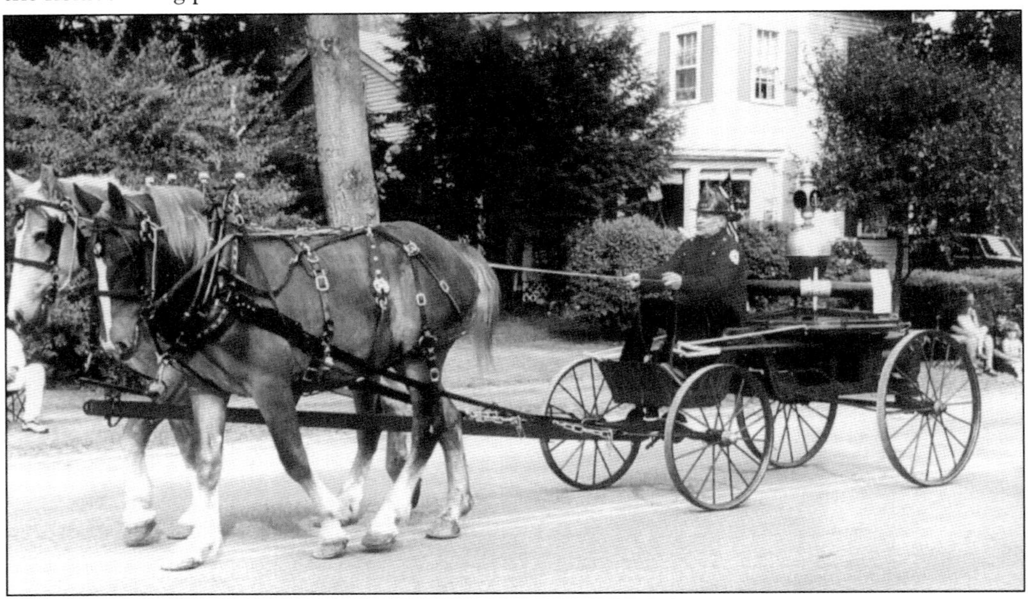

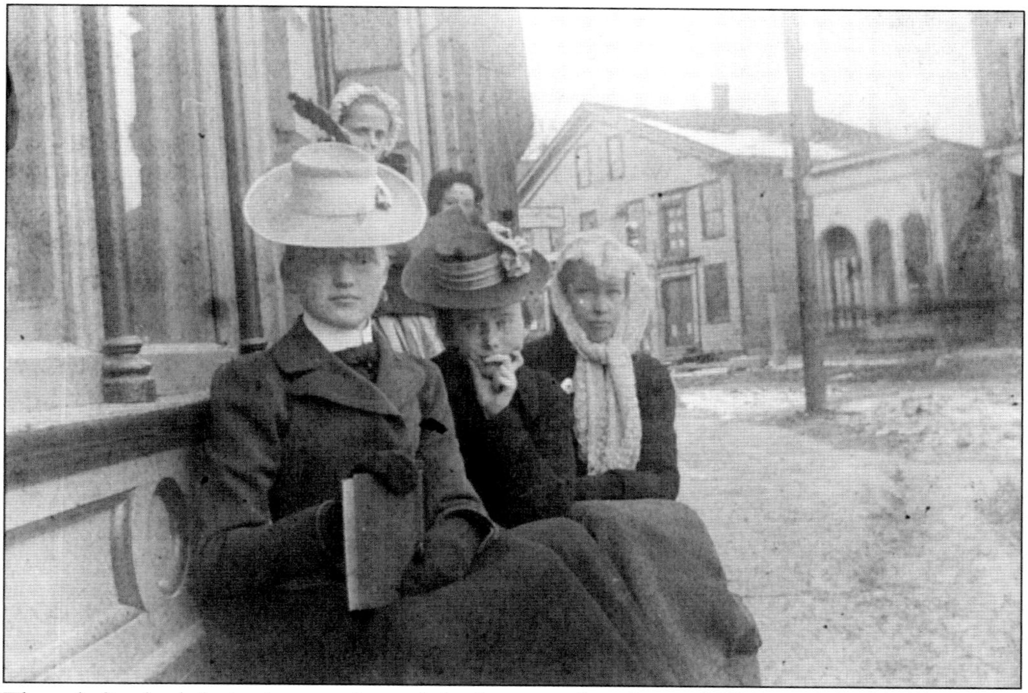

These ladies had their picture taken while they rested in front of Clancy's Grocery Store. The buildings in the background are the livery stable (left) and Kissel barbershop.

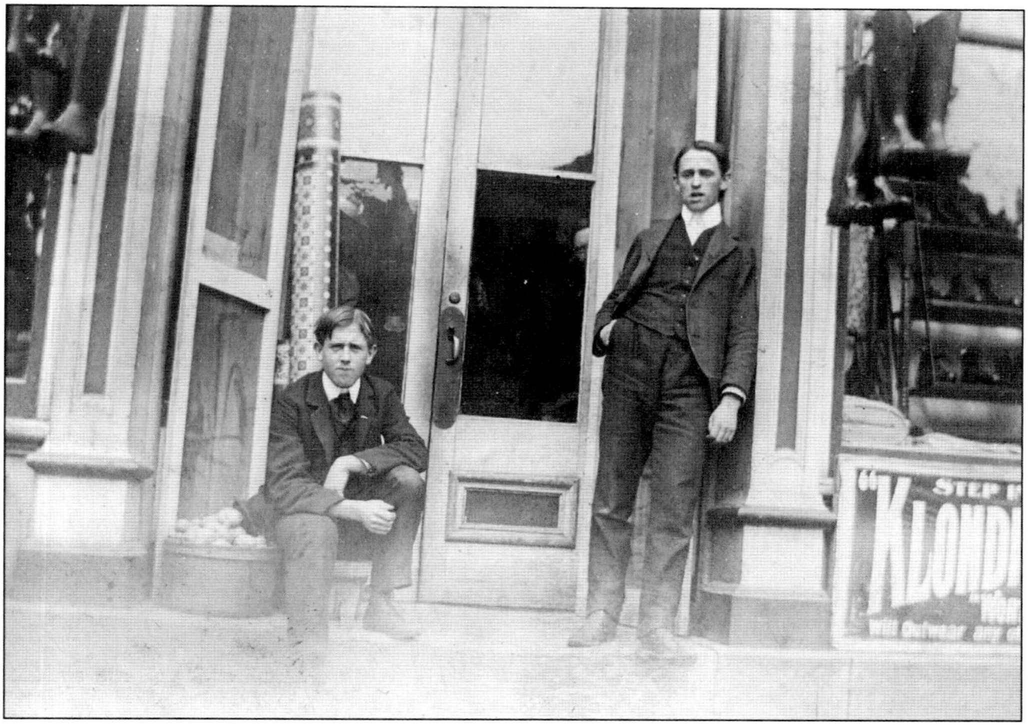

The caption on the back of this image reads "taken in front of store room at Opera Block along Main Street Conneautville."

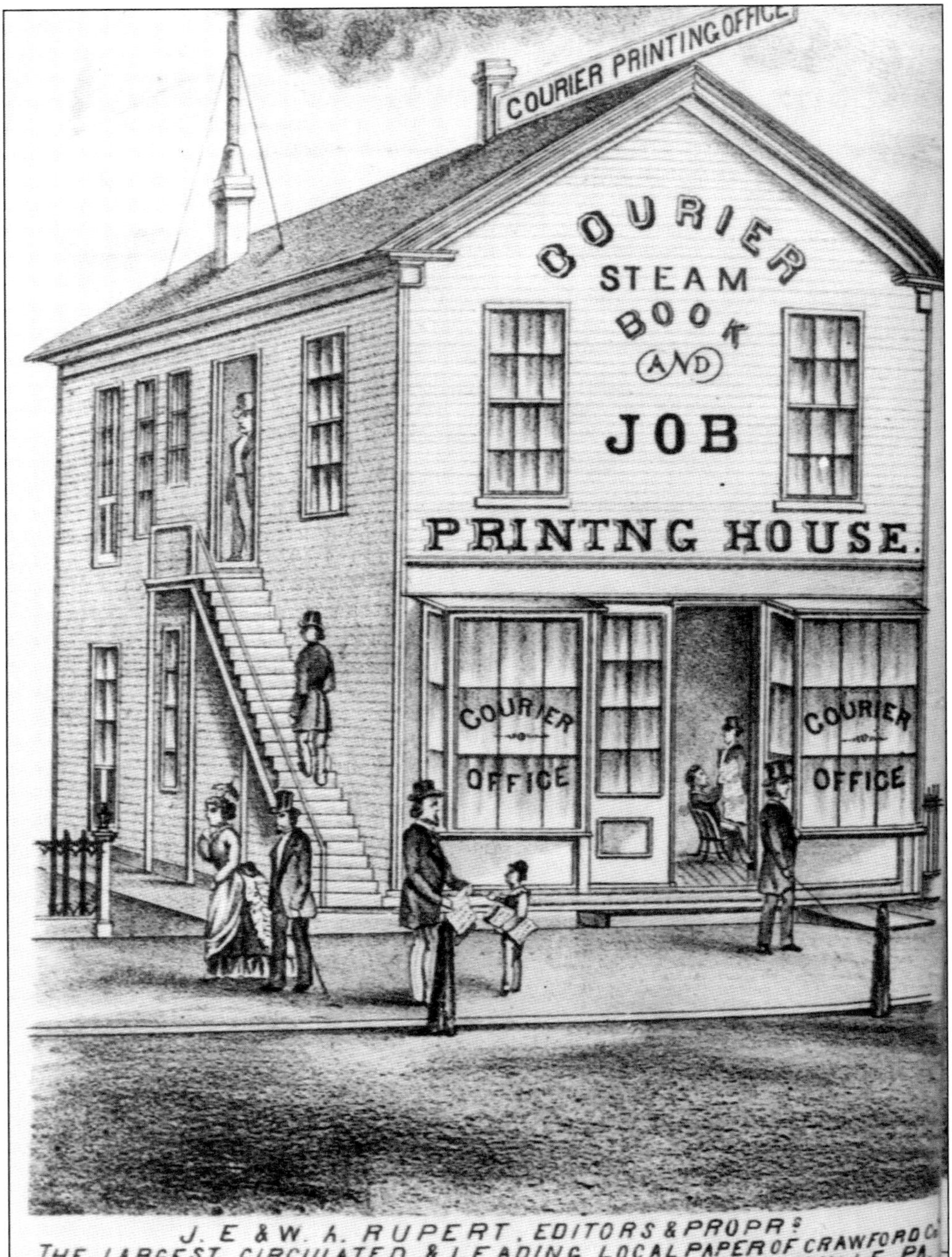

As the population of Conneautville grew, so did the need for local media. The borough's first newspaper, *The Union*, was published in October 1846 and discontinued the following May. On November 14, 1847, A.J. Mead and George W. Brown published the first issue of the *Conneautville Courier* to a readership of 52 people. In 1848, Mead sold his share of the business to Brown, who grew the publication to 200 readers by the end of its first year. The *Courier* was first printed at an office on Main Street (depicted in this drawing), but moved extensively around town in the following decades. In 1854, Brown sold the business and moved to Illinois, where he lived until his death.

A faded copy of a daguerreotype image taken in 1847 is one of the few remaining photographs of George W. Brown. He is seen here the year he started printing the *Conneautville Courier*.

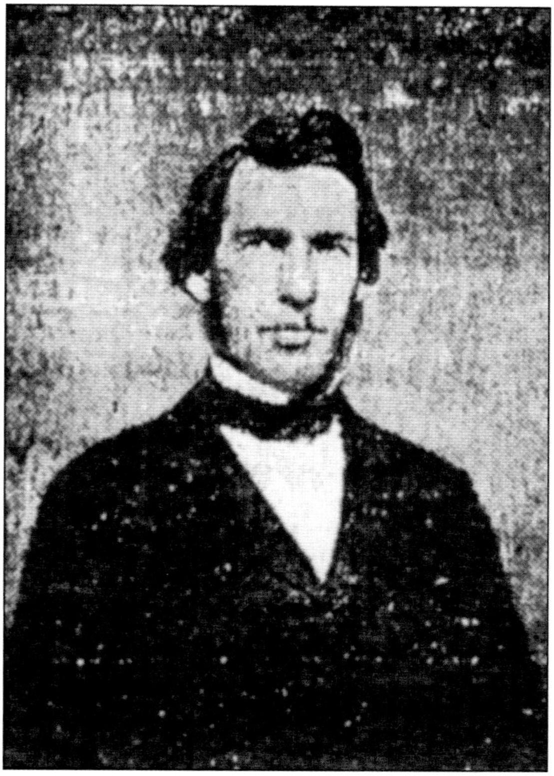

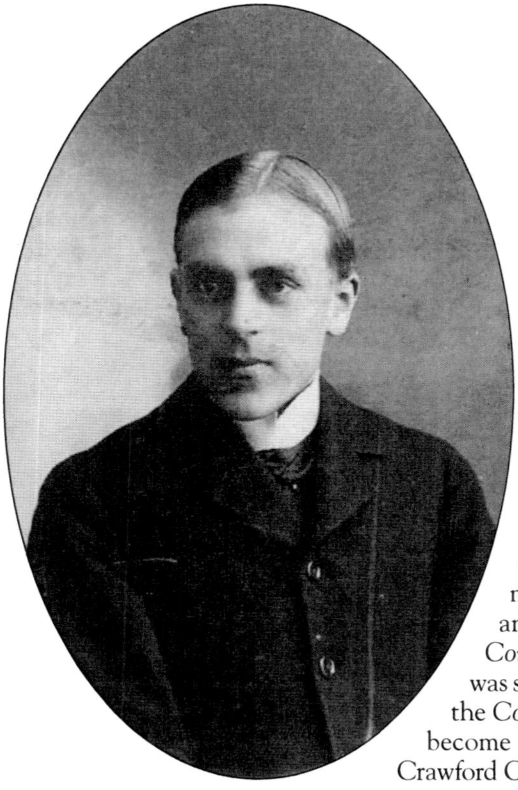

After his brother retired, J.E. Rupert (left) asked his son Lynne to become the *Courier*'s new editor. At the same time, the business underwent many changes in technology, including the addition of a new 10-horsepower steam boiler used to power the printing presses. This technology was made obsolete when electricity allowed for faster and clearer printing. The Ruperts' tenure with the *Courier* ended on April 1, 1918, when the company was sold to Neill Robinson. The Rupert family edited the *Courier* for nearly four decades and saw it grow to become the largest regularly distributed newspaper in Crawford County.

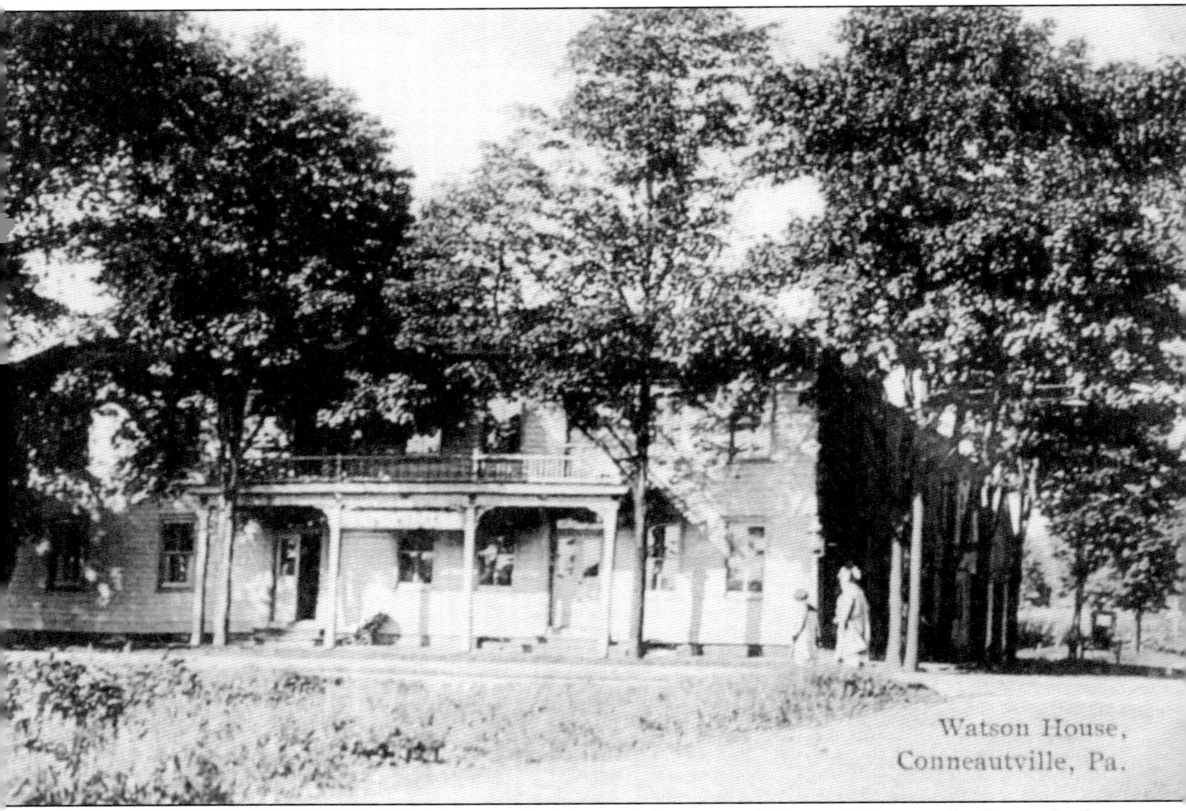

In 1833, a frame hotel was erected on the corner of Main and Second Streets. In the early days, it was known as the Stage House and later as the Conneautville Hotel. In January 1905, Frank C. Watson purchased the property and subsequently had it refurnished. He continued operating the property as a hotel under the name "Watson House" until it was destroyed by fire in the early 1920s. A note found with this picture states that "the bottom floor was half partitioned off with a separate entrance for a saloon." The unidentified author also writes "I recall being in the kitchen, standing on a stool, looking through a porthole in the dining room."

The Conneautville Thimble Club was organized for women who were interested in the business of sewing. Pictured here are, from left to right, (front row) Anna Booth and Pearl Townsend; (second row) Ida Fetterman, Nellie Brennan, and Georgia Fetterman; (third row) Harriette Wilson, Nellie Perrin, Lillian Fish, and Vesta Leet.

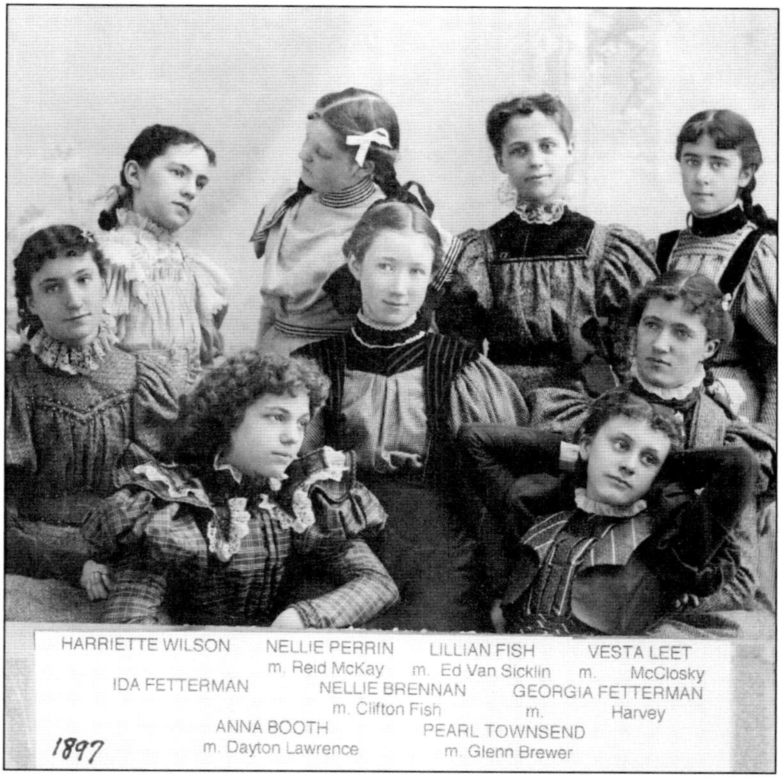

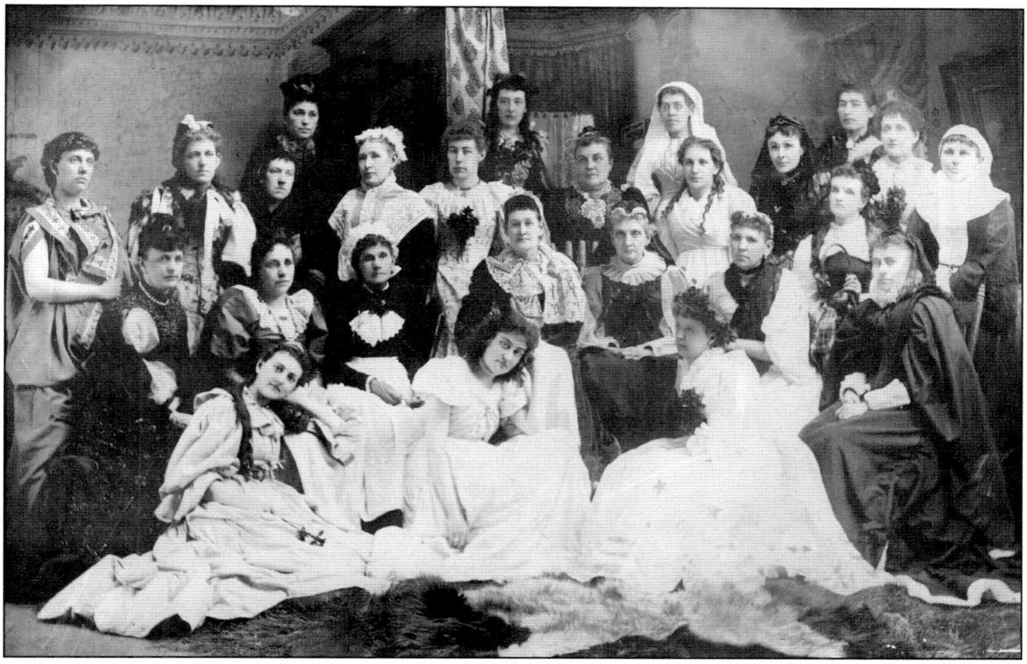

Conneautville's Shakespeare Club was organized around 1900 for the women of town who were interested in studying William Shakespeare. Their weekly meetings consisted of reading passages of plays, discussing characters, and comparing themes. This club also undertook the maintenance of the public park grounds, keeping the area clean and beautiful for many years.

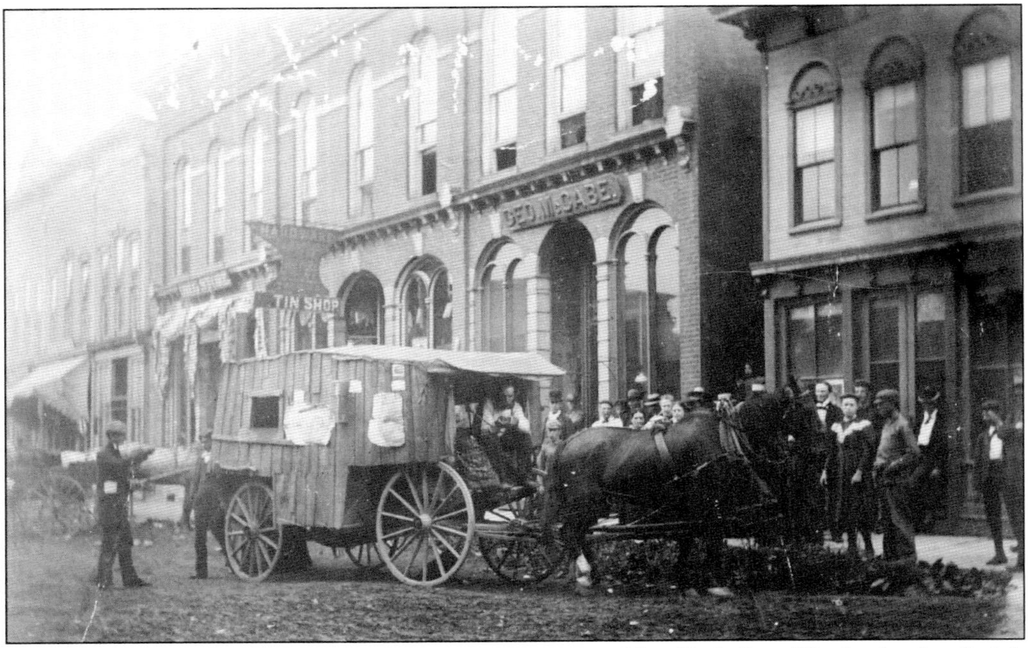

The "House on Wheels" arrives in town on its journey to New York City. The Lasley family left from Port Angeles, Washington, on March 22, 1894, in hopes of making a cross-country trip. The date of their arrival in Conneautville has been lost, but this photograph proves they crossed a significant portion of the country. The Opera Block can be seen in the far left.

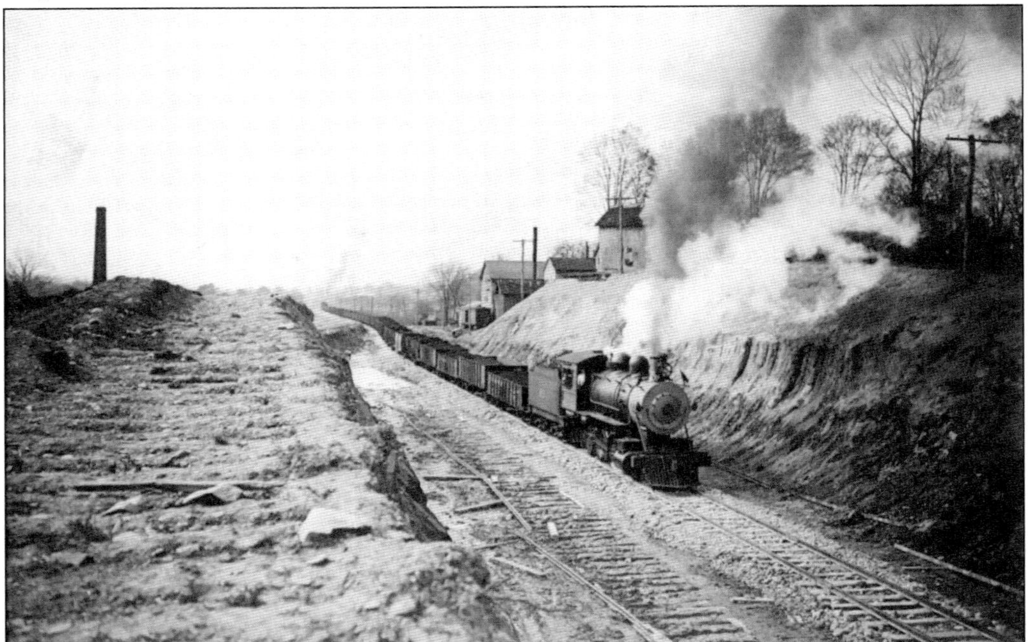

Although the railroad meant the end to the historic Erie Canal, it did connect Conneautville to plenty of other destinations. This image from 1909, taken just south of the borough, shows tracks in the old canal bed. The chimney in the background belonged to Saxton Chemical Works, which burned in 1885.

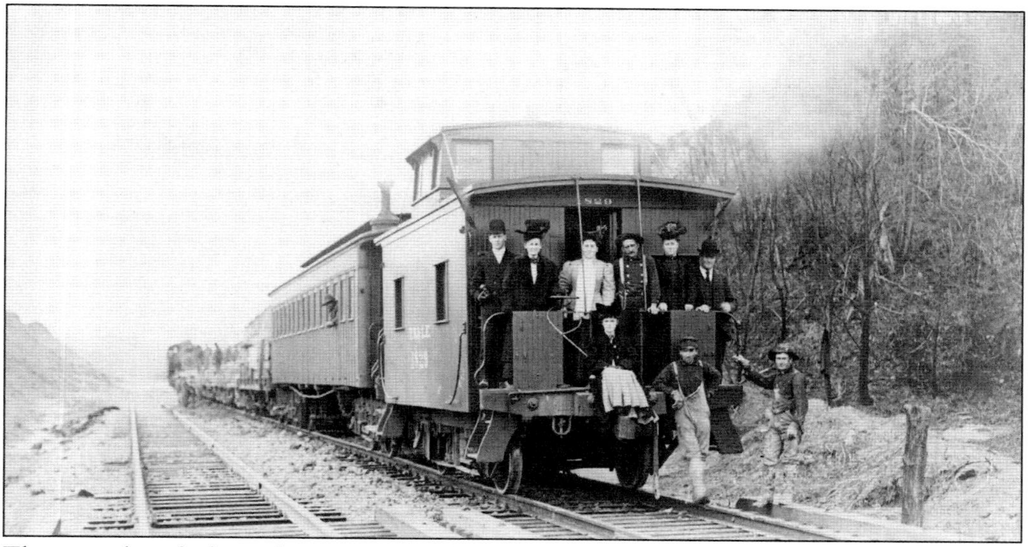

These unidentified people pose on a caboose outside of town. The only description of this photograph is the word "Conneautville," written on the back. Although the canal vanished, the railroad brought numerous opportunities to the area.

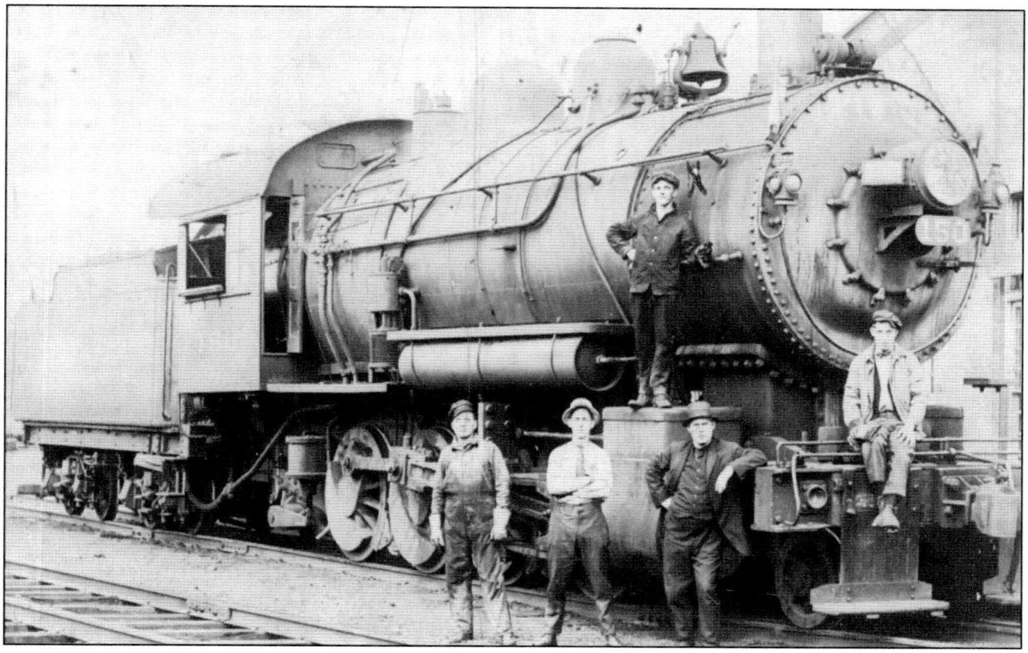

The identification on the back of this photograph reads, "Conneautville" and "Giles Parker and brother." Many photographs exist from the turn of the century depicting scenes of the railroad around Conneautville.

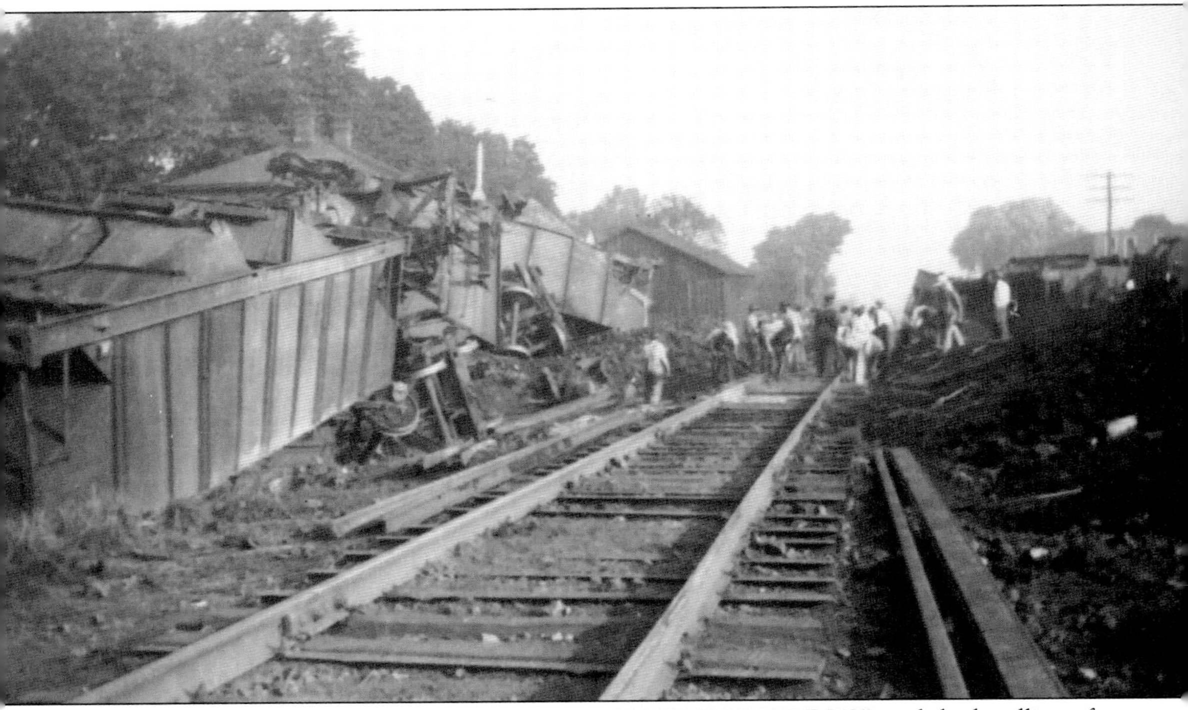

"FOURTEEN CARS CRUMPLED IN CONNEAUTVILLE WRECK," read the headline of an *Erie Daily Times* article. "Twisted and crumpled as though made of tin, coal cars were hurled from the tracks Christmas morning when a broken truck caused one of the worst smashups that Bessemer has ever suffered. More than 400 tons of coal, destined for Canadian export, were dumped beside the track and up against the Penn Furniture Co. with damage to the extent of $5,000. The train was northbound and traveling at a rapid rate on the down grade when a box car, in the center of a long train, jumped the track as the train was passing the Moulthrop Foundry. James Hart, gate tender at the Center Street crossing, where the wreck occurred, says he saw some of the cars hurled as high as the three-story factory of Penn Furniture. No one was reported injured in the accident."

Two

Business and Industry

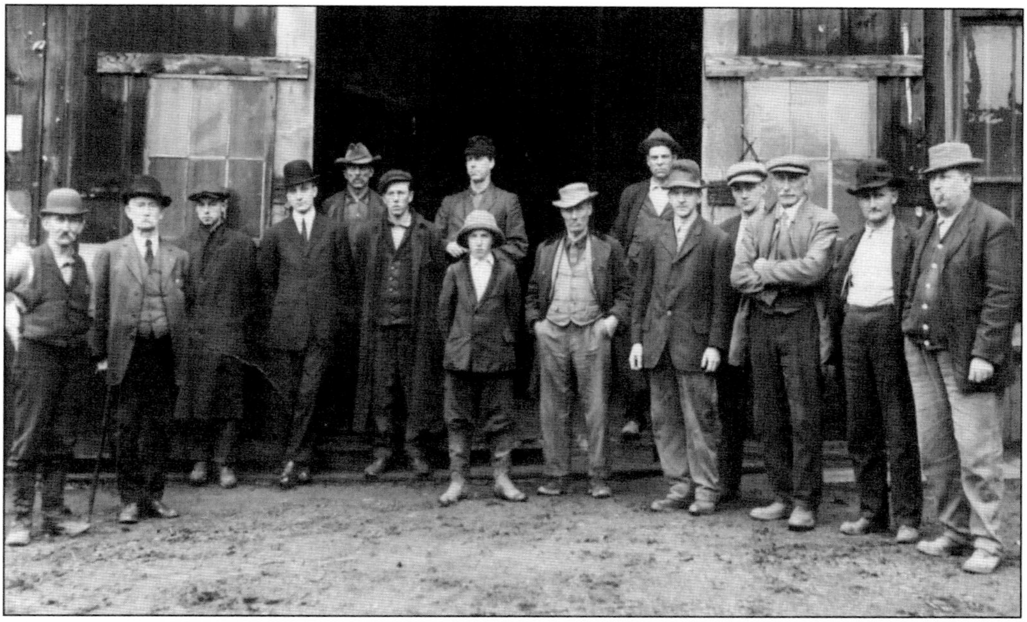

The gentlemen posing for this 1905 photograph are workers from Penn Furniture. From left to right are Dan Matthews, James Gowdy, Harry Hewitt, ? Waride, Dave Shoemaker, George Wright, Orlando Walton, Ed Stark, Jerkey Reed, ? Hills, Harry Gitsen, John Parker, ? Artman, Mert Nilder, and Mart Cleary.

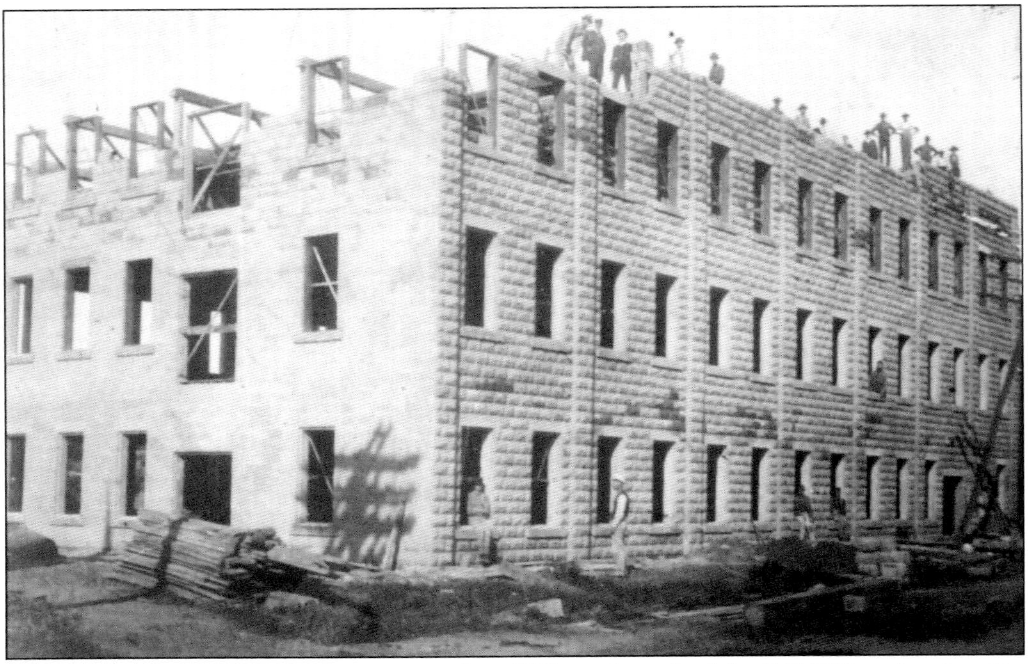

The Penn Furniture Co. was first organized in 1902 as a branch of the R.F. Wilcox Lumber Co. The company moved into a building along Canal Street previously owned by Darby Furniture Co., which had moved to Marietta, Ohio, in 1901. In 1905, the company, needing to expand, began construction of a new factory adjacent to its current one. The company manufactured kitchen and dining room furniture at this location.

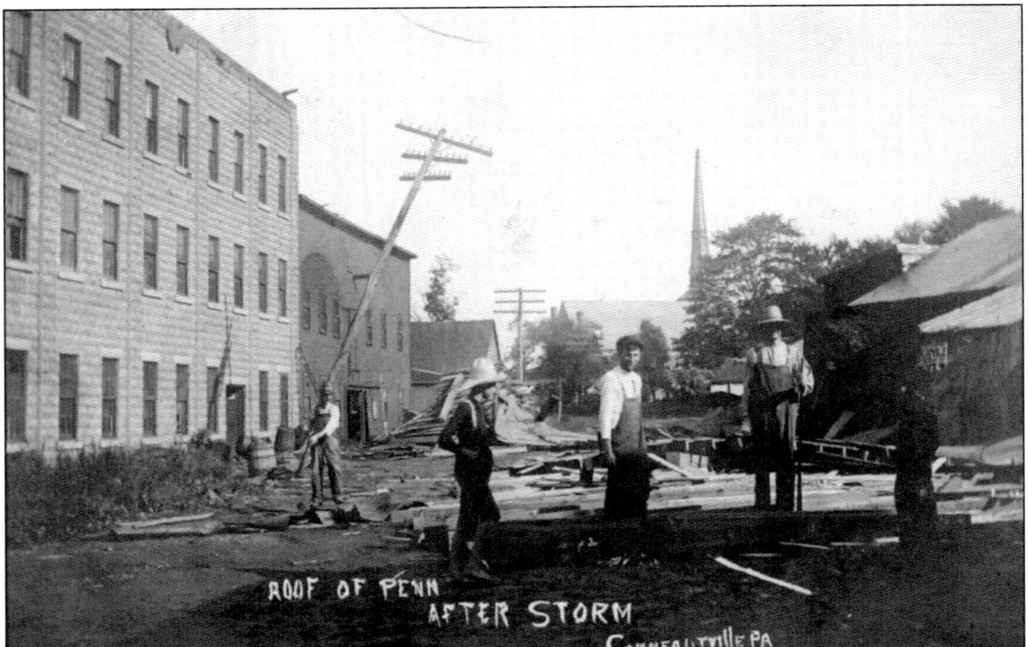

These men standing on Canal Street are cleaning up debris that was caused by a severe storm. As seen in the photograph, the winds were powerful enough to knock down telephone poles and destroy roofs. The steeple of the Presbyterian Church can be seen in the background.

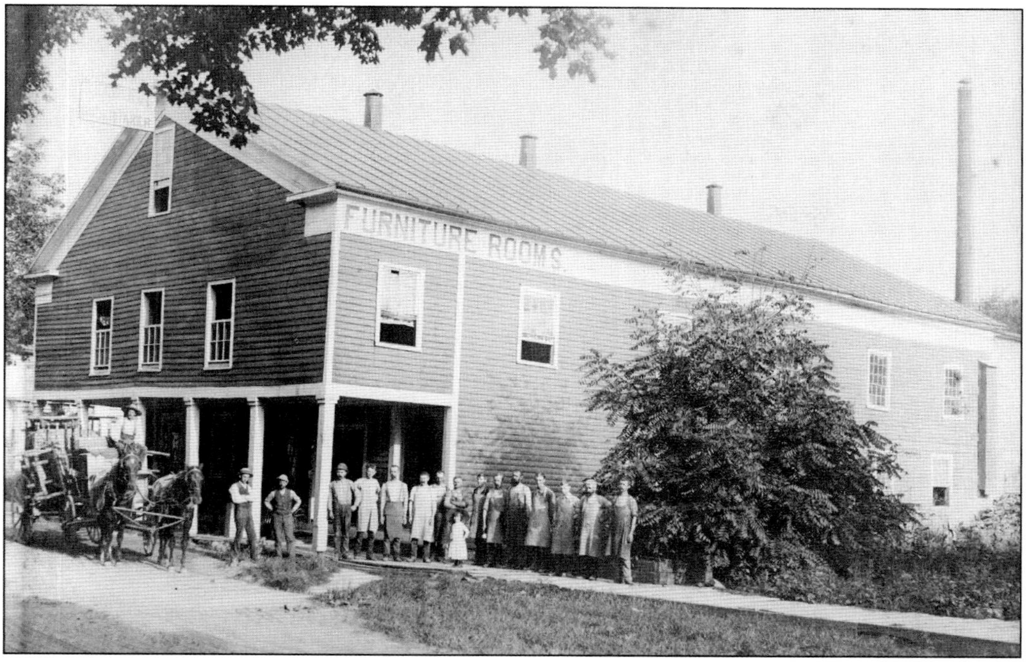

In 1882, William H. Darby purchased the factory he had previously been a partner in and opened the Darby Furniture Co. The business had two locations in town—one along Canal Street and the other on Center Street. These factories produced all types of furniture except chairs. This photograph of the factory on Center Street was taken around 1890.

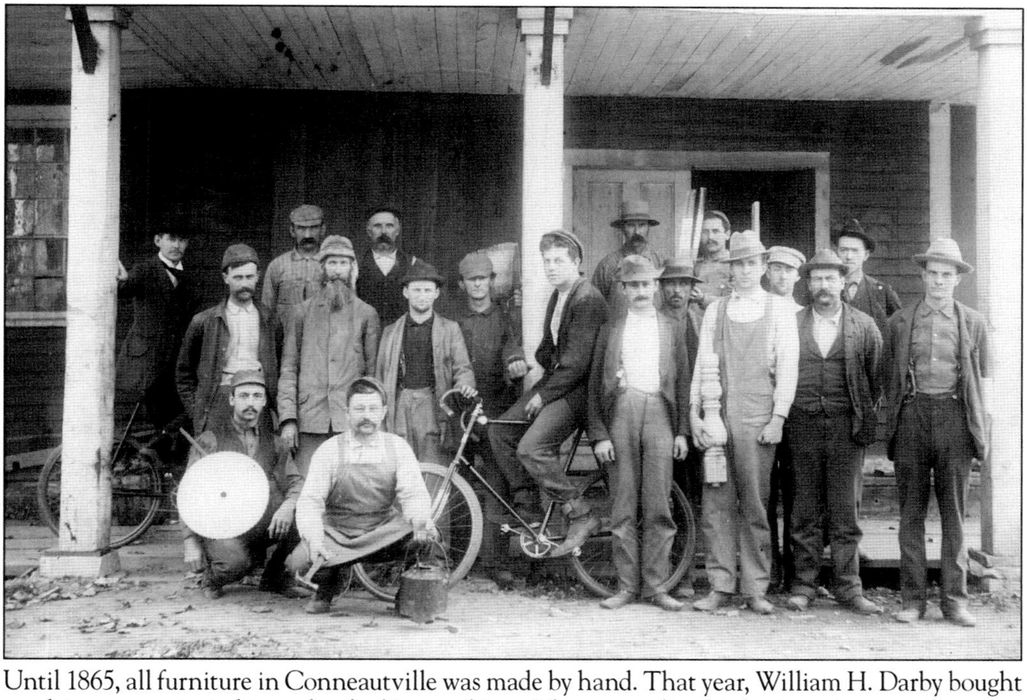

Until 1865, all furniture in Conneautville was made by hand. That year, William H. Darby bought machinery to assist in his trade of cabinetmaking. After expanding his business into two factories, Darby hired a workforce of 40 persons to build furniture. The employees of Darby Furniture Co., pictured here around 1890, produced some of the finest furniture around.

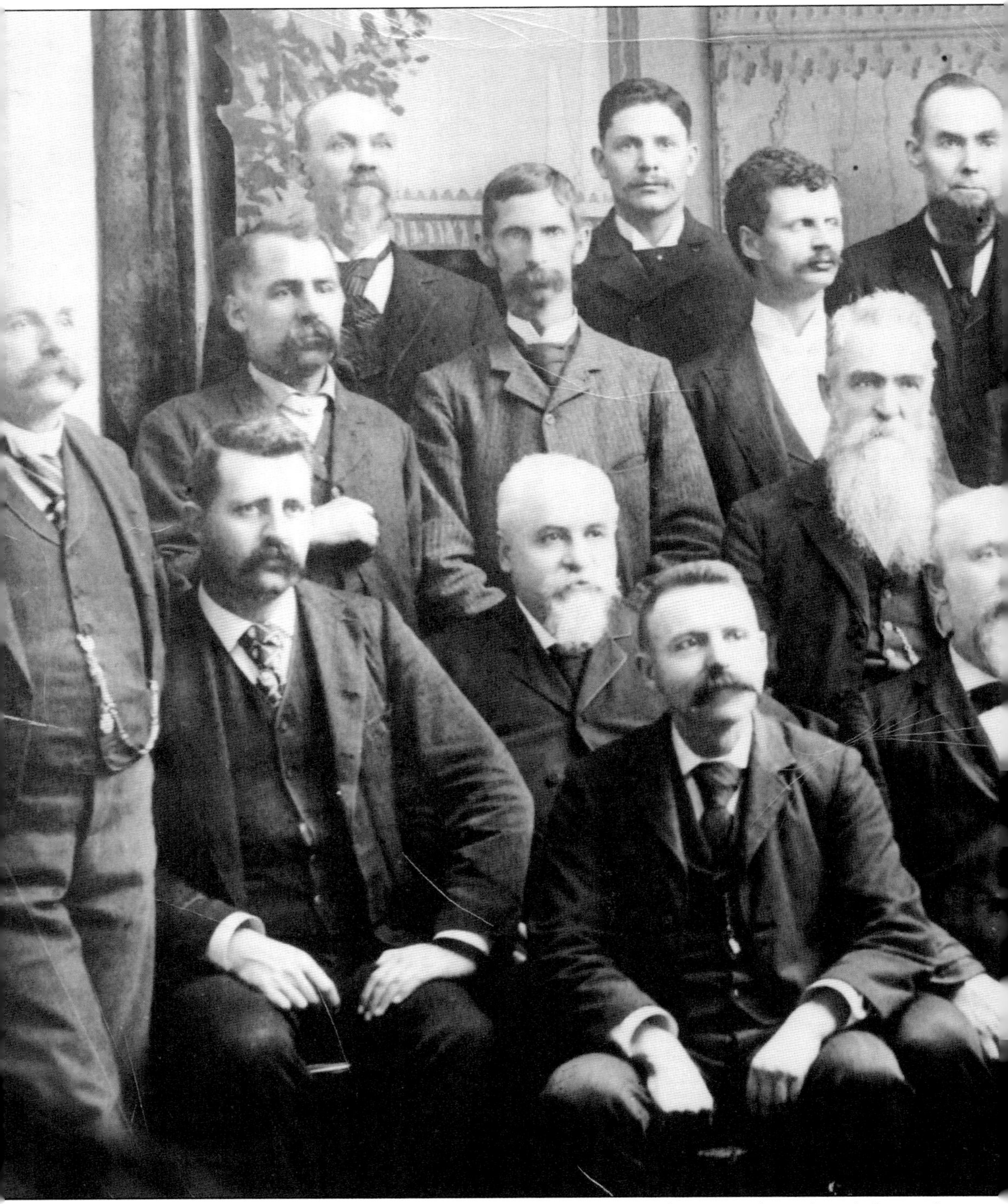

Conneautville's businessmen gathered in 1895 for this photograph. Pictured are, from left to right, (first row) Maurice Fitzgerald (druggist), George McCabe (shoe store), and A. Stage (hotel owner); (second row) W.A. Rupert (*Courier* editor, standing), M.H. Lect (clothing), E.T. Montague (general store), J.B. Frazier (doctor), E.L. Litchfield (flour and feed), J. Brown (banker), E. Robinson (dry goods), and Grant Hopkins (notions); (third row) W.A. Lawrence (tinner), F.L. Lord (grocer),

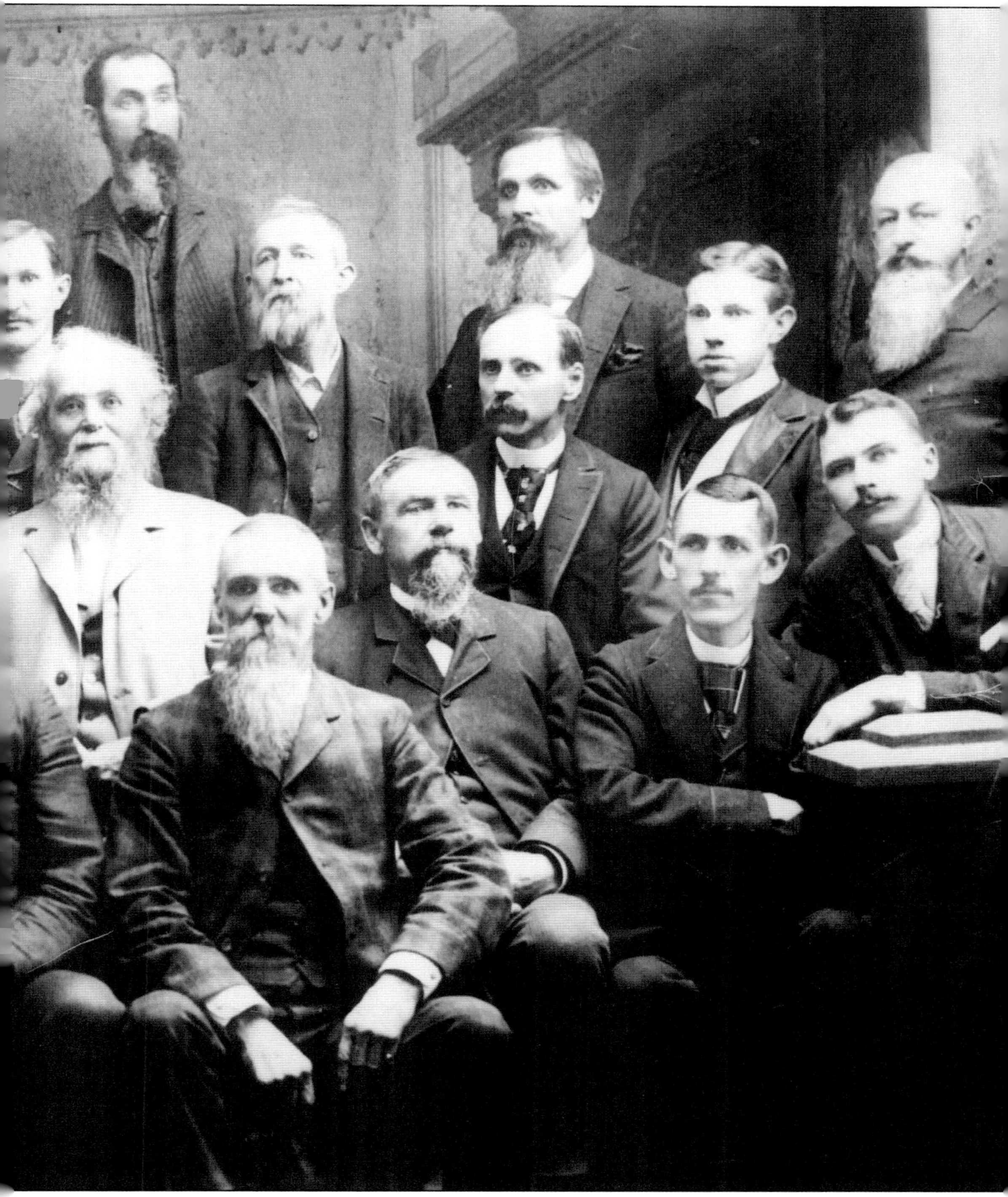

? Marsh (dentist), John Kissel (barber), J. Benjamin (furniture), J.E. Rupert (*Courier* editor), A. Robinson (grocer), and I.S. Krick (hardware); (fourth row) W.P. Frazier (monuments), N.C. Neville (jeweler and watchmaker), J.C. Sturtevant (banker and congressman), E.C. McKay (grocer), and L.G. Leffingwell (druggist and doctor).

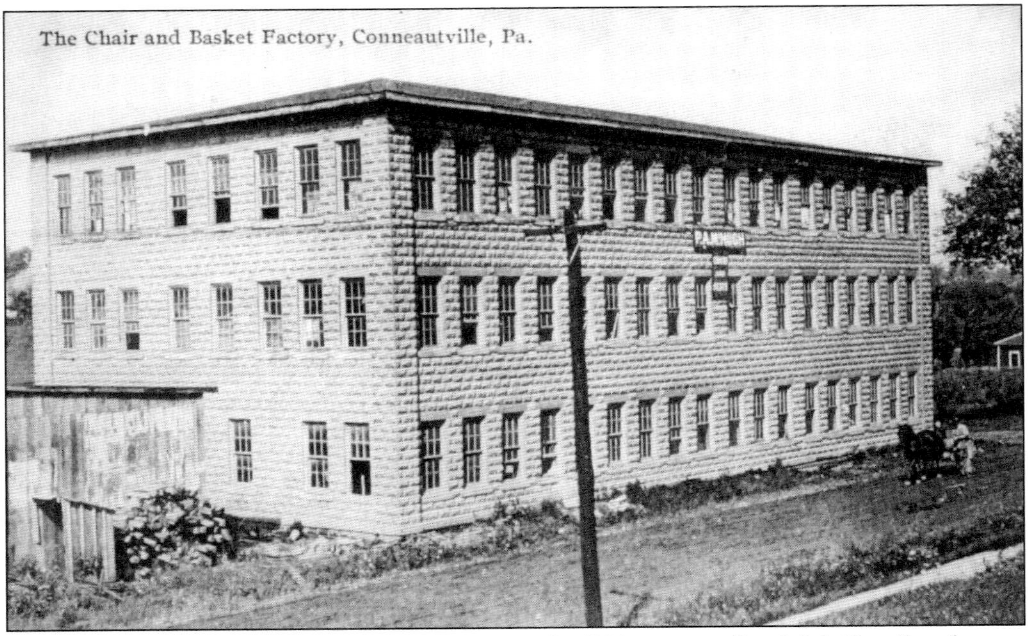

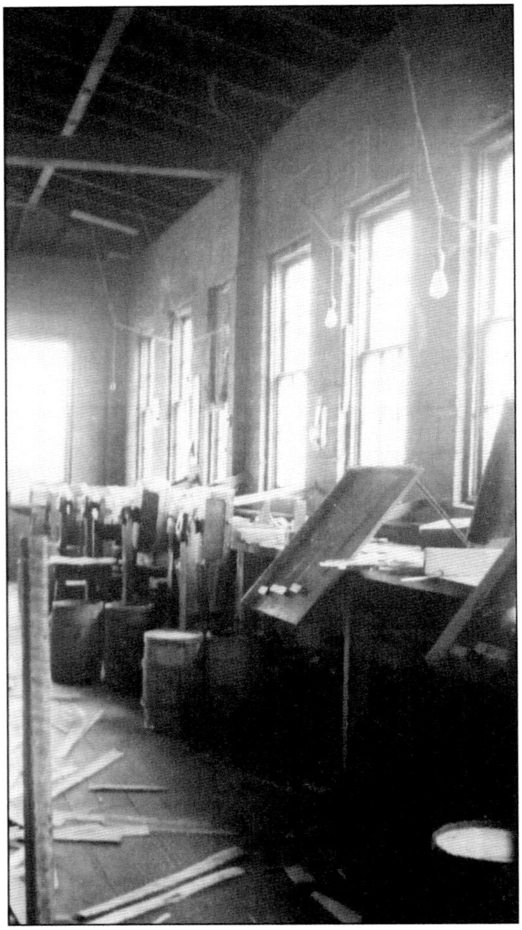

In 1914, partners Frank M. Covell and H. Sherman Pease finalized the lease of half a building on the southern end of the borough where they could grow their already thriving basket manufacturing business. This building already housed the McHugh Chair Factory owned by Patrick McHugh. It was known locally as the Chair and Basket Factory Building.

In April 1916, the town was shocked when a murder-suicide occurred at this factory. Following a fight in the engine room of their shared building, chair manufacturer Patrick McHugh shot and killed Frank Covell, part owner of Pease & Covell Basket Factory. McHugh then turned the gun on himself. The fight broke out when McHugh asked Covell to vacate the building, claiming that he wanted the whole space for his chair factory. This image shows a workroom of the basket factory.

These advertisements appeared around 1880 in a pamphlet that advertised Conneautville's businesses. As storefronts changed, the dates of their previous tenants were often not recorded. However, ads like these offer an exceptional look into the past.

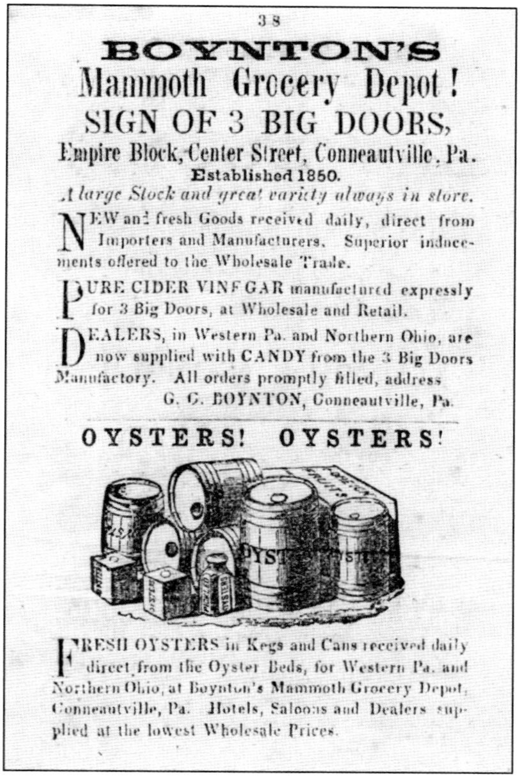

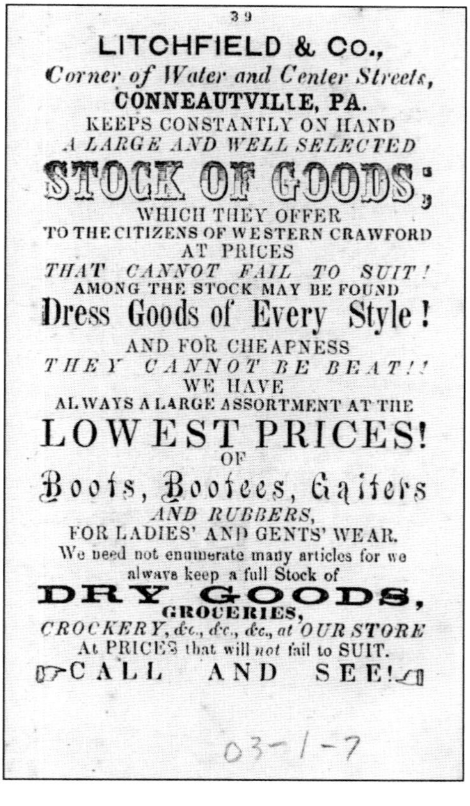

Eli Litchfield was a farmer and partner of O.O. Ticknor, who established a large mill in Conneautville. It's estimated that Litchfield opened a store along Main Street in the 1860s.

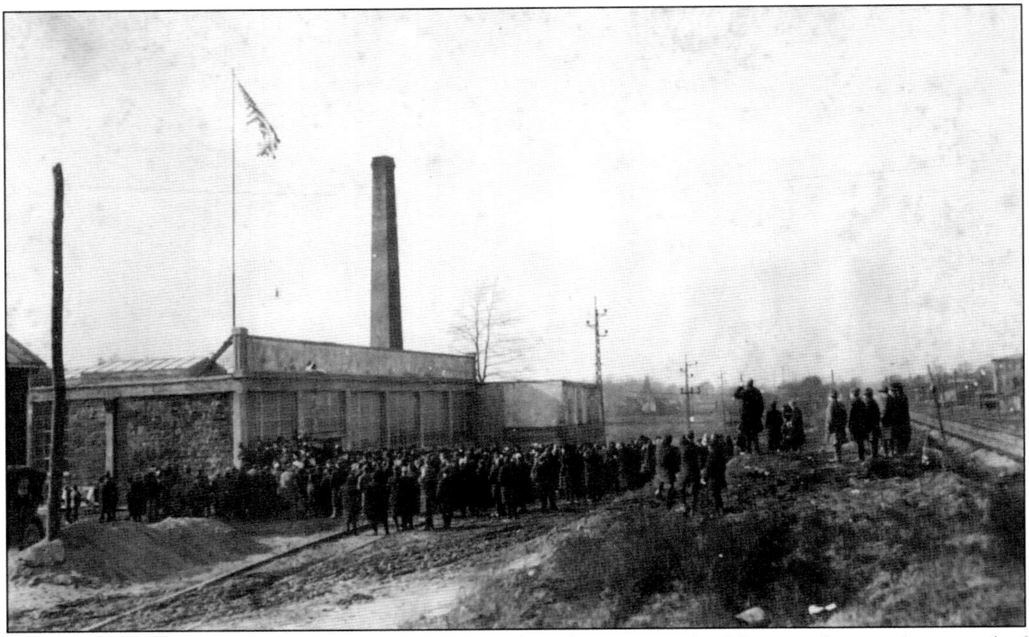

In 1918, the Burke Electric Company completed work on a new building at the southern end of town. After first occupying the third floor of the basket factory, Burke Electric moved into its new facility in November 1918. This picture shows people gathered to listen to a speech, most likely political. Scenes like this were common around town as politicians journeyed from factory to factory.

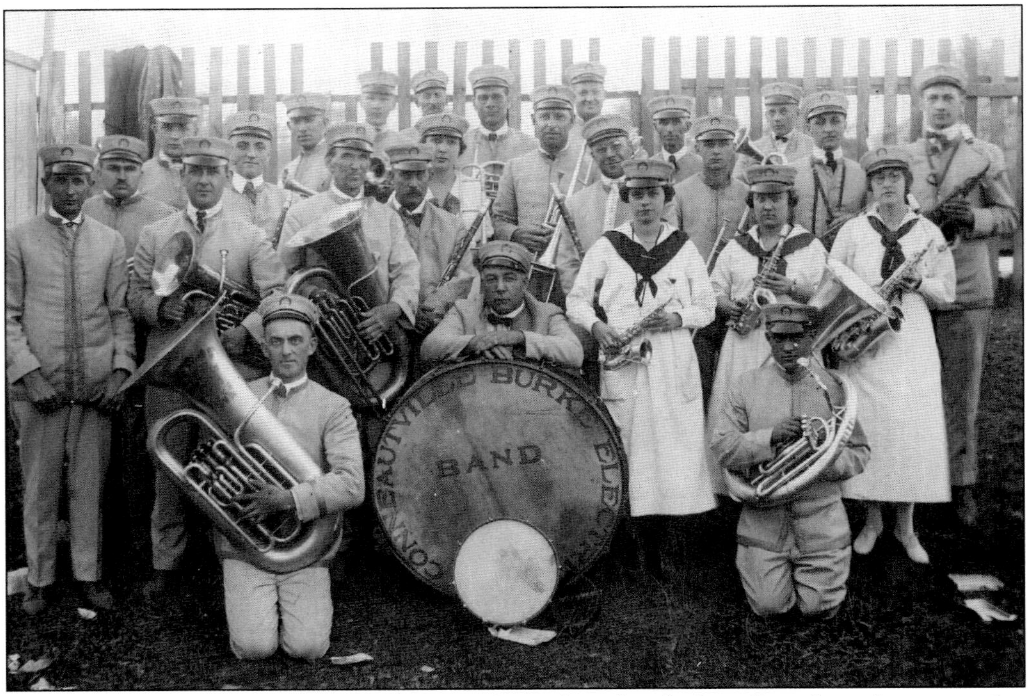

To keep workers' spirits up, factories often had marching bands that allowed employees to relax and entertain. Conneautville's businesses were no exception. This c. 1920s photograph shows the Conneautville Burke Electric band, which would march in parades and play at local events.

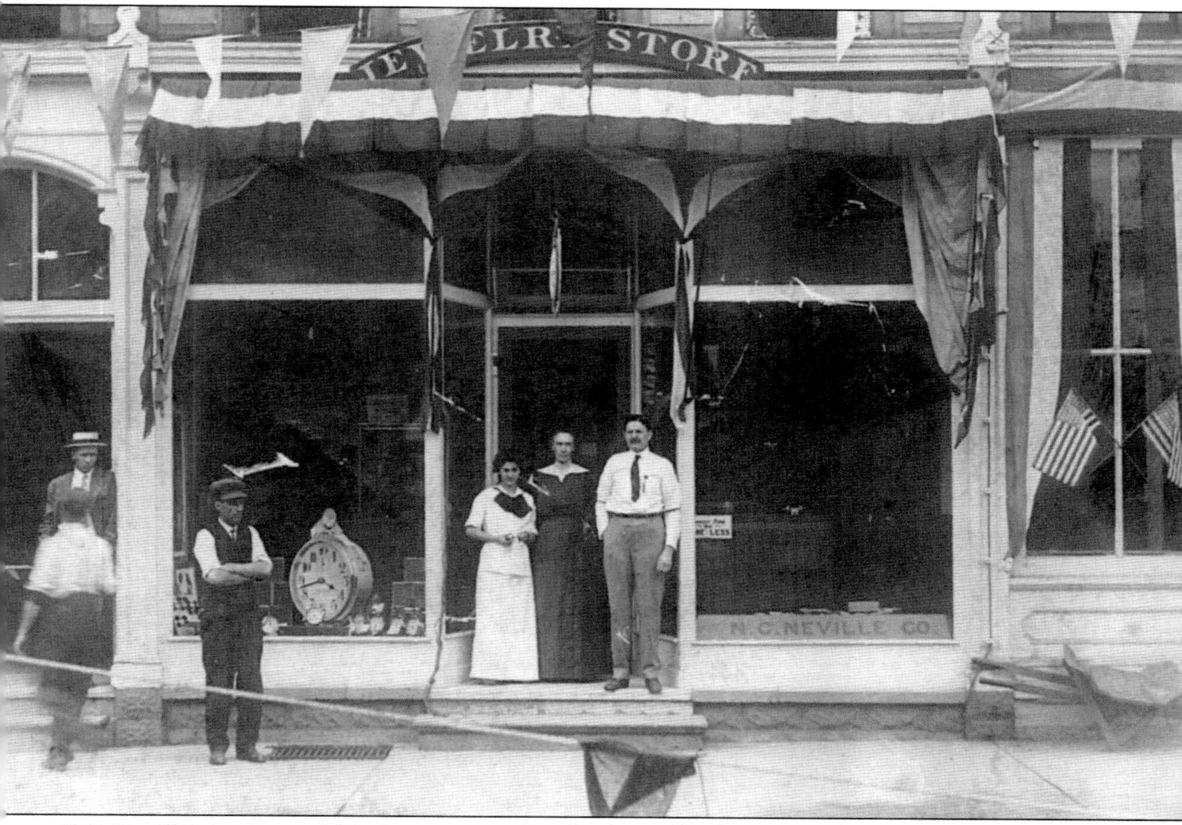

N.C. Neville's Jewelry and Clock store opened in the Opera Block in 1884, playing a significant role in Conneautville's prosperity. The items carried in this store included diamonds, watches, clocks, jewelry, cut glass, and toilet and manicure novelties. Watch and clock repair were also important branches of the business, as well as Mr. Neville's hobby of eye care. The *Courier* writes of the business, "The equipment in the optical department includes an opthalmoscope and retnoscope and in fact all modern facilities for testing and correcting the vision. Mr. Neville gives his personal supervision to this work and his ability as an optometrist is unquestioned. The company is composed of N.C. and his wife Irene Neville. Mr. Neville has always taken a keen interest in public affairs. He has served as a member of the Borough Council, is an enthusiastic member of the Board of Commerce, and can always be found among the foremost in any progressive movement."

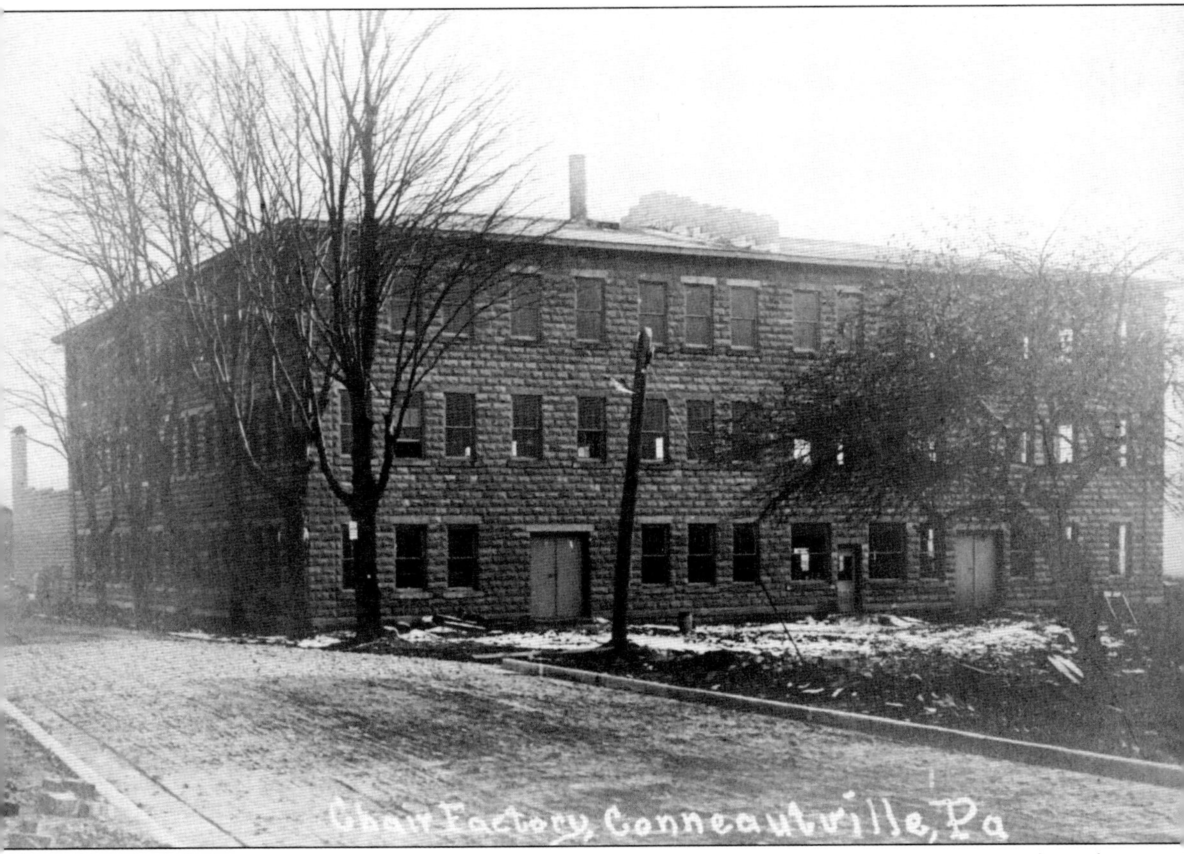

Around 1920, Frank Snyder purchased the basket factory and continued the production of wooden folding chairs, which had become popular around 1900, during Patrick McHugh's ownership of the facility. In 1922, Snyder bought a building along High Street, moved his chair-making business, and soon after began construction on a building that would double the size of his current factory. A *Conneautville Courier* article from June 28, 1922, reported that "Mr. Snyder took up some time ago the making of a chair similar to the McHugh folding chair and has made improvements upon his product until he has now what is considered the best non-tippable small folding chair in the entire market. He expects soon to close one contract for 10,000 of the chairs."

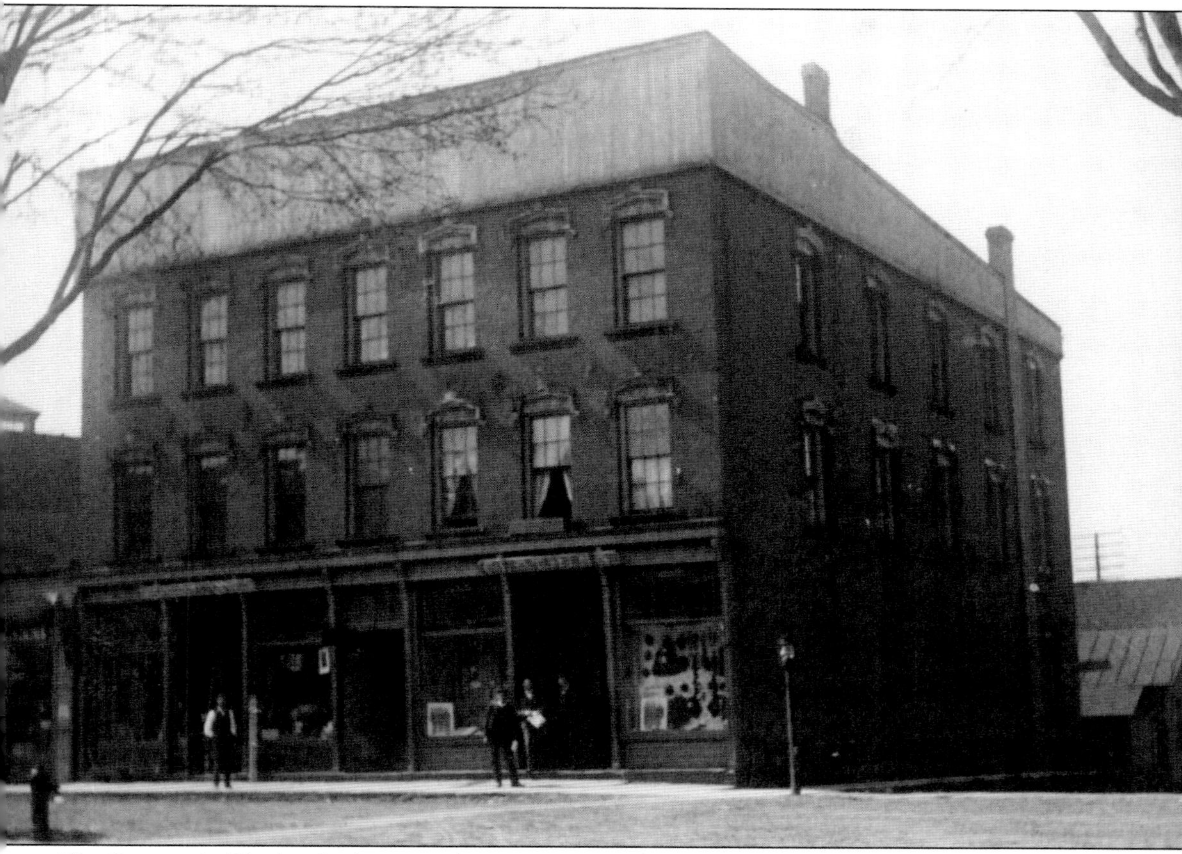

The Courtright Block, which sits on the intersection of Main and Pearl Streets, has a mysterious history. The deed states that Cornelius Courtright sold the property to F.A. Temple on November 23, 1849, at a price of $100. However, the date of the building's construction was not noted. In 1947, owner Charles G. Melcher had the third floor removed because it was causing the building to lean. This third floor once housed the Masonic Lodge and Independent Order of Odd Fellows. Dinners, dances, and celebrations were often held in the space.

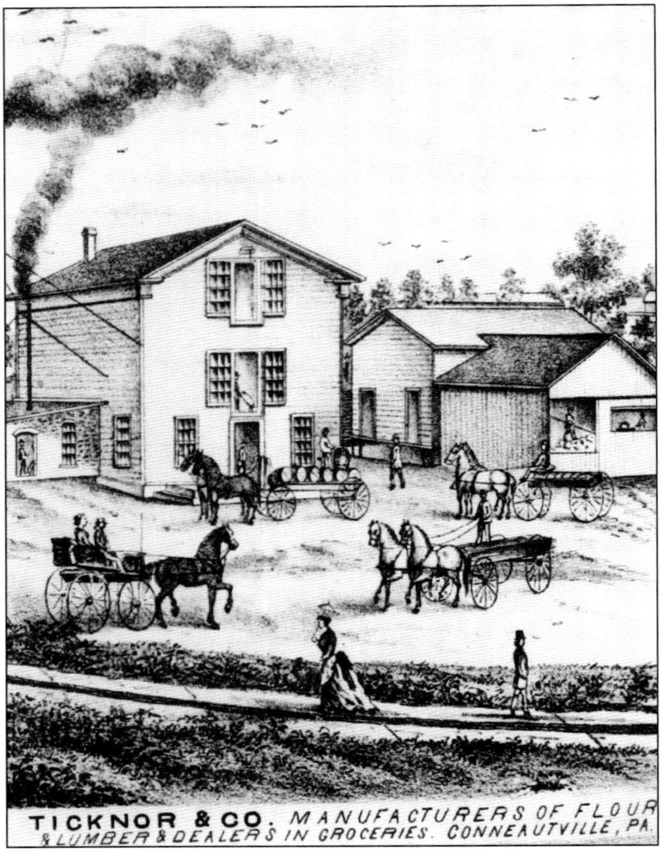

O.O. Ticknor and E.L. Litchfield purchased the Forest Grist Mill in 1857, enlarging its operation as a flour and sawmill. The property contained a brick engine house—capable of producing 80 horsepower—that supplied water and steam to the milling wheels. The mill flourished during the days of the canal, with lumber becoming its most lucrative product.

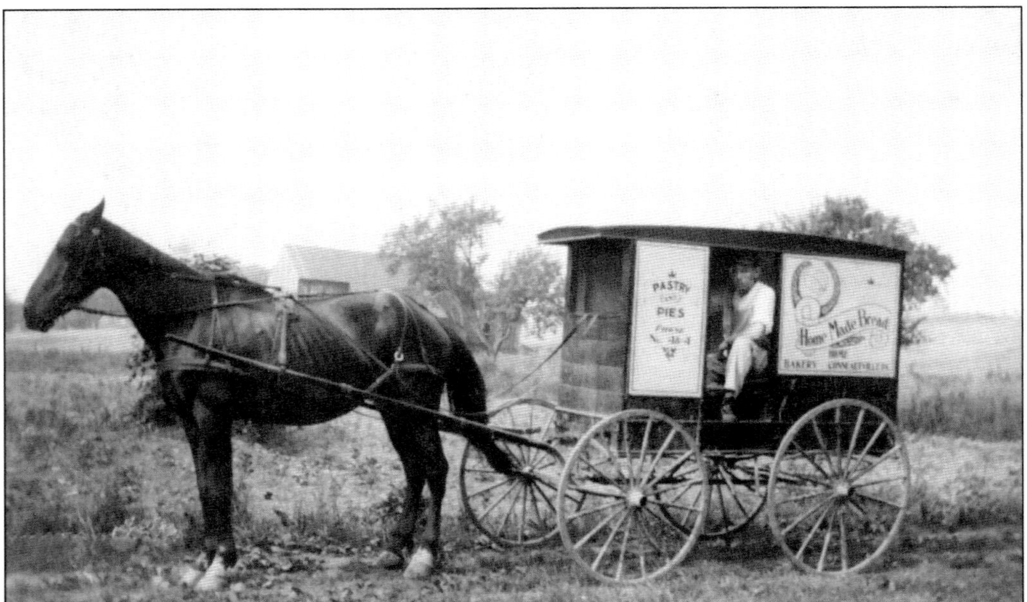

Prior to the advent of the motor vehicle, businesses relied on horse-drawn carriages to reach their customers. Lowell "Shorty" Adkins, pictured here, traveled the Conneautville area delivering bakery items from Adkins Bakery.

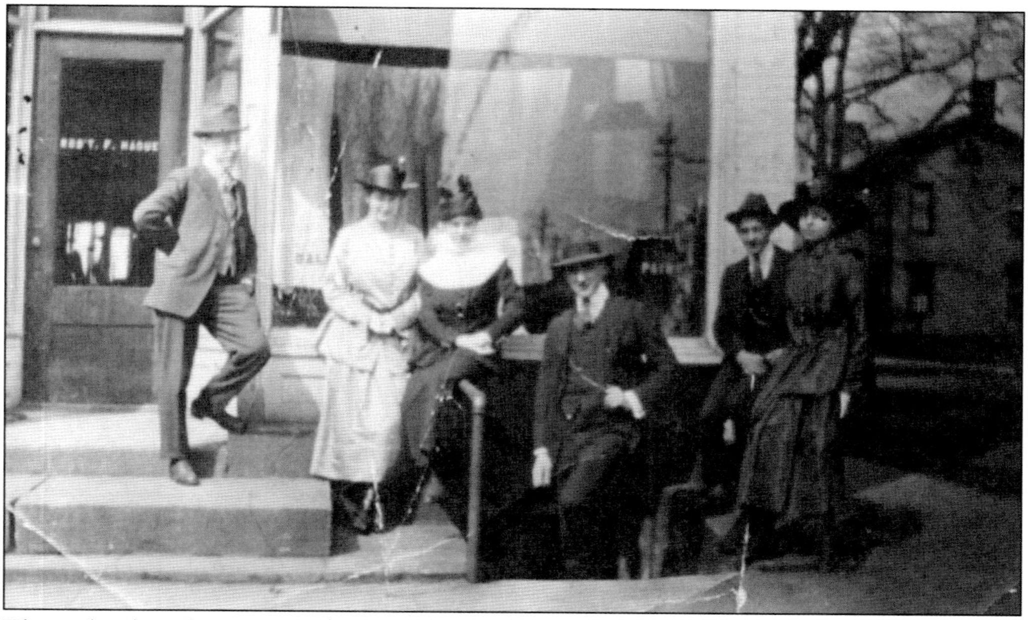

The only identification on this picture reads: "photographed in front of Robert P. Hague Furniture." Robert P. Hague was a Conneautville businessman who occupied a storeroom in the Robinson Block around 1915. He sold numerous household items at this location, including furniture and appliances.

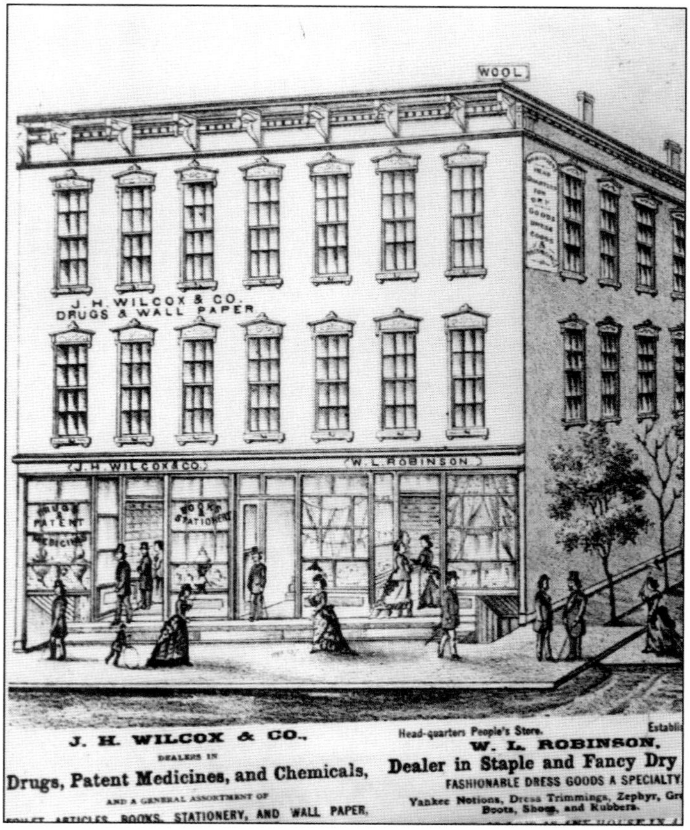

The Robinson Block has been home to numerous shops, restaurants, and social organizations. It was built around 1860 and has changed little over the last 150 years.

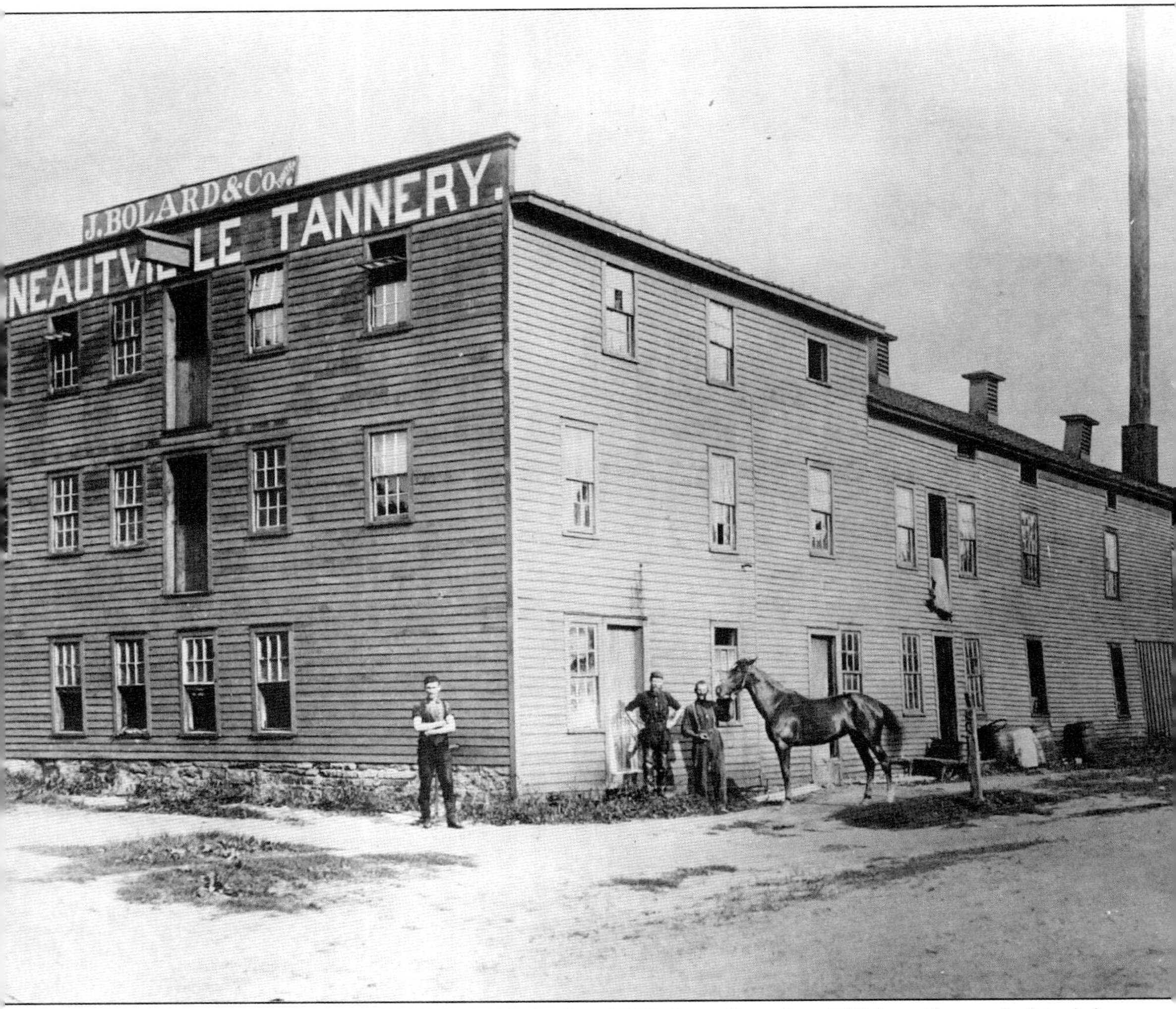

Jacob Bolard & Co. Tannery was established in 1868 along Canal and Walnut Streets behind the present Valley United Methodist Church. A large factory for the time, the tannery stood three stories high and was capable of producing 4,000 hides per year. Jacob Bolard had an excellent reputation among leather dealers and his sales reached as far east as Boston. Having become successful, Bolard opened a second tannery in Springboro in 1875 and a third in Cambridge Springs in 1897. Although the business in Conneautville was his first, Bolard's Cambridge factory soon grew to become his most successful. Since it was necessary for Bolard to spend a majority of his time in Cambridge, the Conneautville Tannery began to decline and was soon abandoned. This photograph of the Conneautville tannery was taken around 1880.

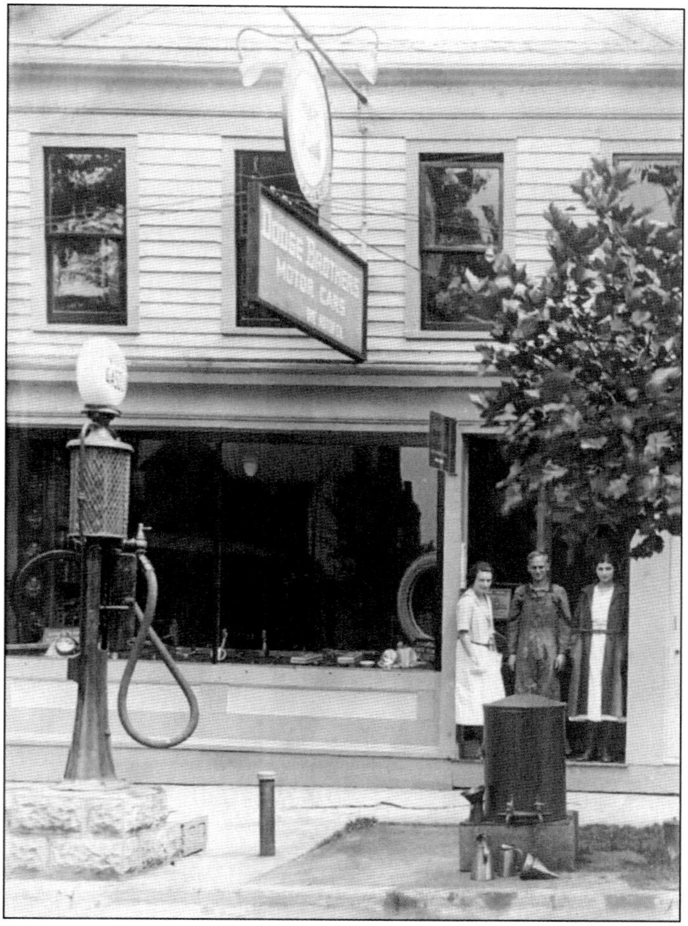

The Dodge Brothers car parts store and gas station operated out of a frame structure along Main Street. The place where this building stood is now the vacant lot to the right of the American Legion. The Ben Dye family, pictured, occupied the second floor apartment.

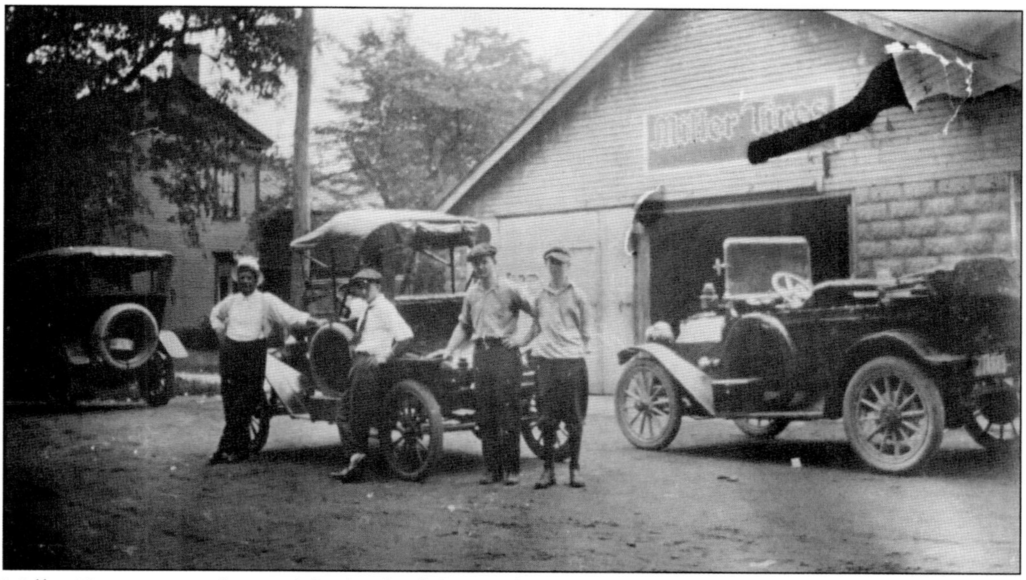

Miller Tires operated out of the back of the Dodge Brothers building. The company specialized in tires but also repaired motor vehicles. This image was taken sometime in the 1930s.

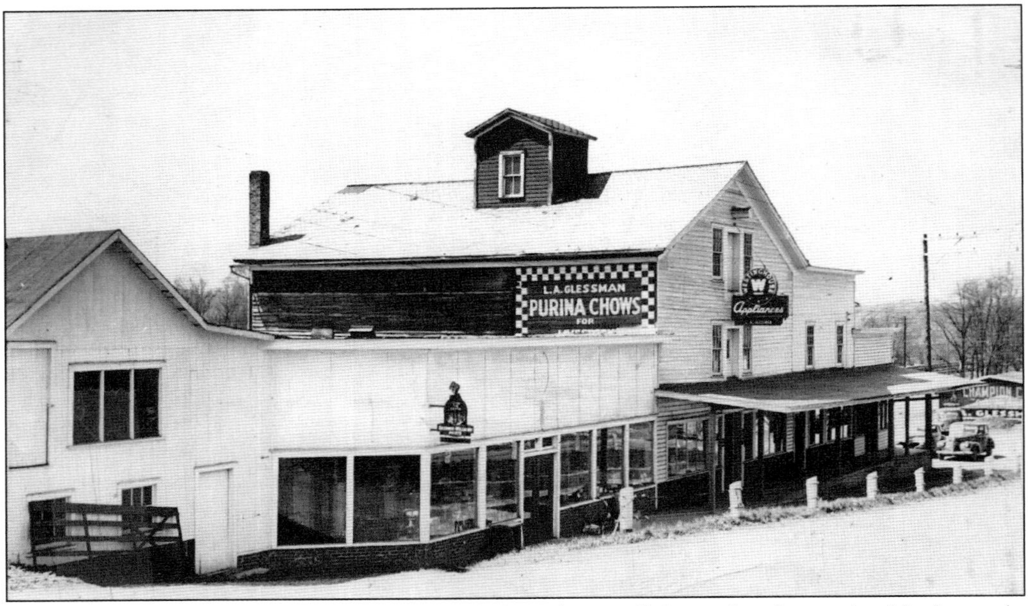

In 1918, L.A. Glessman purchased the former O.O. Ticknor mill, located in the south of the borough. Along with his sons Howard and Alton, Glessman operated this business as both a mill and a general store. They sold coal, mixed feeds, fertilizers, paints, tools, and eventually electric appliances. On the night of July 6, 1977, the building was destroyed when a lightning strike set it on fire.

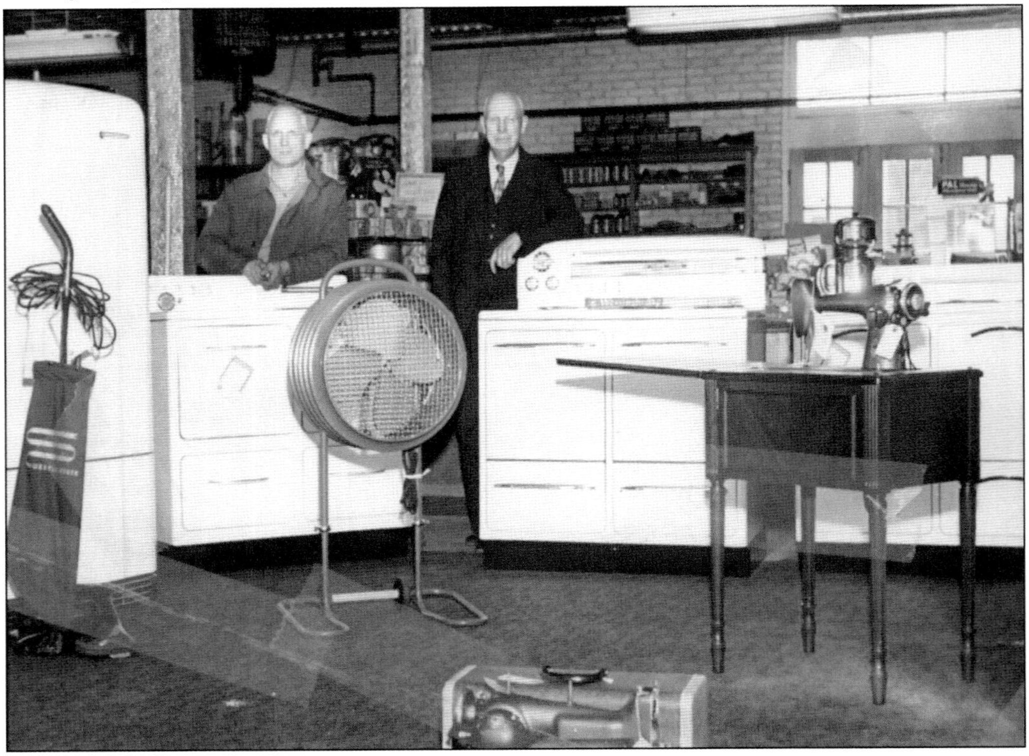

Owner L.A. Glessman (right) and an unknown man stand in the store among Glessman's plentiful appliances. For many years, Glessman's was the trusted place to purchase household and farming equipment.

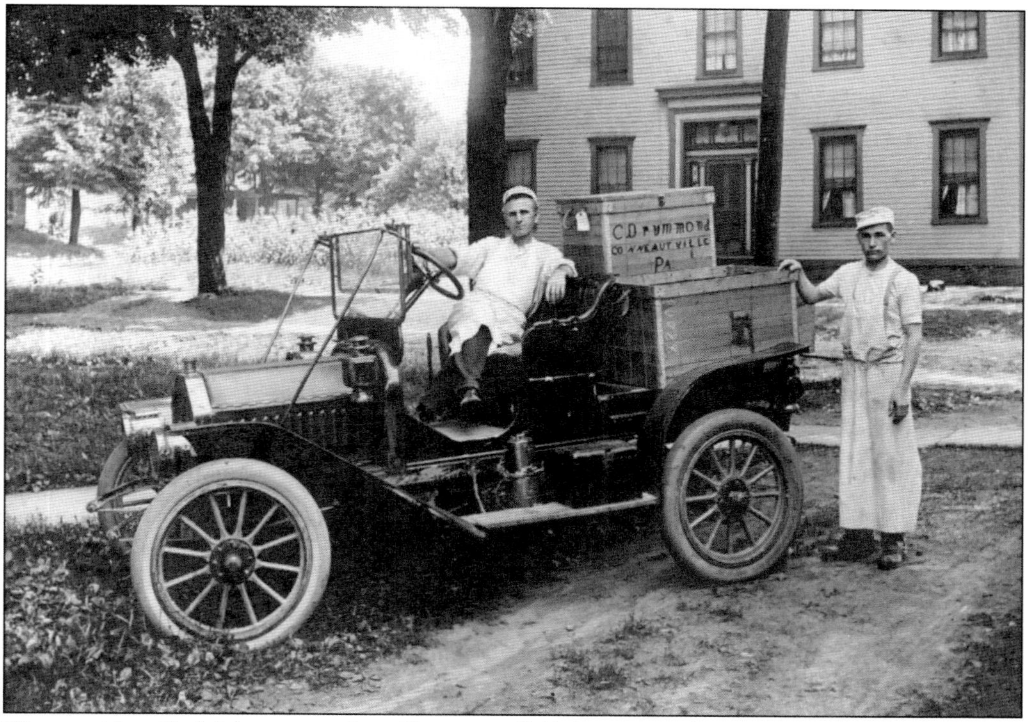

These unidentified deliverymen from Drummond's Bakery were photographed after loading their vehicle in 1916.

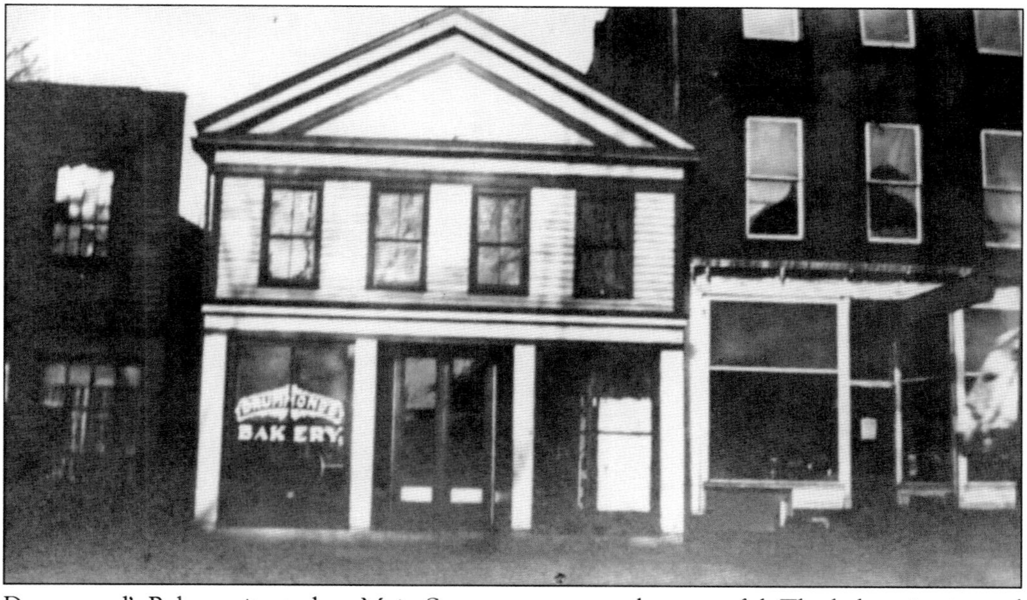

Drummond's Bakery, situated on Main Street, was extremely successful. The bakery is pictured here in 1916.

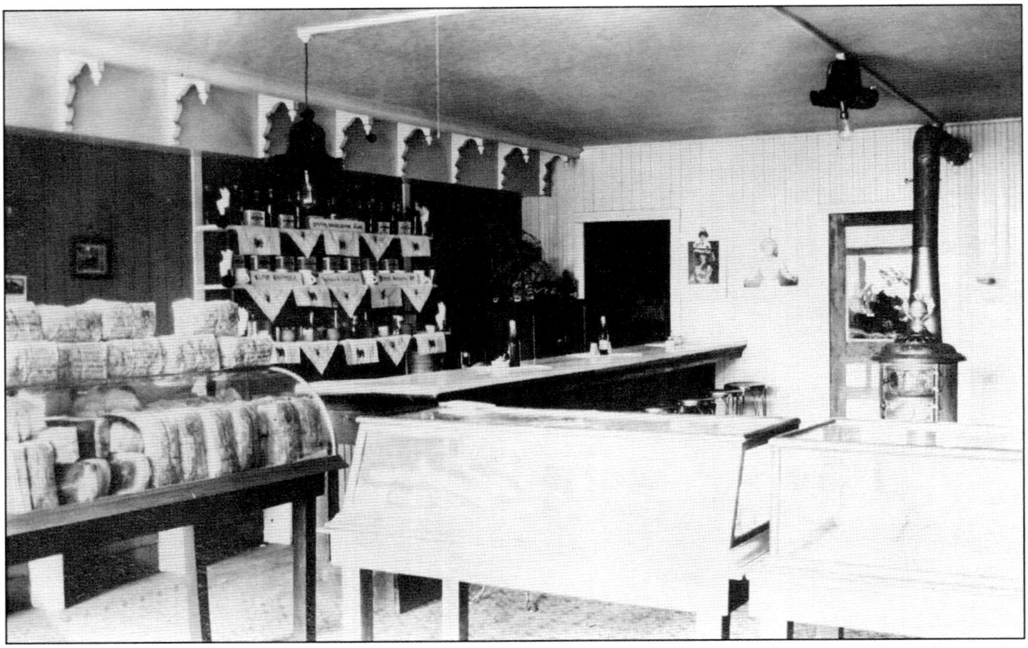

The inside of Drummond's featured all the necessities of a typical bakery. This 1916 image shows the display cases stuffed with breads ready for sale. Today, this building is home to the Valley Inn.

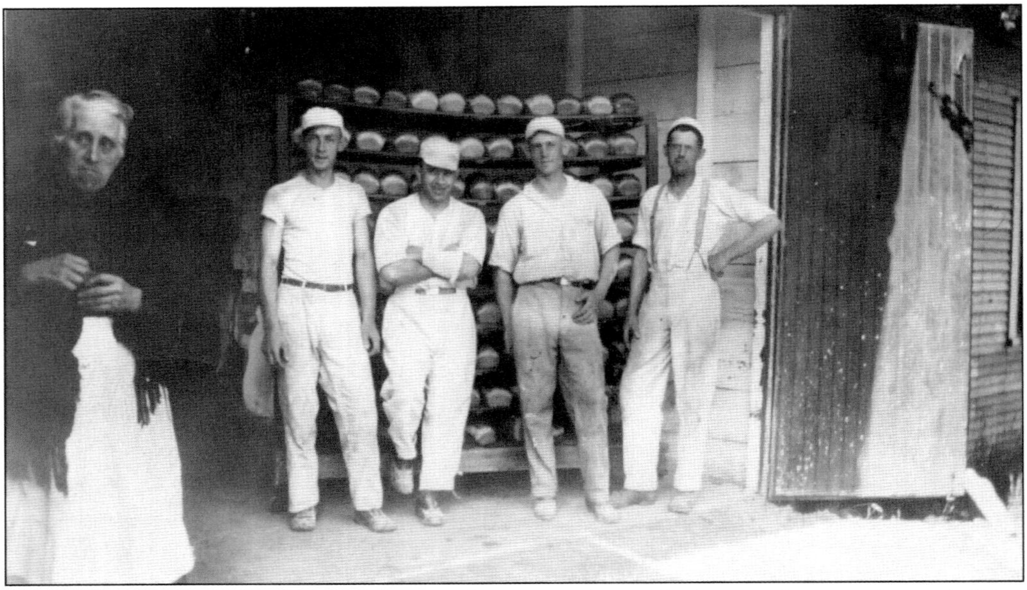

Conneautville has been home to a significant number of bakeries. Among them, Adkins Bakery has been the most famous. The business began in a structure along Shermansville Road where items were exclusively made for home delivery. Pictured here are, from left to right, unidentified, W.H. Adkins, Leo "Mike" Adkins, and two unidentified employees outside the bakery on Shermansville Road.

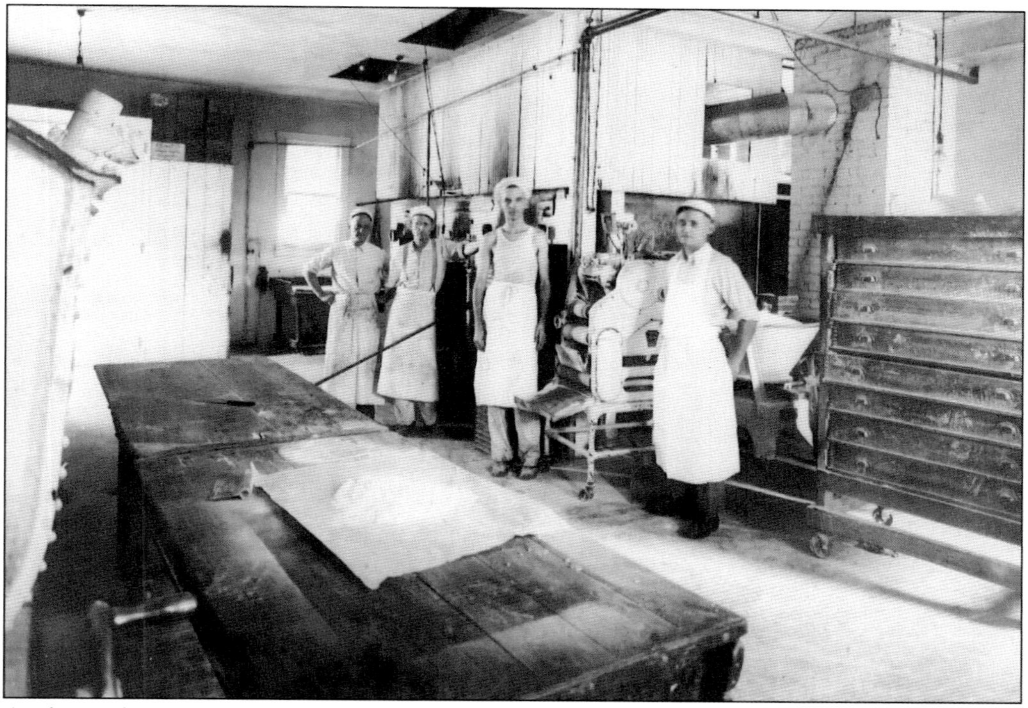

As demand increased, Adkins moved production to a new facility on Main Street where they could sell their items in a retail environment. Pictured above, from left to right, are Mike Adkins, Elton Ellis, Pat Sheehan, and Leland Adkins. Between Pat and Leland is a new rolling machine used to shape loaves of bread. Below, Leland Adkins and Gladys Ford are ready to serve customers in the bakery's storefront.

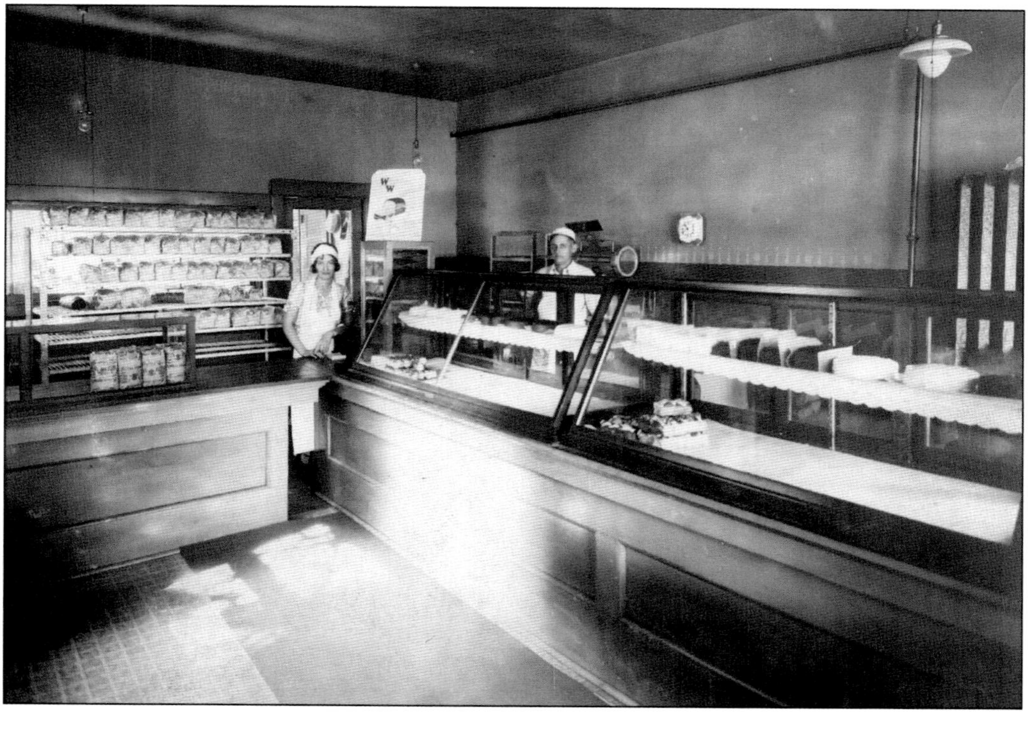

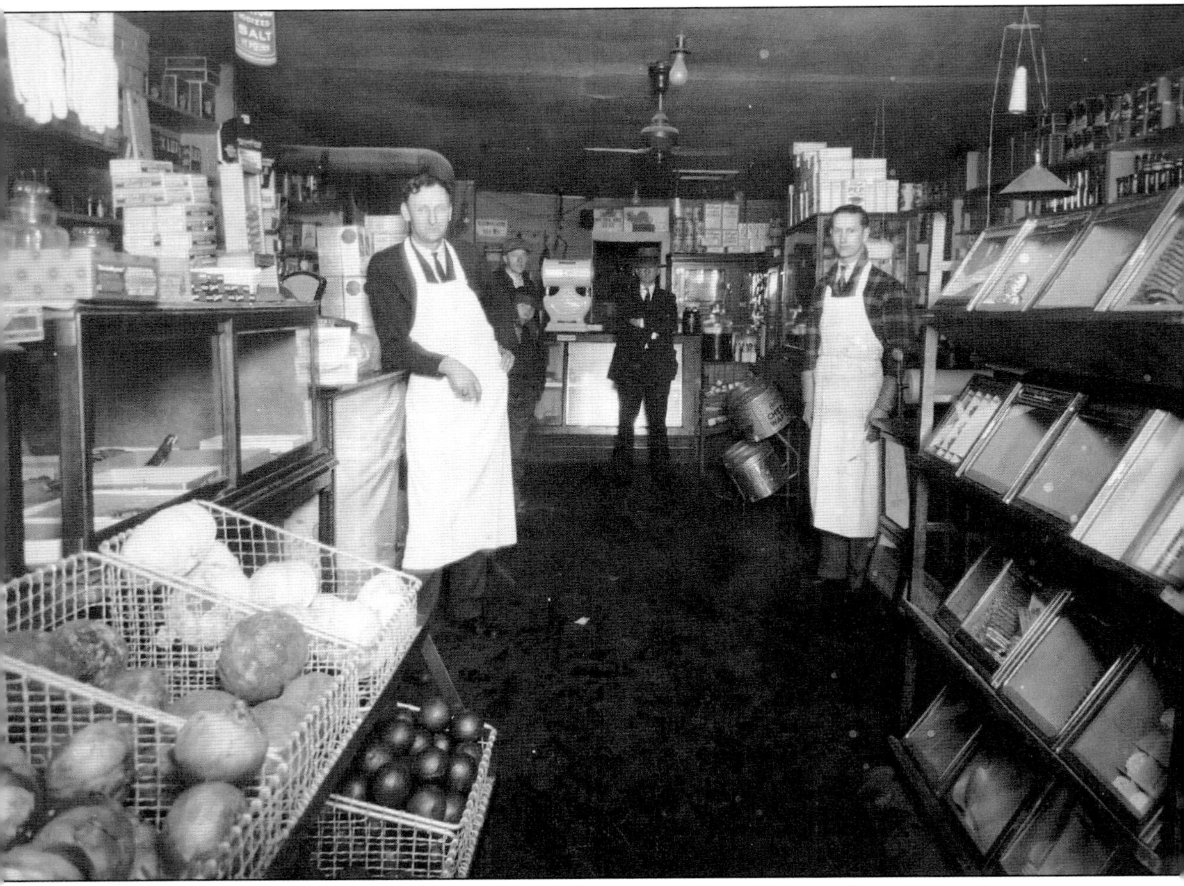

The Klinginsmith Meat Market was located next to Adkins Bakery along Main Street, an area that is now a vacant lot. This market offered a wide variety of foods and specialized in selling bulk quantities. Pictured in this image are Harry Sherlock (left) and Mr. Klinginsmith (rear center); the others are unidentified.

Three

School and Church

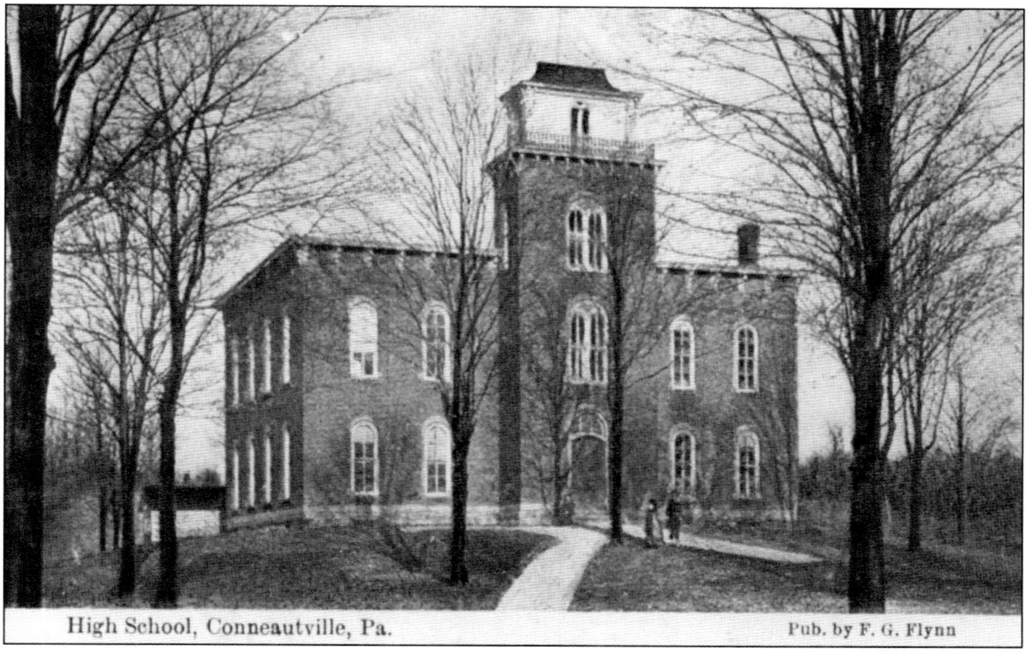

On April 11, 1849, a charter was granted by Crawford County Court to Conneautville for the purpose of opening an institution of higher learning. The Academy, as it came to be known, occupied a four-room building on the present site of Saint Peter Church. The Academy served as a school until 1867, when this structure was built at the intersection of Washington and Center Streets at a cost of $20,000. Conneautville High School, as it was known, was situated on the present site of Lord-Mason Memorial Park, and first consisted of seven rooms. In 1916, the building had a large, two-story addition tacked on.

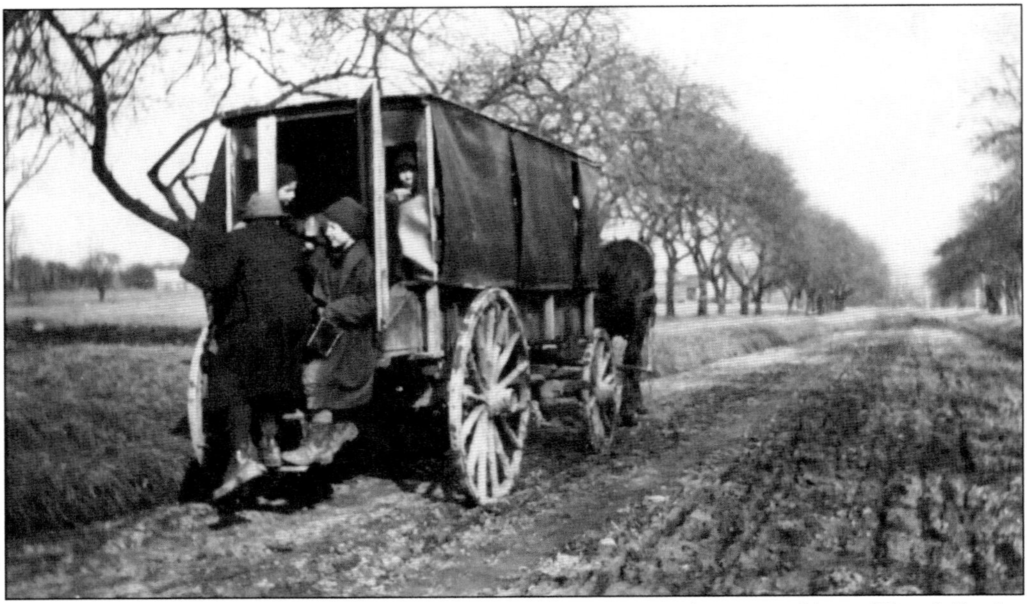

In education, getting the students to school has sometimes caused many problems. This difficulty was enhanced in rural areas where many students lived on farms far away from their school buildings. Conneautville's school would have certainly utilized a horse-drawn carriage similar to this to pick students up. This image shows a "school bus" taking students to Rundell's School outside of Conneautville's borough.

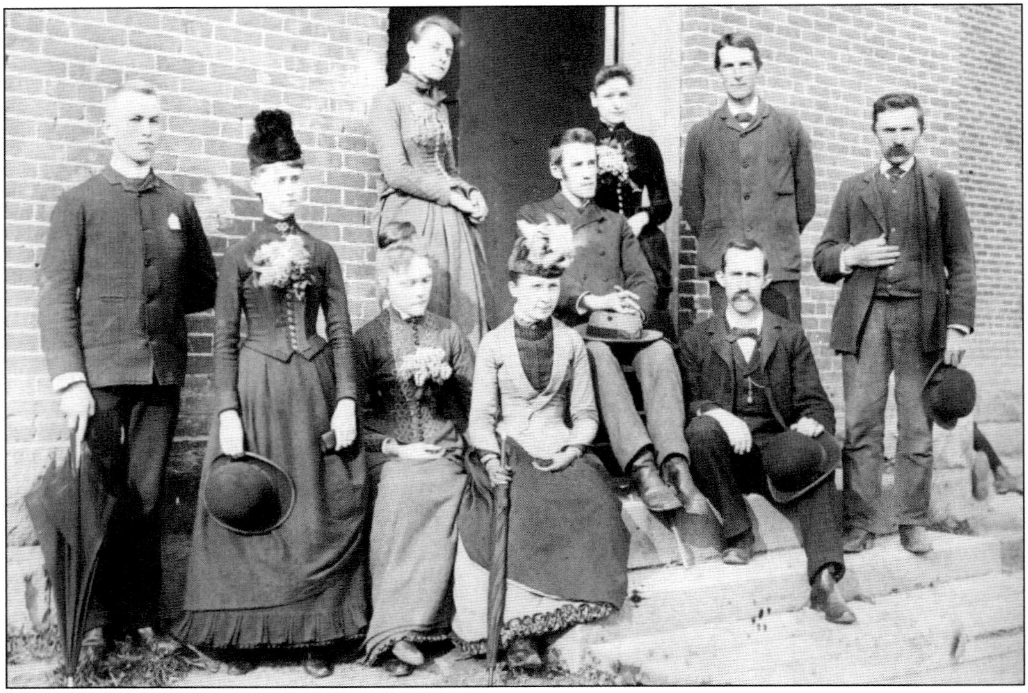

The three graduating seniors of Conneautville High School in 1889 pose here alongside faculty. The graduates are (front left) John Brooks, Daisy Derby, and Lulu McGuire. Faculty include Professor Edwin T. Mason (principal), Professor Carlisle (assistant principal), Professor J.G. McBride, and teachers with last names including Billings, Robinson, Clancy, and Moore.

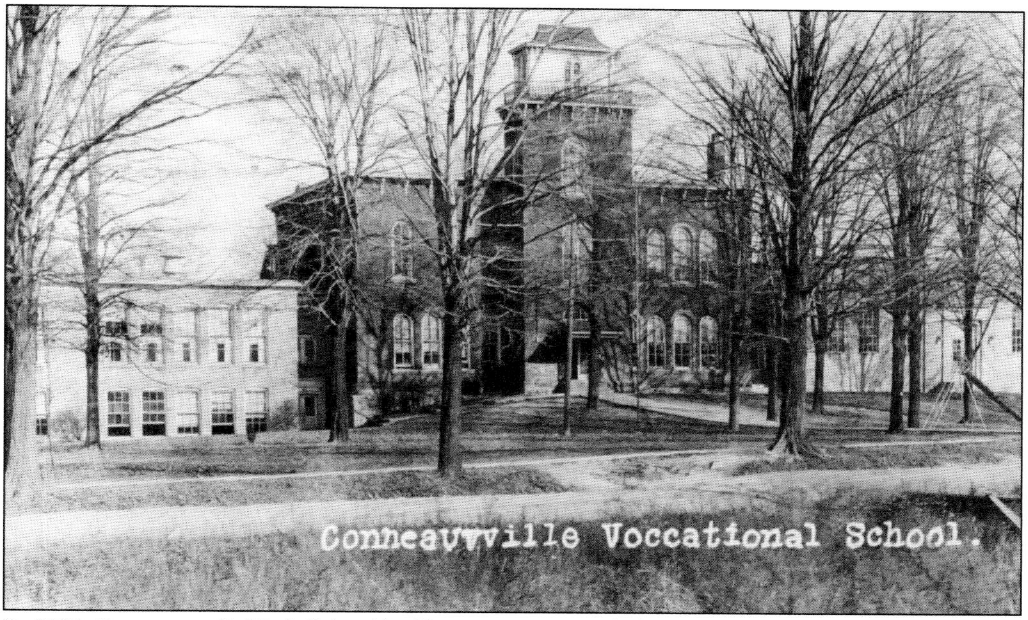

By 1916, Conneautville High School had become overcrowded. A steady rise in the local population had increased the need for a more spacious and modern school building. A significant change occurred that year when ground was broken for a two-story addition that would be situated on the northern side of the existing structure. This new wing would house the vocational and specialized trade departments as well as modern larger classrooms. The building is pictured above in 1950; below is an aerial view of the grounds with the football field.

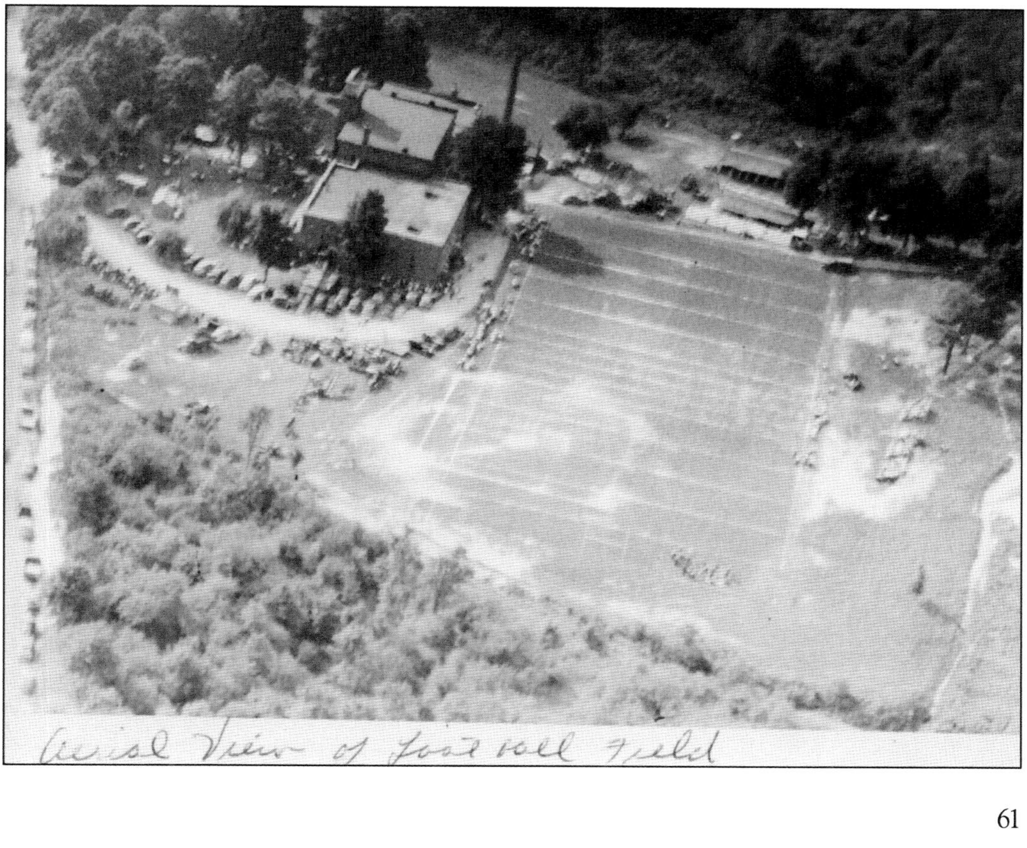

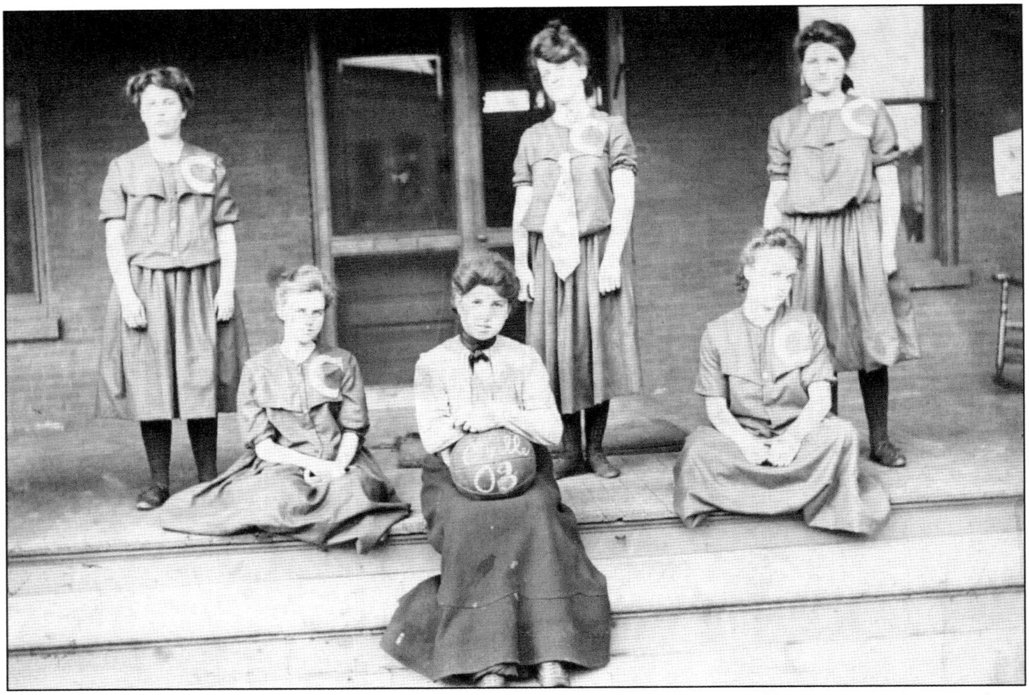

An early Conneautville High School girls' basketball team is pictured here in 1903. Listed on the back of the photograph are the names Frances Hewitt, Fida Hewitt, Edna Nichols, Hayes Neville, and A. Clair Penfield.

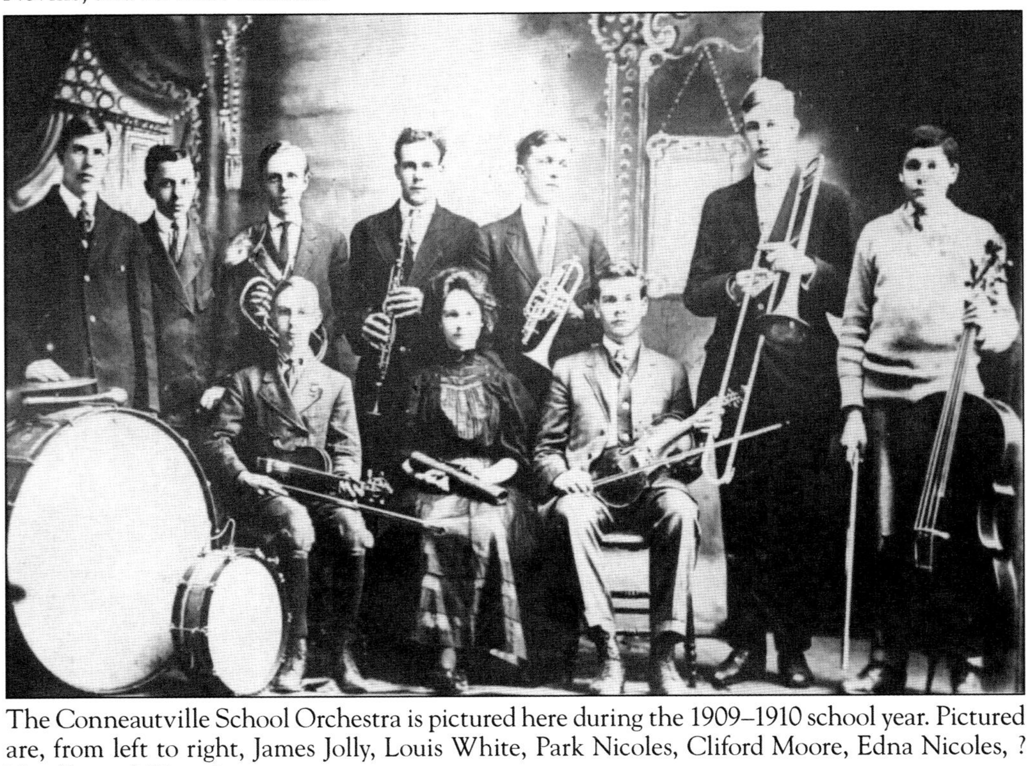

The Conneautville School Orchestra is pictured here during the 1909–1910 school year. Pictured are, from left to right, James Jolly, Louis White, Park Nicoles, Cliford Moore, Edna Nicoles, ? Neville, and Clare ?.

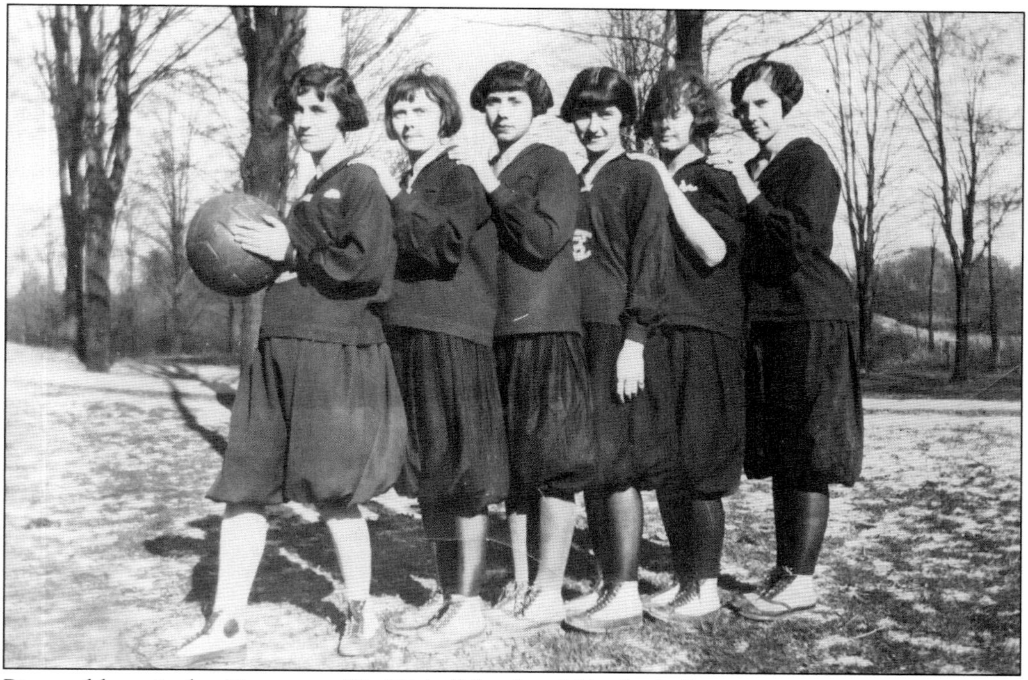

Pictured here is the Conneautville High School girls' basketball team in 1925. They are, from left to right, Anita Morell, Georgia Awald, Mable Townsend, Anna Phelps, Esther Bauer, and Hazel Jones. At this time, the school had yet to build a gymnasium. These women practiced and played in the Opera House. After clearing the seats, the space was large enough to fit a court. However, they also had to dodge the columns that supported the structure.

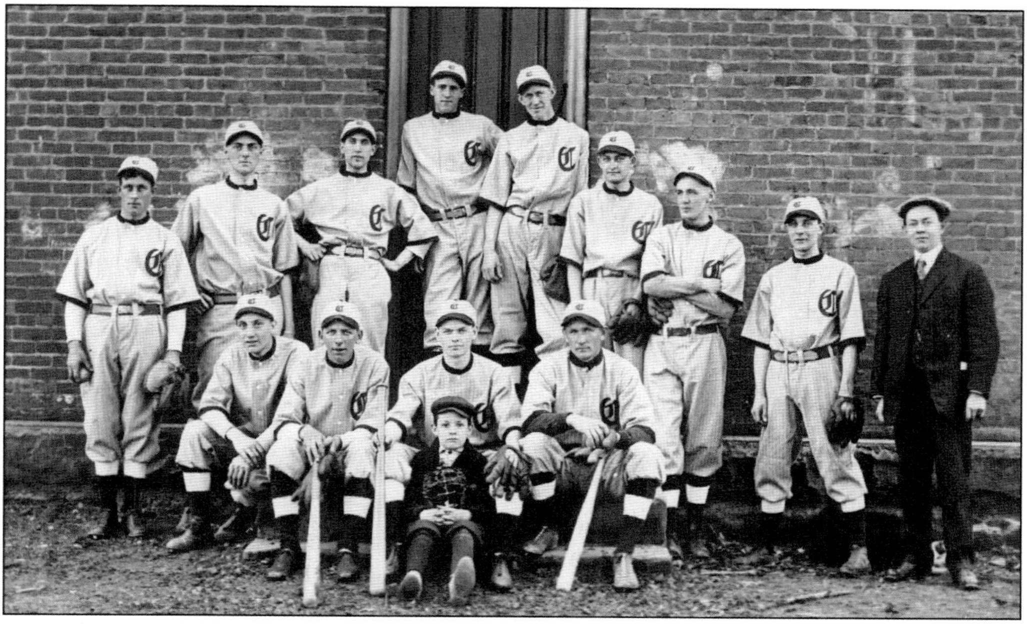

An early Conneautville School baseball team poses for an undated photograph. The photograph is captioned with the names R.B. Davids, Scoop Rager, Owin Kirk, Lars Hagerstrom, Ned Fuller, Carson Clancy, Clifford McKay, Nelson Ross, Carl Dove, John Carr, Marr Hammond, Paul Maxler, Harry Correy, and Byron Knapp.

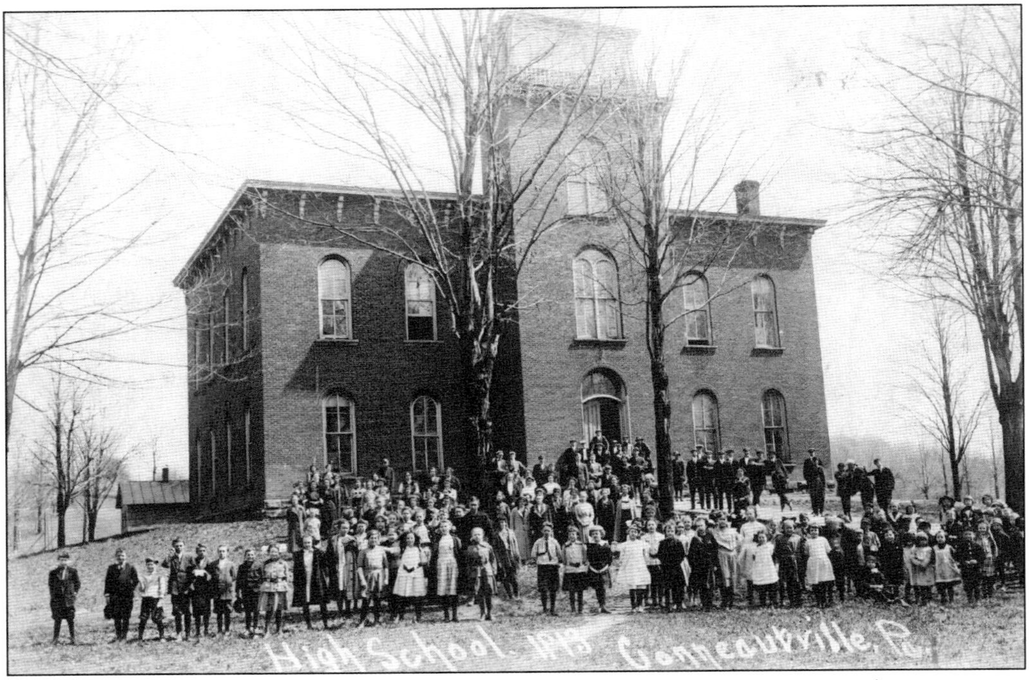

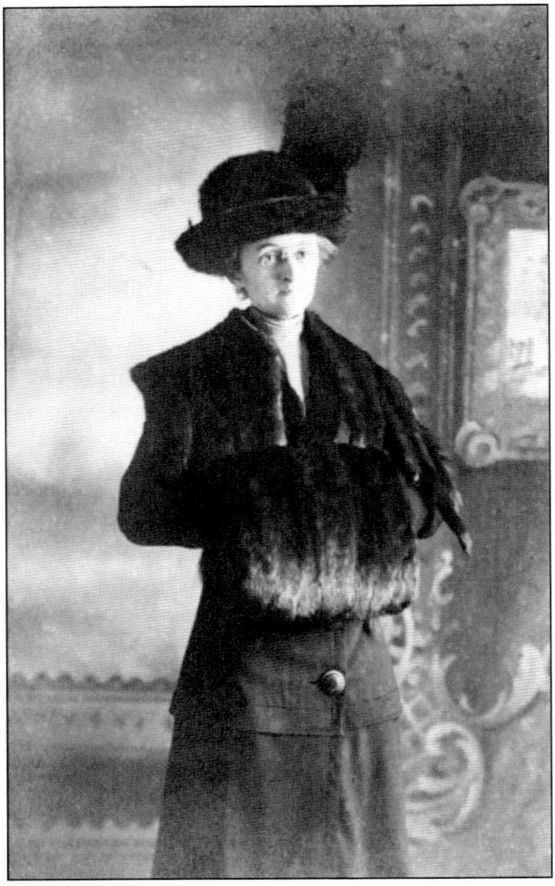

Throughout its existence, the Conneautville School held classes for children of all ages. This picture shows the entire school on the front lawn in 1913–1914. This structure could safely accommodate 150 students.

In 1906, Sadie Johnson began teaching third and fourth grade in Conneautville. She worked as a teacher for the next 40 years and was a beloved figure in the community. She retired on May 30, 1946.

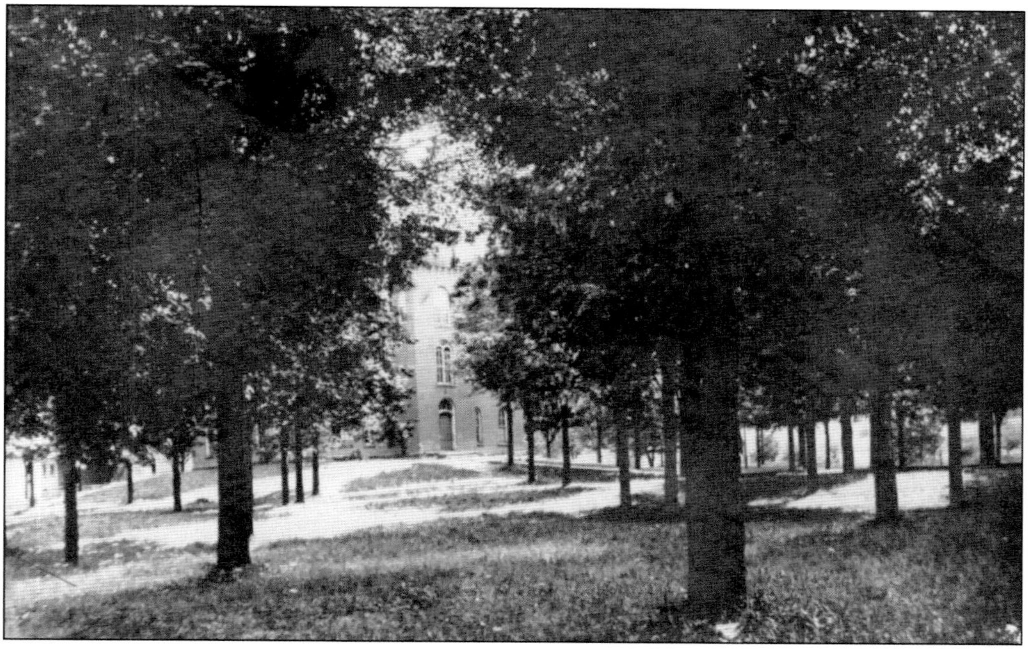

Around 1850, students were planting trees on the school grounds when Thomas Henretta stopped by and asked if he could help. Holding a hickory sapling, Henretta proclaimed that he was planting the tree in honor of "Old Hickory," the nickname of Pres. Andrew Jackson. The tree, which once stood in the north corner of the park, is believed to be the only monument in Conneautville to a U.S. president. Above, the school is nearly invisible through the trees. Below, students enjoy a beautiful day outside while playing under the many trees on the school grounds.

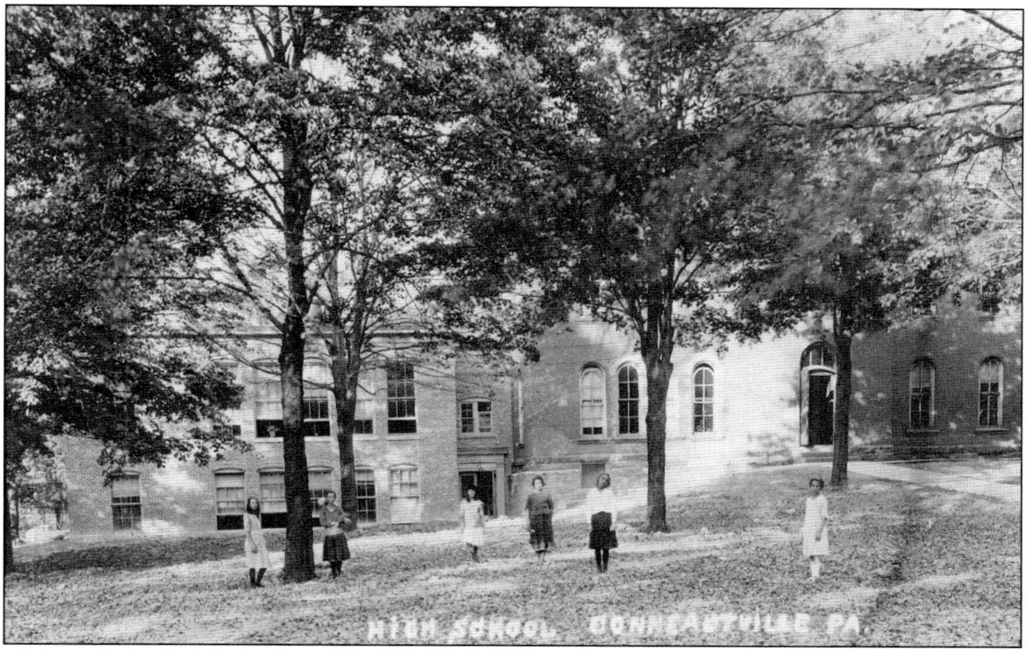

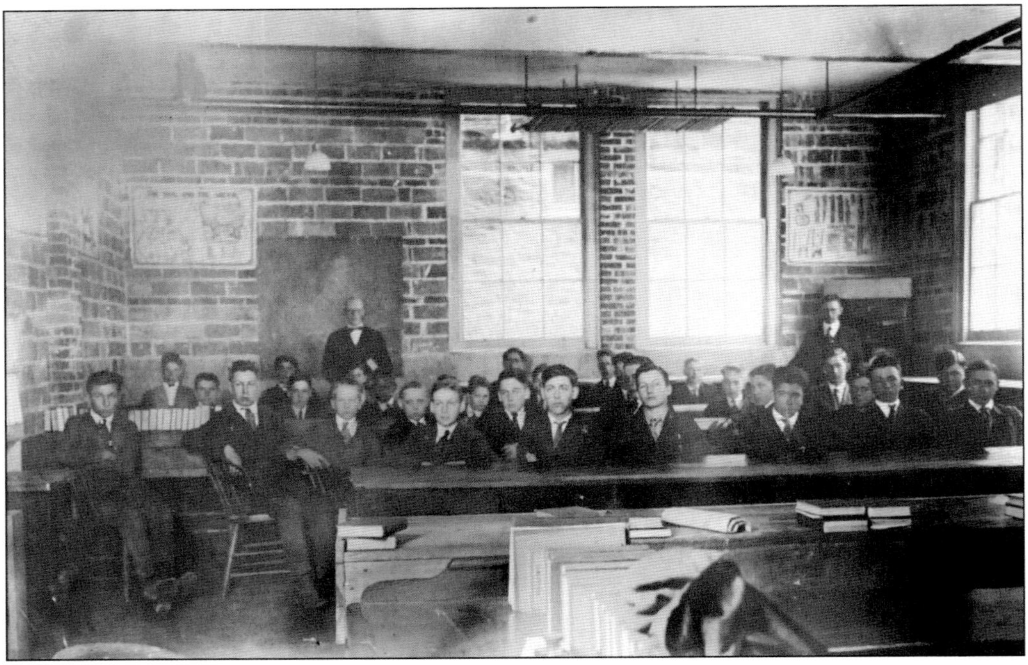

The fact that photographs were taken of this agriculture class suggests that the rooms were state of the art for the time. It was customary, in early years of education, to separate male and female classes depending on the trades that were studied.

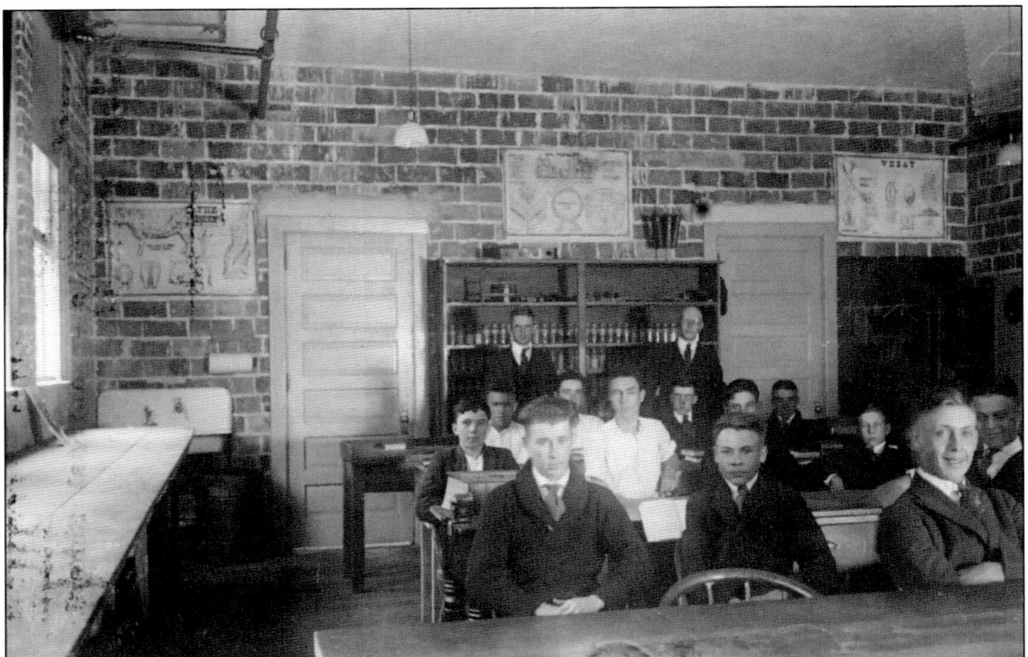

At first, Conneautville High School lacked the need for specialized classrooms. However, after the addition of the vocational wing, new agriculture classes offered these students a more focused curriculum.

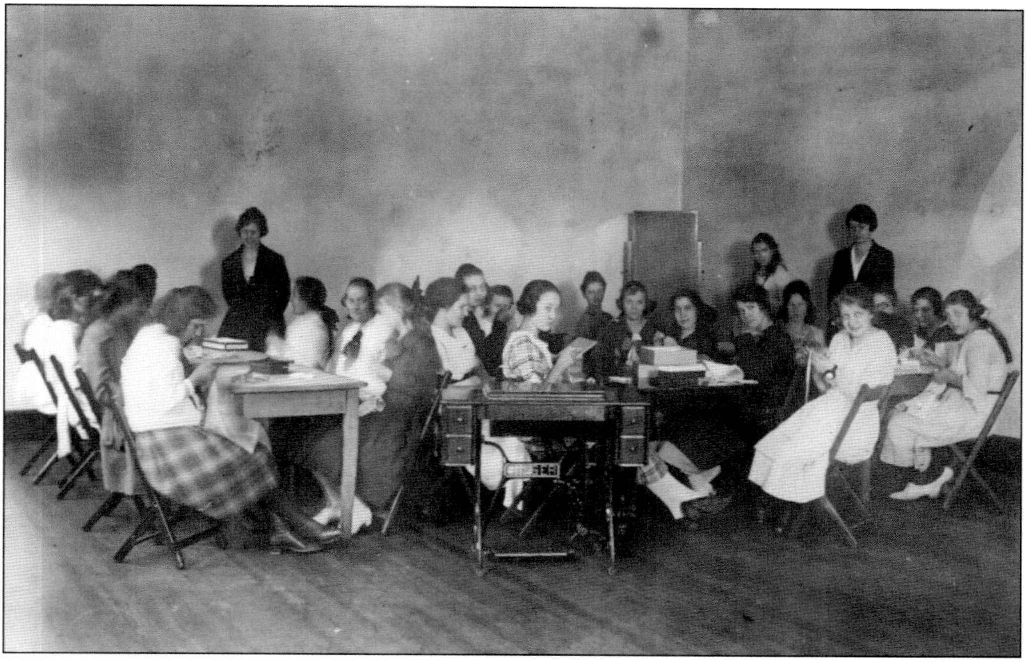

Sewing was an important aspect of home economics education. The students seen here had the luxury of a single sewing machine.

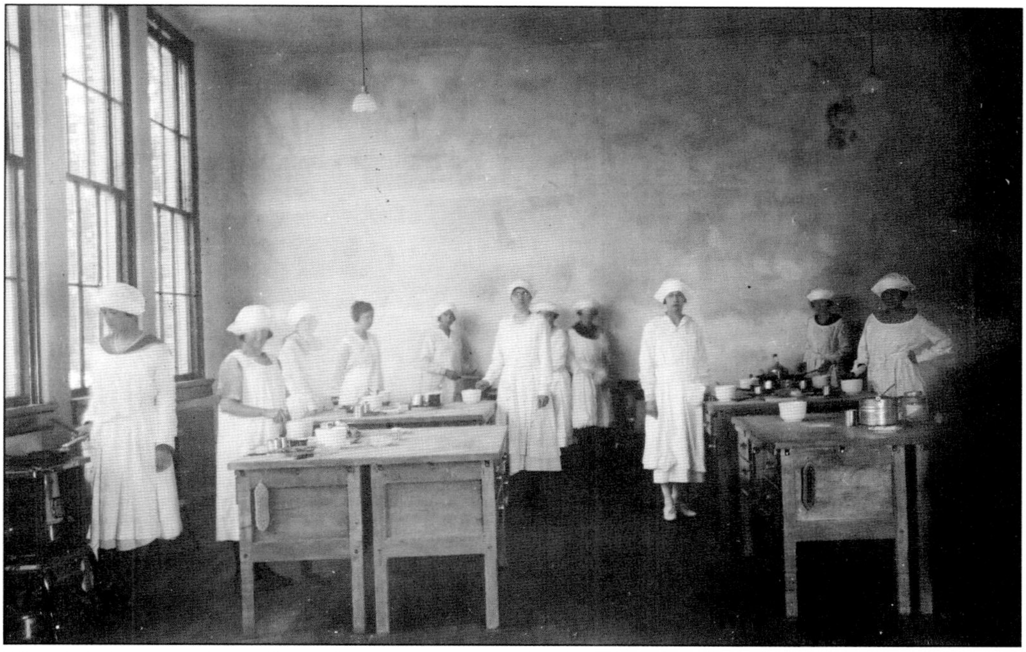

This faded image of a cooking class gives a unique look into the world of early culinary education. A caption on the back of this image reads: "The ultramodern home economics room in the vocational school."

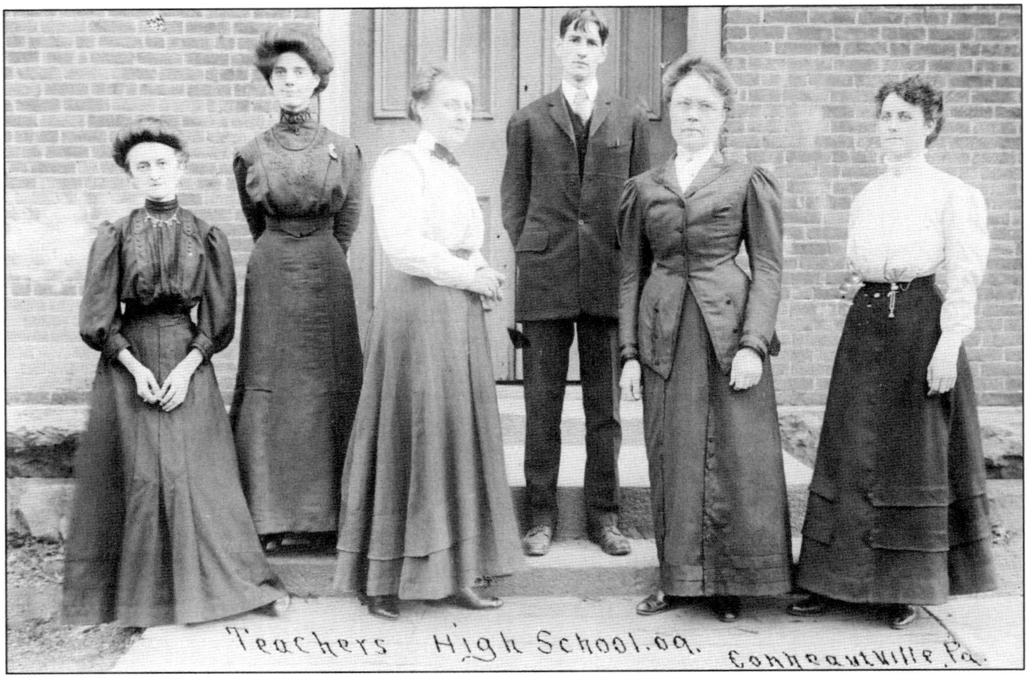

The Conneautville High School faculty of 1909 posed for this picture outside the school building.

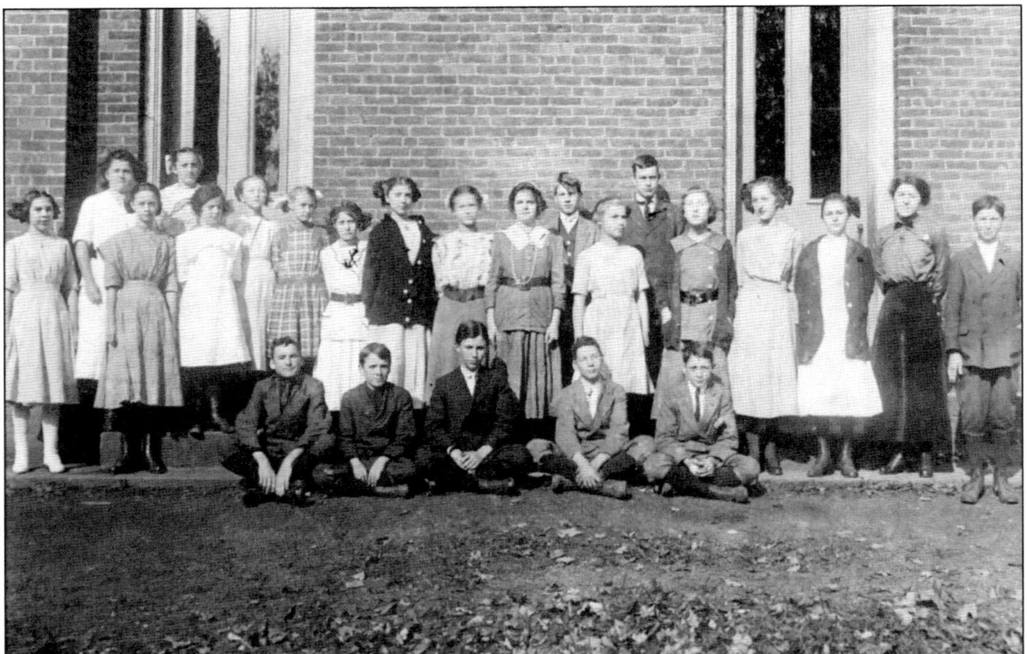

The seventh and eighth grade classes posed for this picture during the 1912–1913 school year. Pictured here are, from left to right, (first row) Nelson Flynn, Clifford Thompson, David Fraizer, Tom Logan, and Osmond Slayton; (second row) Estella Butterfield, Myrtle Breese, Faye Johnson, Clara Walton, Nellie McCabe, Gladys Fish, Mable Wilder, Myrtle Weisman, Martha Neville, Virginia Higley, Eva Parker, Ralph Butterfield, Hazel Bryson, Gordwn Beebe, Maye Pletcher, Kathleen Penfield, Edith Perrin, teacher Hazel Breese, and Allen Butterfield.

Seen here in his later years, Dr. Edwin T. Mason (right) could look back on a long life of personal achievement and community service. Having been crippled with polio, Mason was unable to attend college but received a degree through correspondence. He also organized the first meeting of Conneautville school alumni in 1894—a tradition that continues today. Dr. Mason passed away in October 1934 at the age of 74.

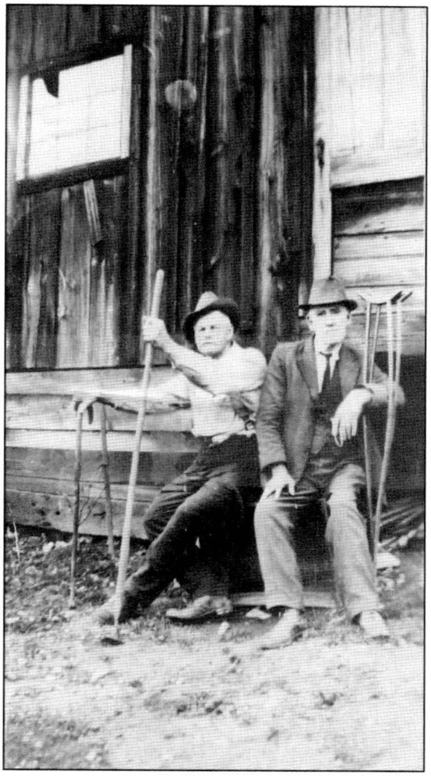

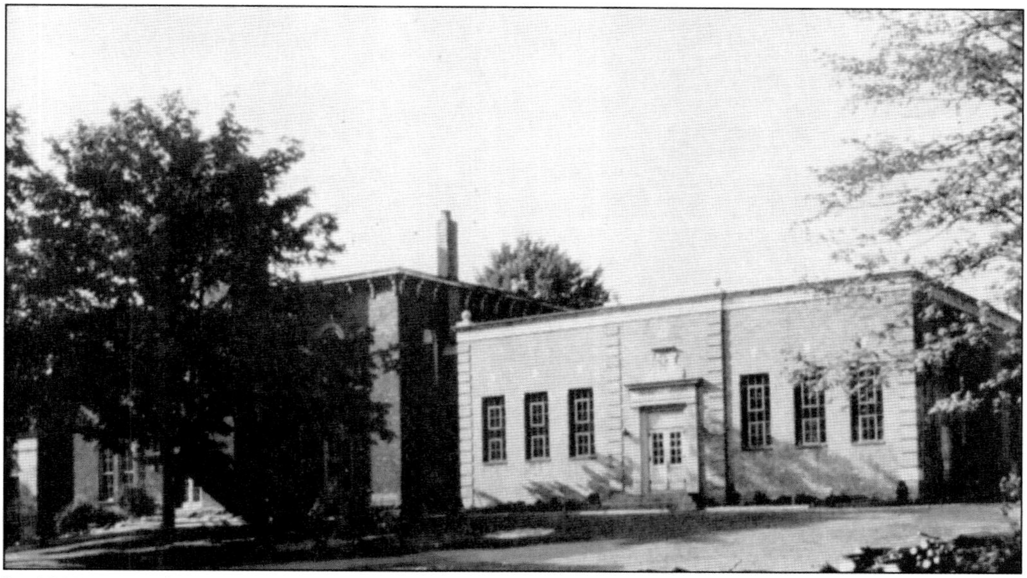

In 1929, an auditorium-gymnasium addition was built onto the school. Known as Mason Hall, this addition was a tribute to Dr. Edwin T. Mason, who played a significant role in education in Conneautville. Mason was a Conneautville High School graduate who later became a teacher and eventually the school principal. Townspeople and alumni raised funds for the building. The amount raised was matched dollar for dollar by Raymond S. Lord, an alumnus of the school, in memory of his brother. A grand total of $30,000 was raised for the building. Lord-Mason Memorial Park is also named in honor of these two individuals.

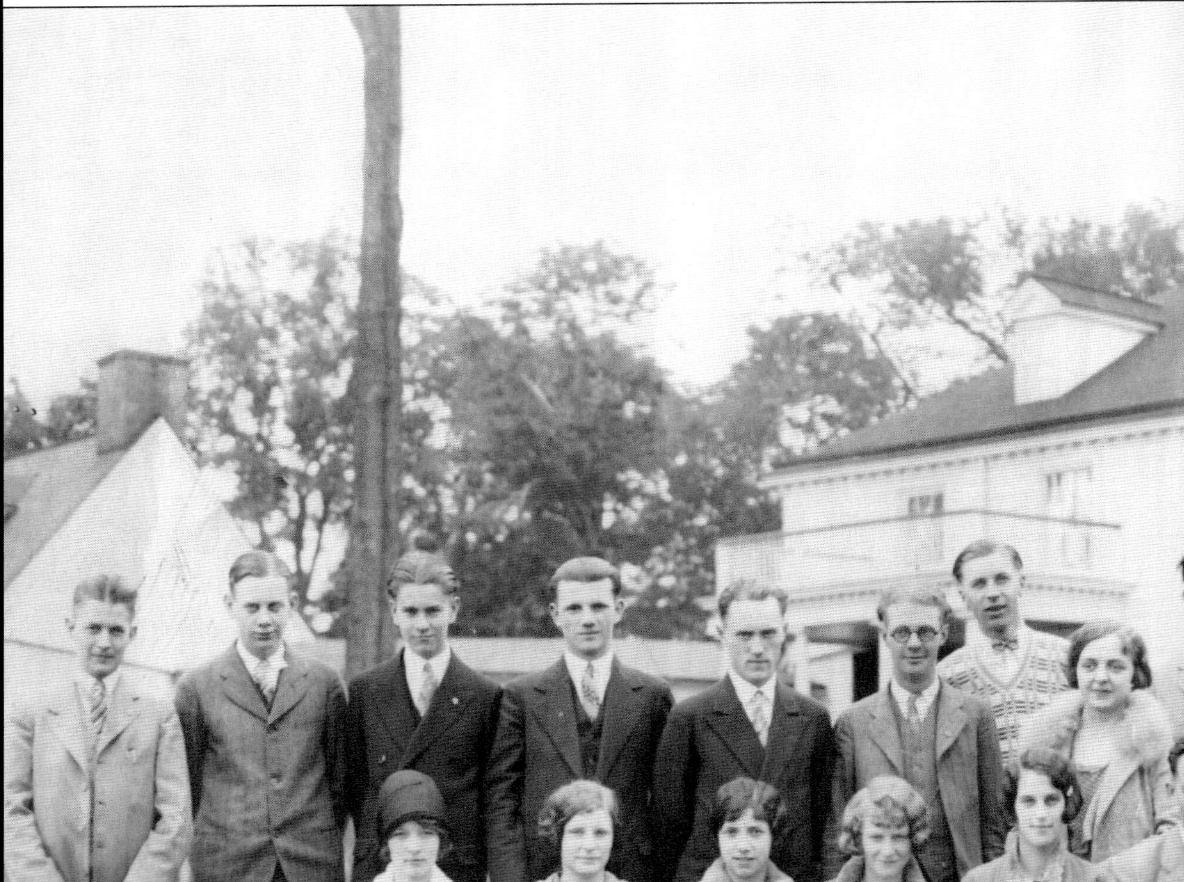

In May 1927, the senior class of Conneautville Vocational School took a trip to Washington, DC, and posed for this picture in front of Mount Vernon. Pictured here are, from left to right, (first row) Katherine Hites, Regina Lasko, Mabel Townsend, Gertrude Nicolls, Charlotte Connick, Fred Wing, Olive Beers, Leonard Biggs, Albert Ellsmore, Floyd Boyles, Robert Ransom, and

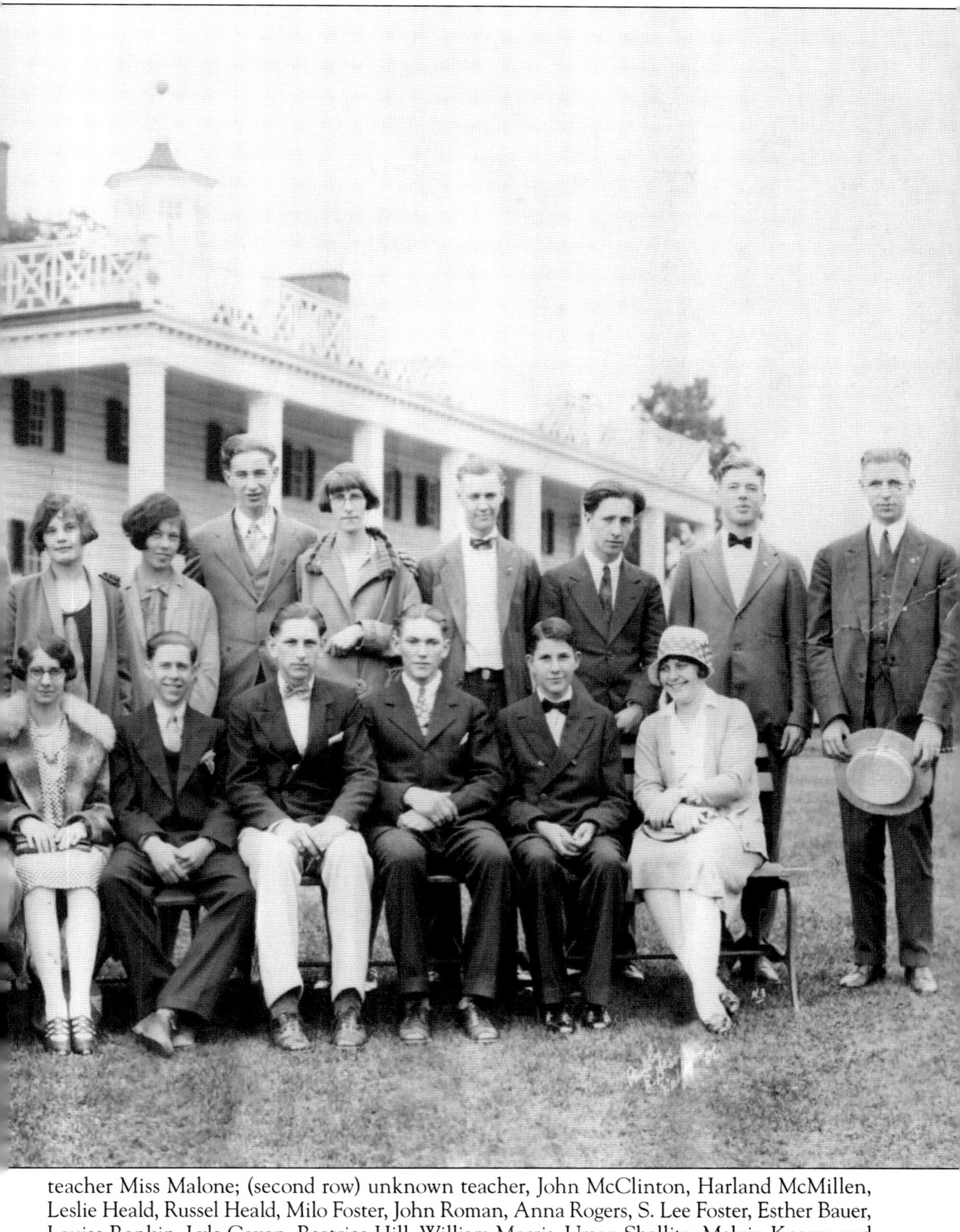

teacher Miss Malone; (second row) unknown teacher, John McClinton, Harland McMillen, Leslie Heald, Russel Heald, Milo Foster, John Roman, Anna Rogers, S. Lee Foster, Esther Bauer, Louise Rankin, Lyle Coxan, Beatrice Hill, William Morris, Urson Shellito, Melvin Knapp, and teacher Mr. Fisby.

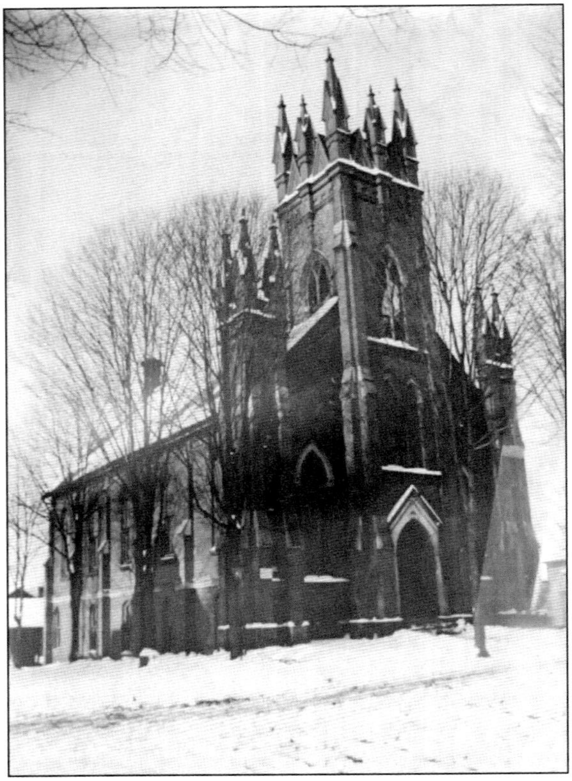

In the spring of 1829, seven people—Jesse Danley and his wife; Thomas Landon, his wife, and his daughter Ester; and George Nelson and his granddaughter, Margaret Nelson—became the original members of the Conneautville Methodist Church, organized by Rev. Joseph Davis. Services were held in the schoolhouse until enough funds were raised to construct their first church, which stood on Walnut and Main Streets. The current church (pictured here) was built in 1877 and featured beautiful stone trimmings. It was completed for a grand total of $8,300. (Courtesy of Patricia Vedner.)

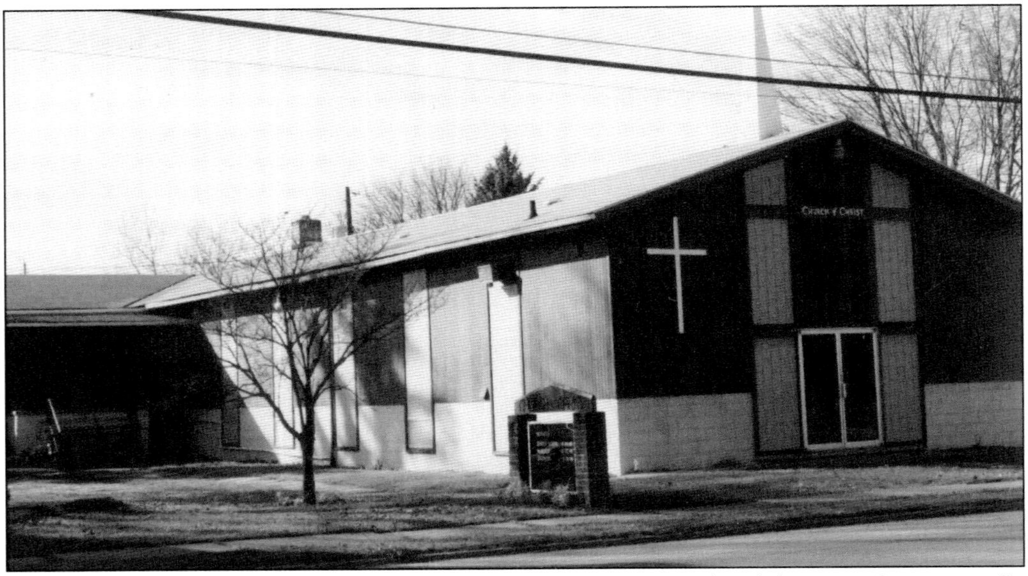

During the summer of 1956, members of the Meadville Christian Church living in Conneautville met and discussed the possibility of opening a church in town. Having secured a two-story house along Main Street, the congregation used this as a meeting spot until plans were organized for a church to be built on the house's location. Construction began on the Conneautville Church of Christ in 1957. The elders of the church called upon Harry K. Orn of Paris, Illinois, to lead this new congregation and become its first minister. The church is pictured here in 1970. (Courtesy of Patricia Vedner.)

The First Presbyterian Church of Conneautville was organized with nine members on October 31, 1835, by Rev. Peter Hassinger. For several years the congregation was divided into two branches that were united in 1865 and worshiped in a wooden church built on Mulberry and High Streets. This structure was consumed by fire in 1867. A newly built church (right) was dedicated on June 14, 1871, with a seating capacity of 400. (Courtesy of Patricia Vedner.)

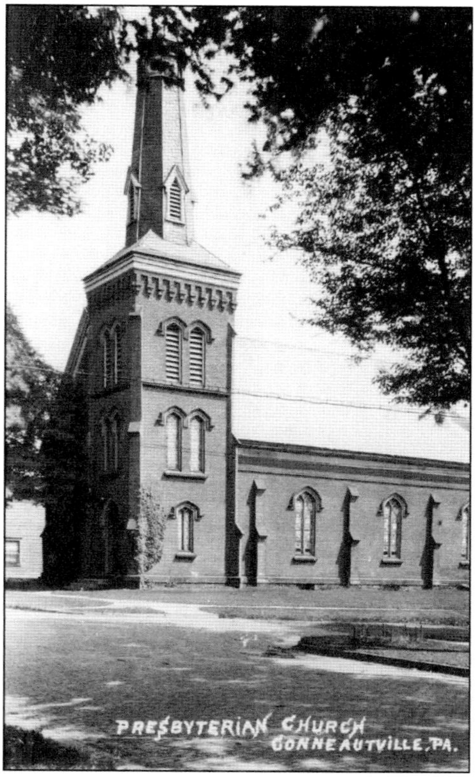

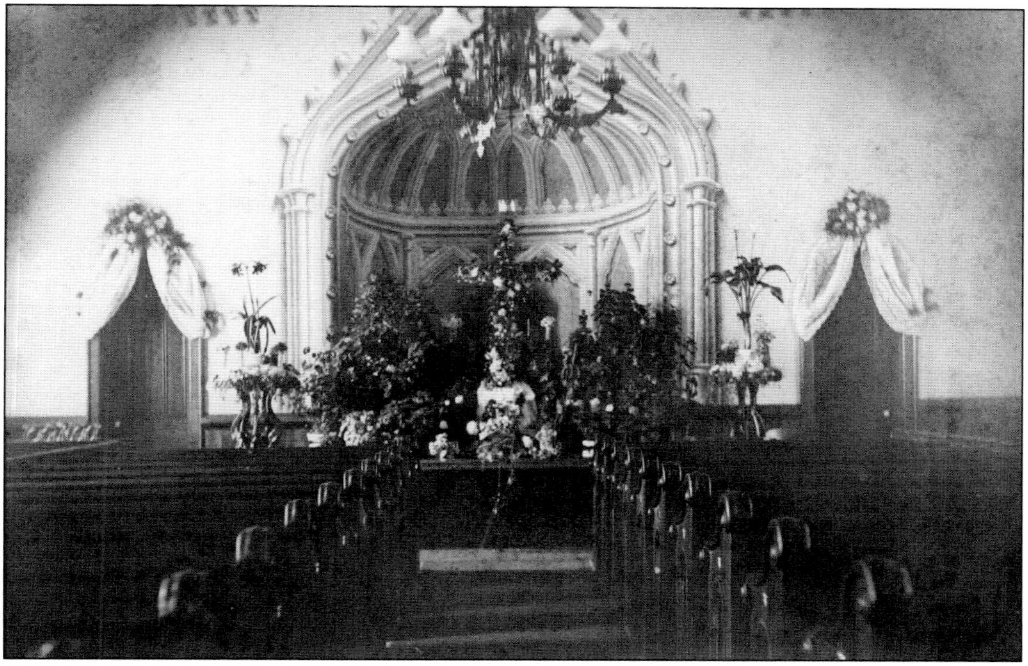

The cost of construction for the new Presbyterian Church was a remarkable $17,000. It was a brick structure featuring large stone window caps and corners and a spire that rose 140 feet high. The church occupied the lot of the current Samuels Market. The inside of the church is pictured here around 1890.

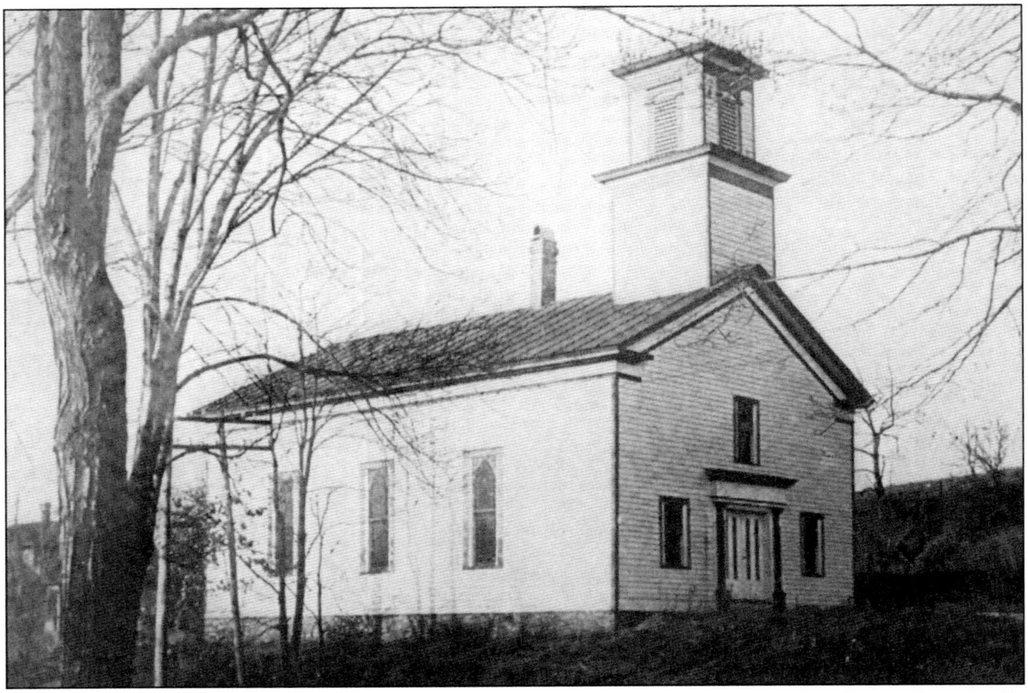

The First Universalist Church was organized on May 13, 1843. It began with 19 members and originally held its services in the schoolhouse. Around 1846, the building of a frame church began on the uppermost extremity of Pearl Street. First services were held there in 1848 with Rev. B.F. Hitchcock. With such a large congregation, the church was able to purchase a bell and the first pipe organ in town.

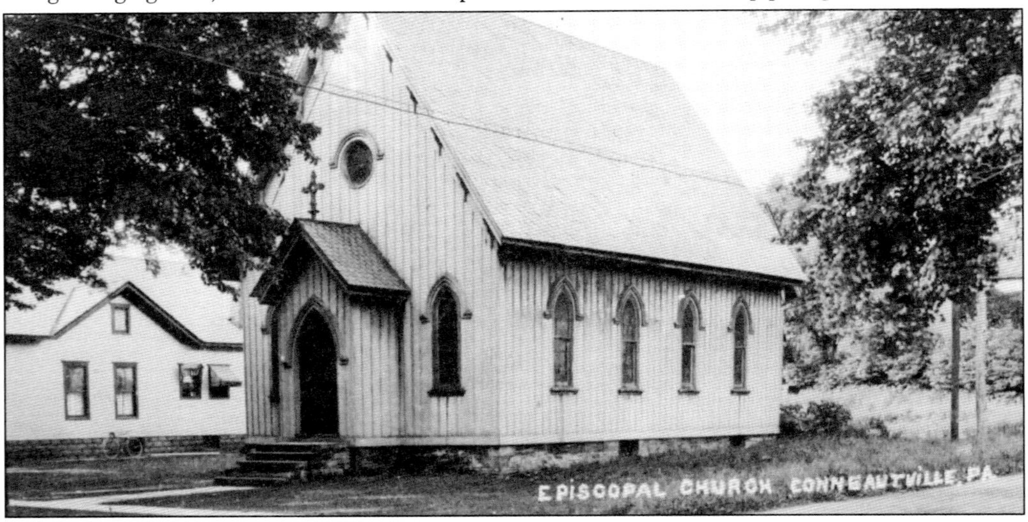

In 1838, the Conneautville Baptists built a small church on the corner of Second and Church Streets, which sat at the back of the Universalist Church. The membership was small and over the years the services began to cease. As religion played a large part of Conneautville life, the vacant Baptist Church was bought by the Seventh Day Adventists, who moved the building across town to a lot on West Street. This church building has welcomed different faiths over the years but has changed little itself. Today it is the Conneautville Baptist Church. It is shown here around 1890 when it was the Conneautville Episcopal Church. It was built in 1870 at a cost of $5,000. (Courtesy of Patricia Vedner.)

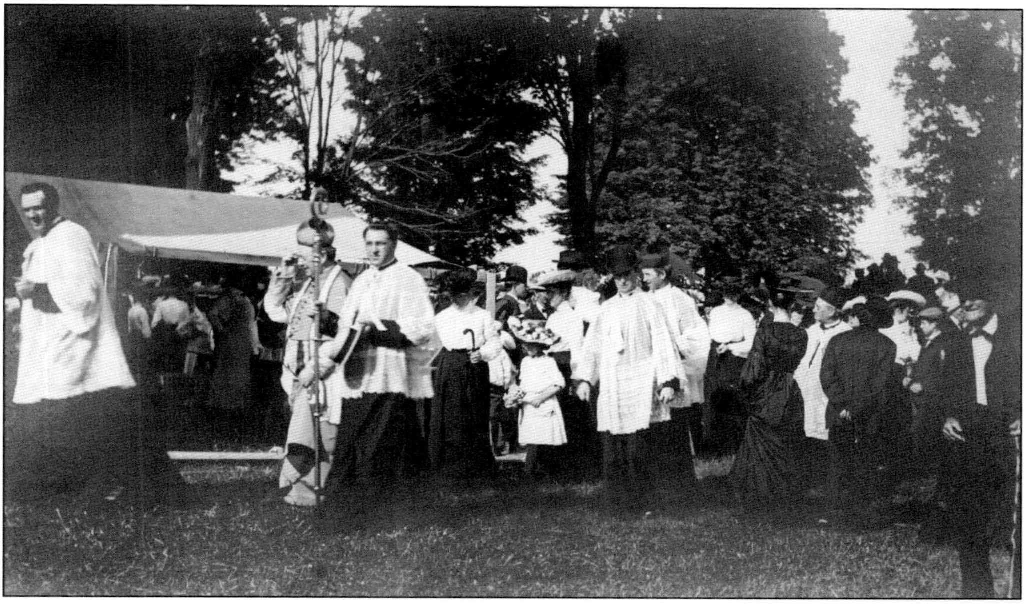

After fire destroyed Saint Peter Church in 1903, planning began on the construction of a larger building that would occupy the same grounds as the previous structure. This image shows the ceremony that accompanied the laying of the cornerstone on July 10, 1904.

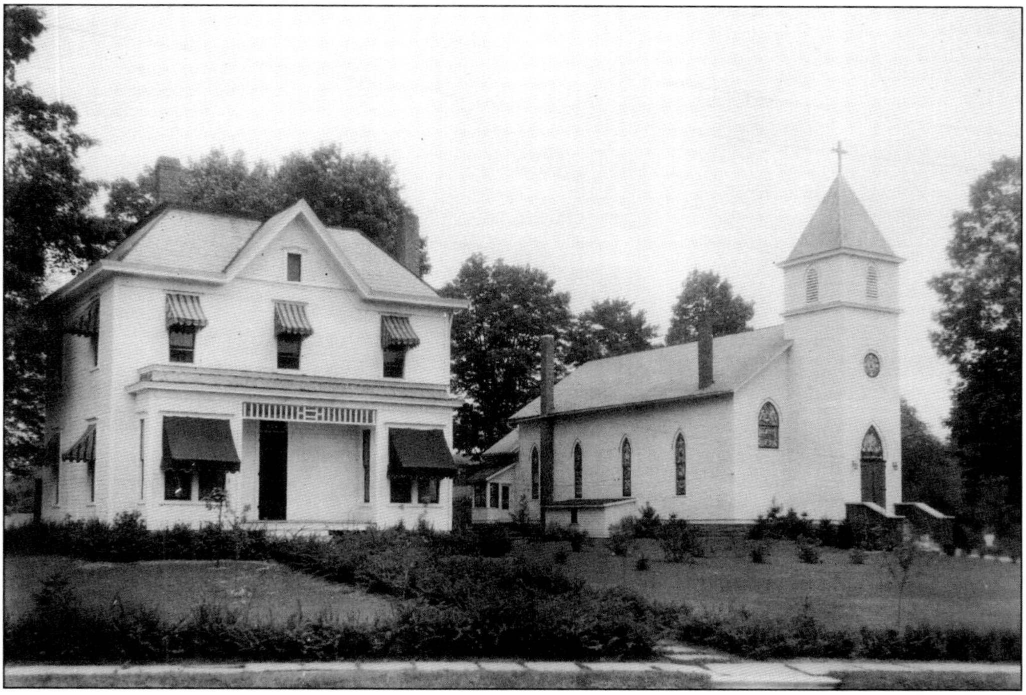

Saint Peter Roman Catholic Church held its first meetings in 1850 in Thomas Henretta's barn. Services were held in private houses until 1871, when church members bought an old schoolhouse known then as the Academy. Services were held there until the church was destroyed by fire in 1903. The present church building was erected on the same foundation and dedicated in 1905. This image from the 1950s shows the church grounds and rectory, which once stood in the lower left corner of the lot. (Courtesy of Patricia Vedner.)

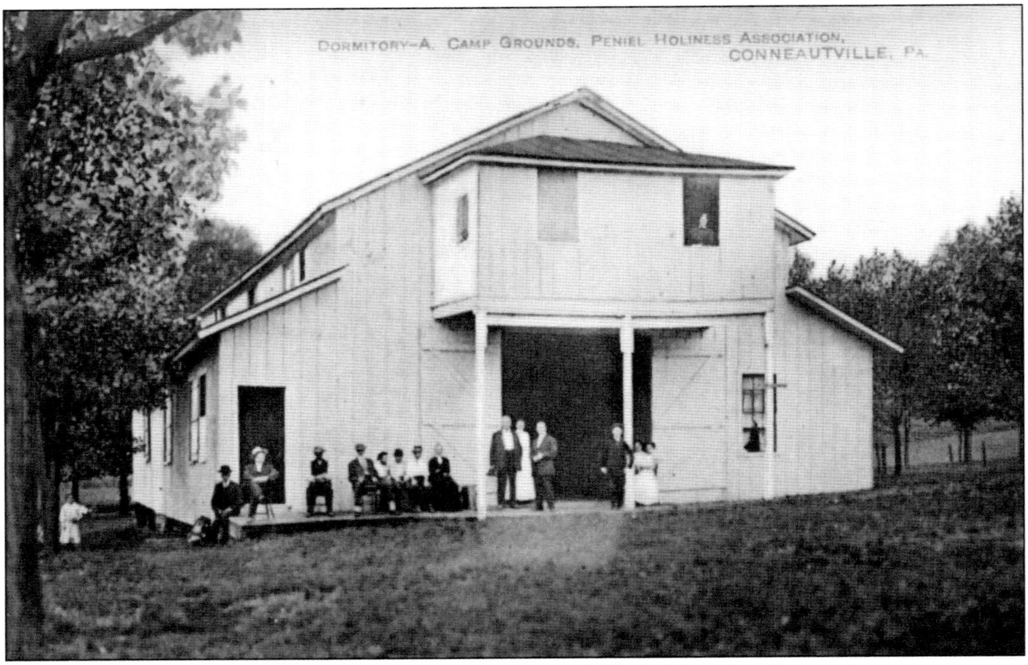

The Crawford County Agricultural Society, formed in 1853, held its first fair in November of that same year on land along Conneautville's southern end known then as Lowry's Grove. In 1887, the fair moved to new grounds just north of the borough and constructed many buildings. Being heavily in debt, the fair association sold its land to the Shenango Valley Holiness Association in 1900. The association was renamed the Peniel Holiness Association and began holding yearly religious camps at the property in 1901. Many of the existing structures at this camp are the original structures used by the Fair Association as exhibit halls. The camp and grounds remain in use to this day. The camp dormitory and dining hall is shown above, while the Tabernacle, formerly the fair's home show building, is seen below.

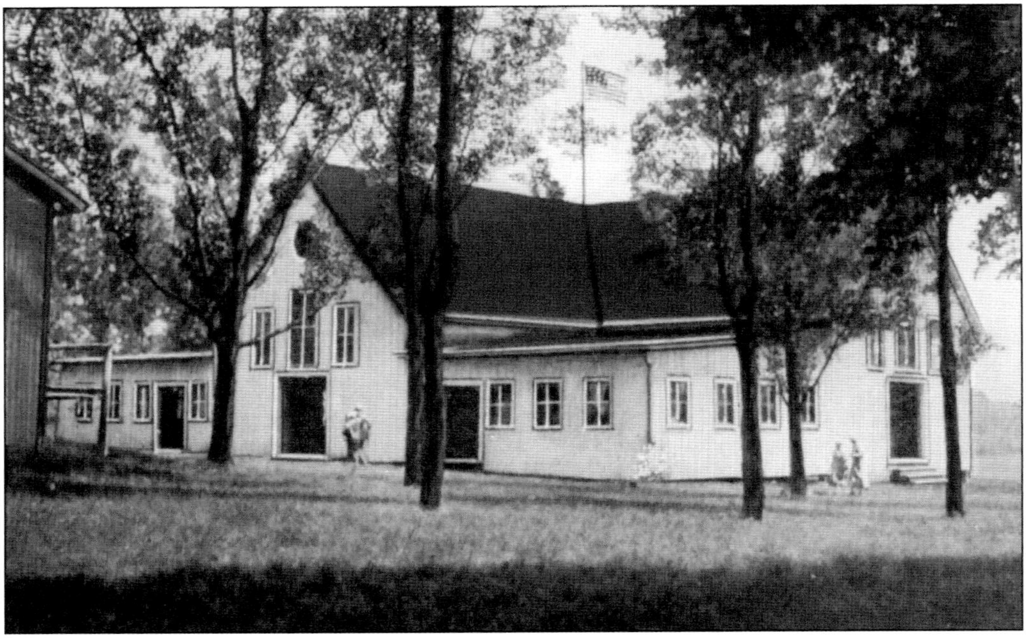

Four

A Centennial Celebration

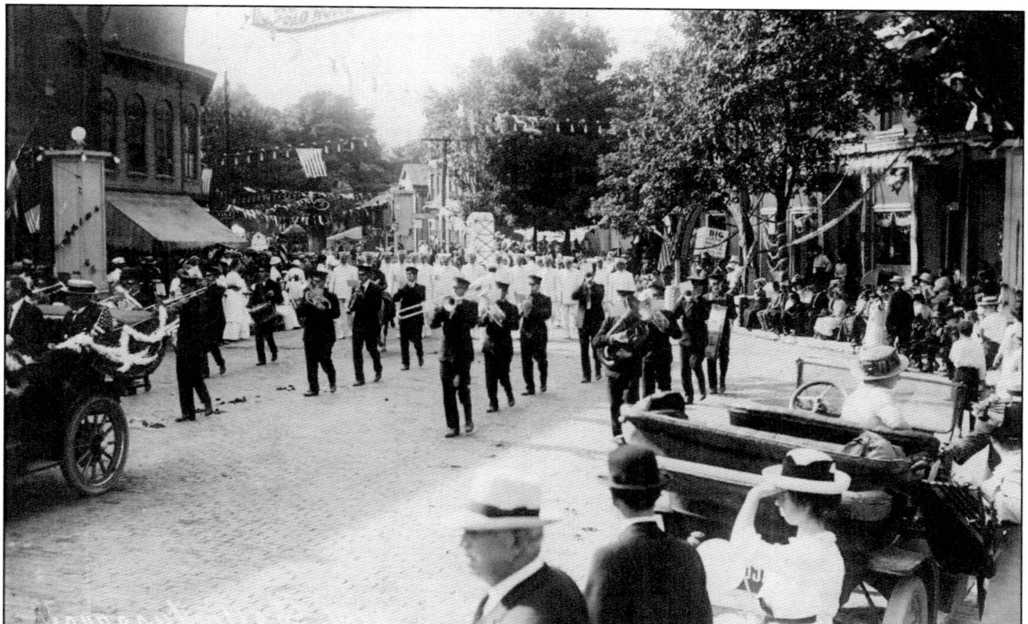

Over a year of planning went into the preparations for Conneautville's celebration of its 100th anniversary, held August 16–22, 1914. This weeklong event is recorded as one of the grandest in Conneautville's history and was well documented. Much of what happened that week was photographed, including an astonishing parade full of floats, motor vehicles, and bands.

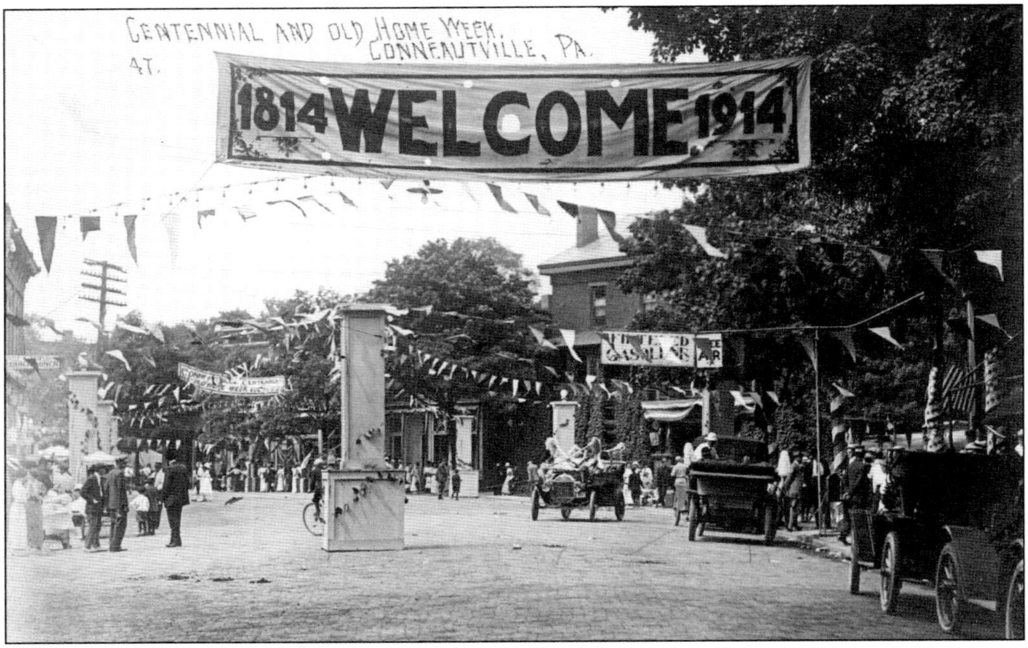

Banners hang over Main Street welcoming people to Conneautville for a week of celebration and activities. Like the homecoming celebrations of today, Old Home Week was also celebrated in late summer. The centennial celebration was an enhanced version of this annual tradition. In the preceding weeks, the town was cleaned, decorated, and renovated. Buildings were draped in decorations and the town was abuzz with activity. The events of the week included special church services, campfires, concerts, picnics, a carnival, a baseball game, and a Grand Ball at the Opera House. At that time, it was recorded that Alexander Power had 64 living descendants, with 40 being present at the celebration.

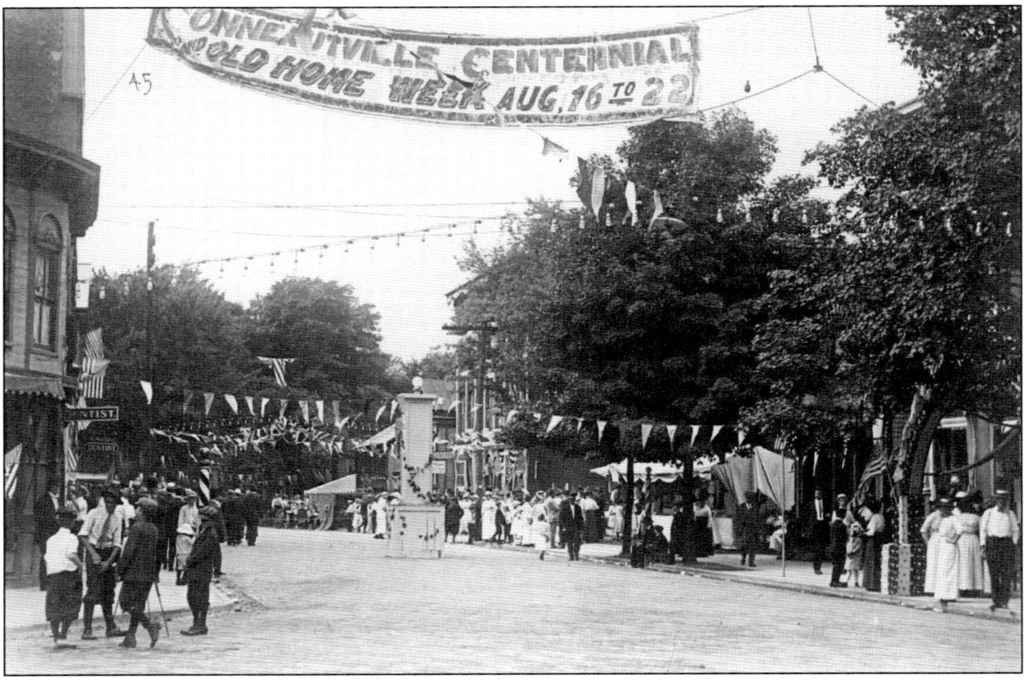

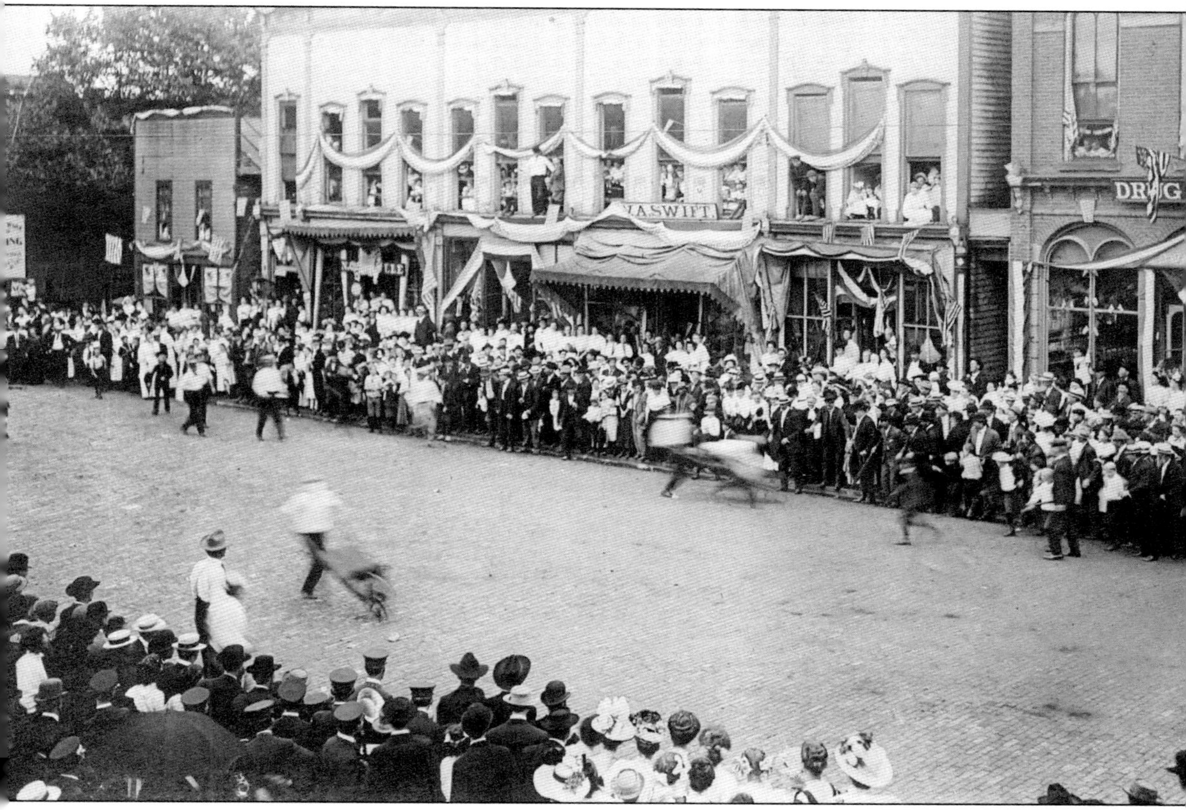

Thousands came out to witness the spectacular display of the parade. Spectators from as far away as Erie gathered for a chance to see some new and curious sights. The motor vehicle itself, fairly new at the time, was remarkable enough to gather a crowd. However, motor vehicles were just a part of the excitement. People lined the streets 10 and 15 deep to watch the parade pass by. Buildings such as the Opera Block, seen above, were overflowing with those who wanted in on the action. Nearly all the windows lining Main Street were packed. Rooftops became dangerously overloaded as any space above the street became a valuable platform to catch a glimpse. This picture taken from the balcony of the Hotel Power appears to show wheelbarrows either being raced or maneuvered in patterns.

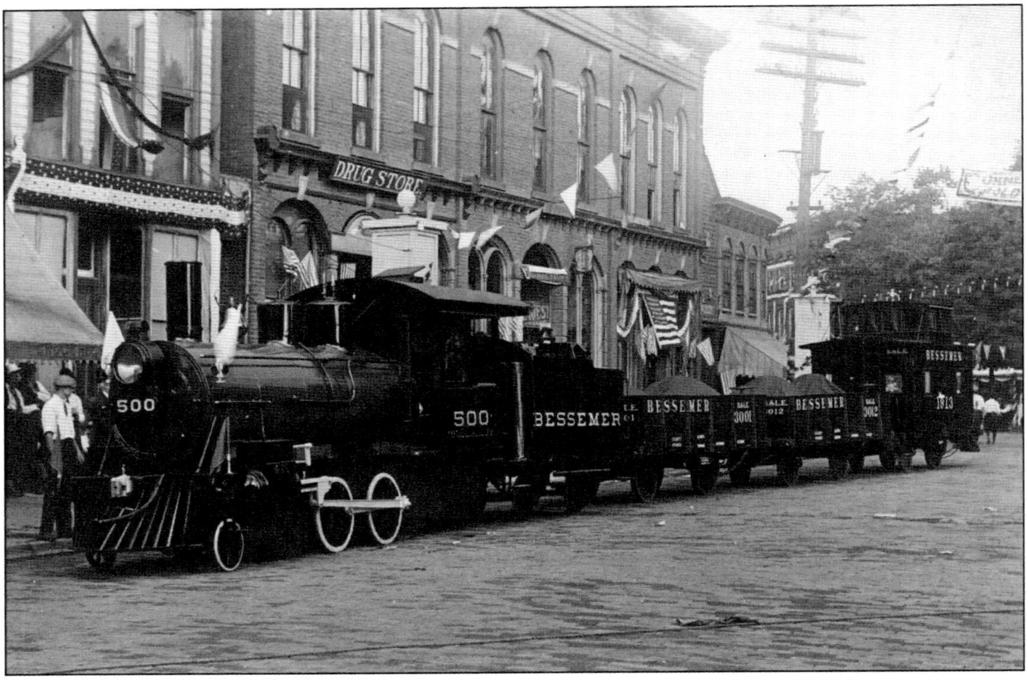

The centennial parade featured this train, which was brought and handled by the Bessemer Railroad Company. The most expensive and interesting entry in the parade, this miniature ore train consisted of an engine and tender, two ore cars, and a caboose. It was run under its own generated electric power but had the appearance of an actual steam train.

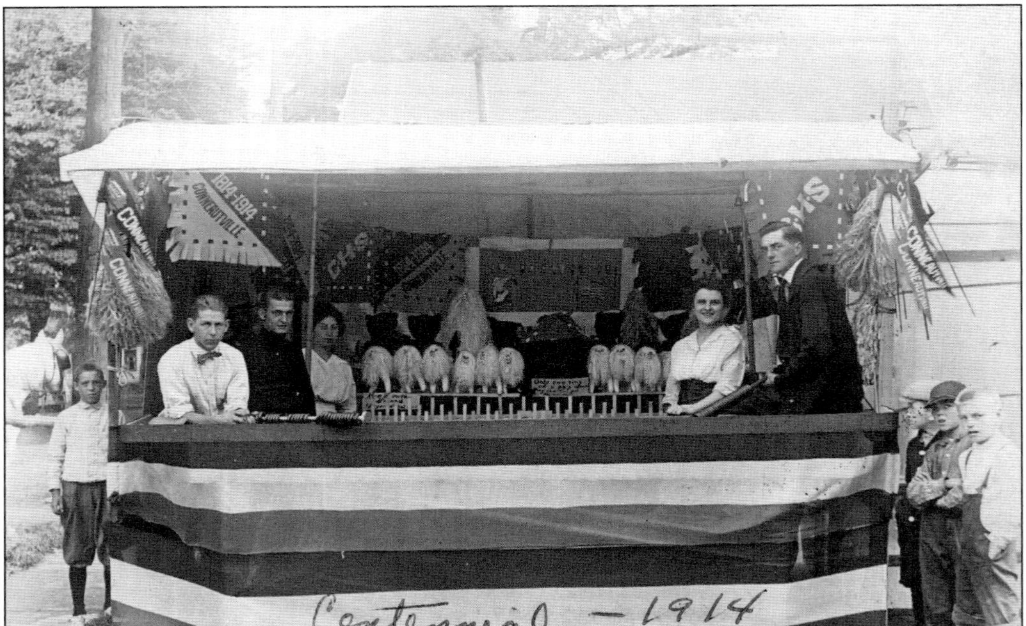

The carnival featured many games and activities for children. Here, workers at one booth pose for a picture alongside children hoping to win a prize. The prizes visible here are all Conneautville-themed and included flags, pennants, and buttons.

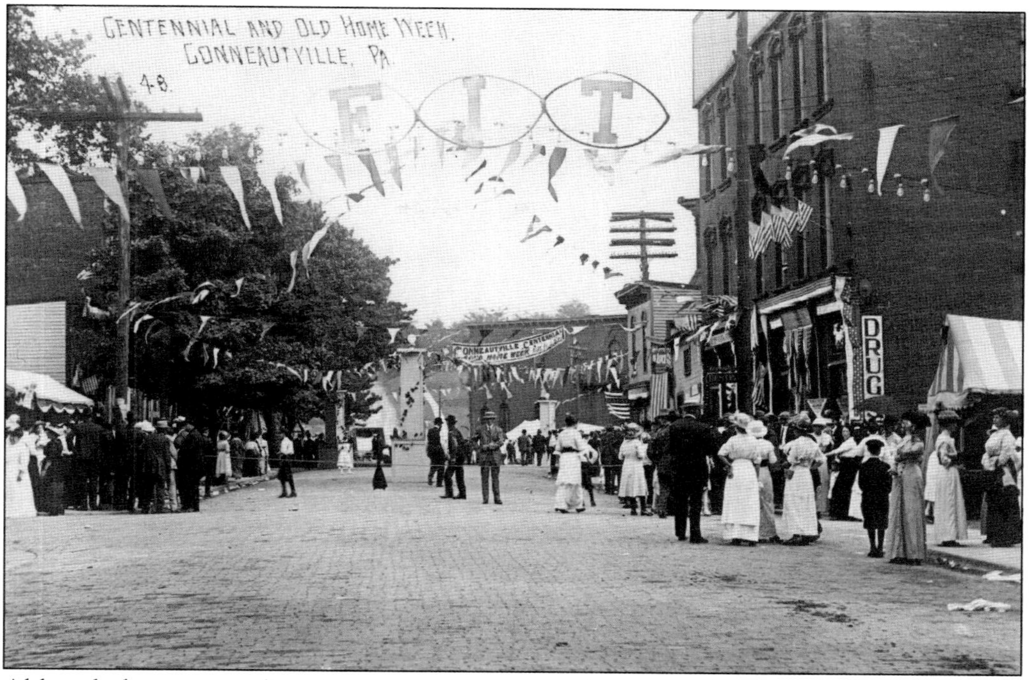

Although the centennial's activities were focused mainly in the public park, the entire town was involved in the celebration. Businesses along Main Street offered their products on the sidewalk and food vendors presented their cuisine to the easily accessible crowd. The street seen here, by the Courtright Block, is bustling with people. The F.L.T. spanning the roadway is the motto of the Odd Fellows—Friendship, Love, and Truth.

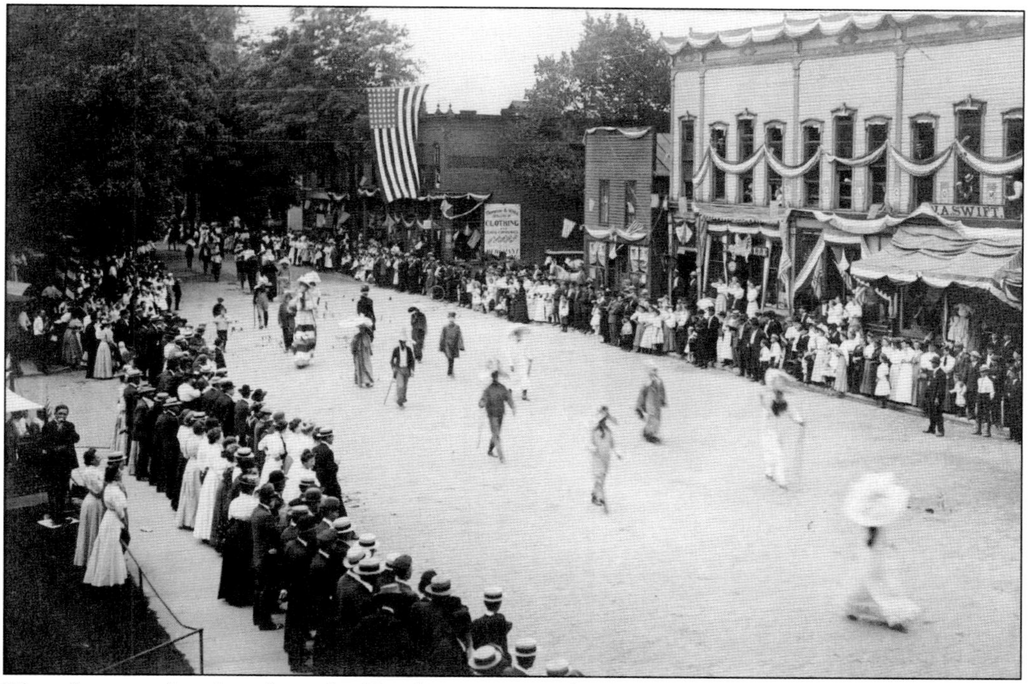

This photograph, taken from the Hotel Power grounds, shows the Merry Widows as they passed parade-goers.

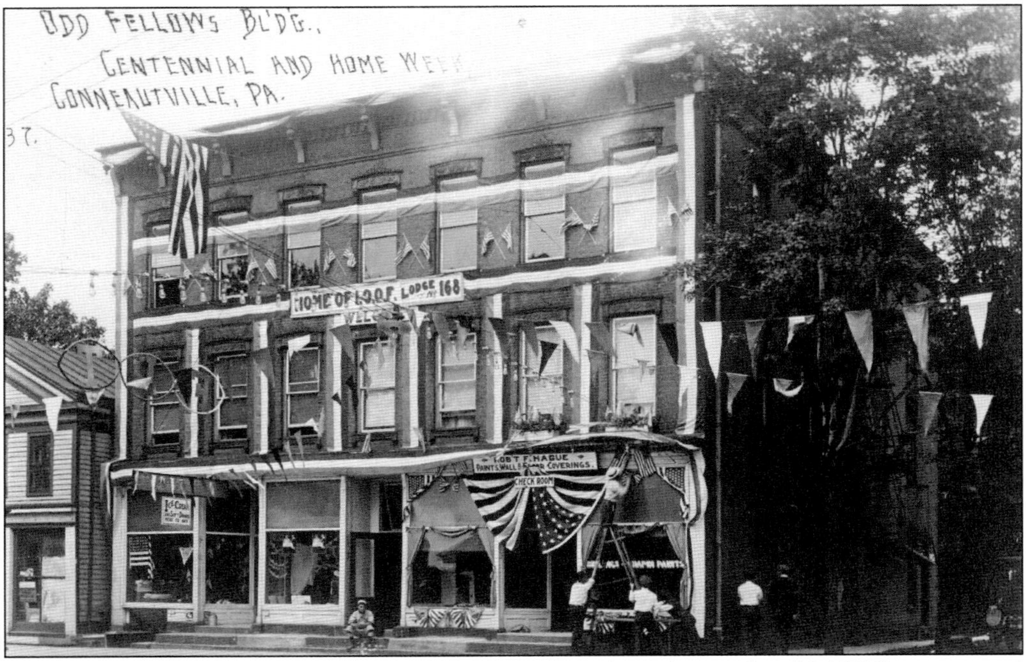

Decorations adorn the Robinson Block. At the time, the Independent Order of Odd Fellows occupied this building. The Odd Fellows society was organized to meet the needs of local communities prior to the advent of national help organizations. Their main goals were to provide charity to individuals when they needed it and fundraising and contributing to the growth of town.

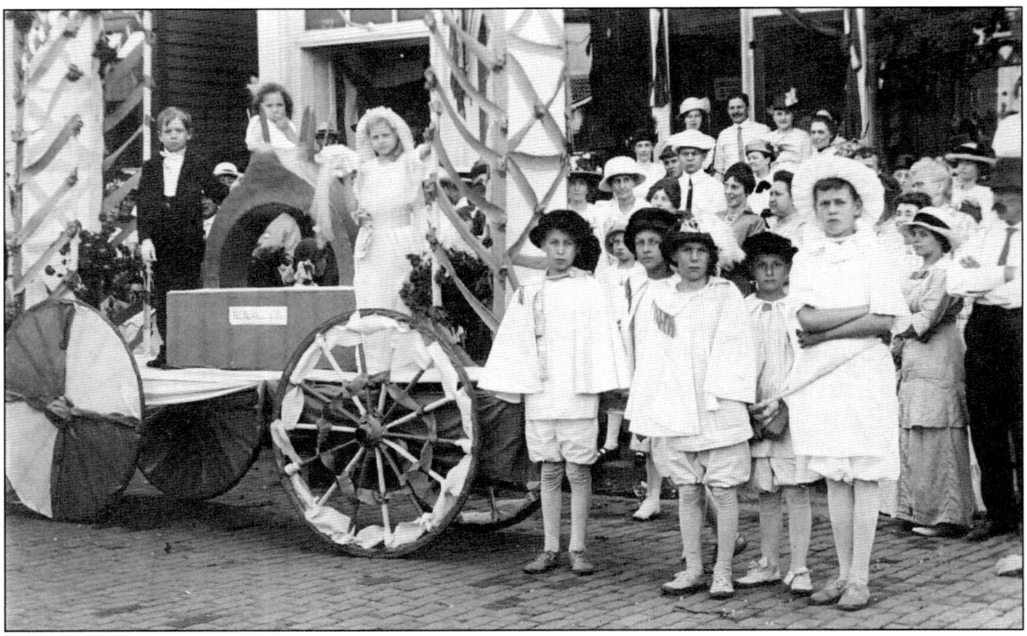

One of the more popular events of the centennial celebration was a Tom Thumb wedding. A popular tradition during the early 20th century, a Tom Thumb wedding featured young children portraying all of the regular wedding roles, including the bride, groom, and minister. Occasionally, the attendants were also children. This ceremony was usually well rehearsed and featured intricate costumes and choreographed movements. This "wedding" was held at the Presbyterian church.

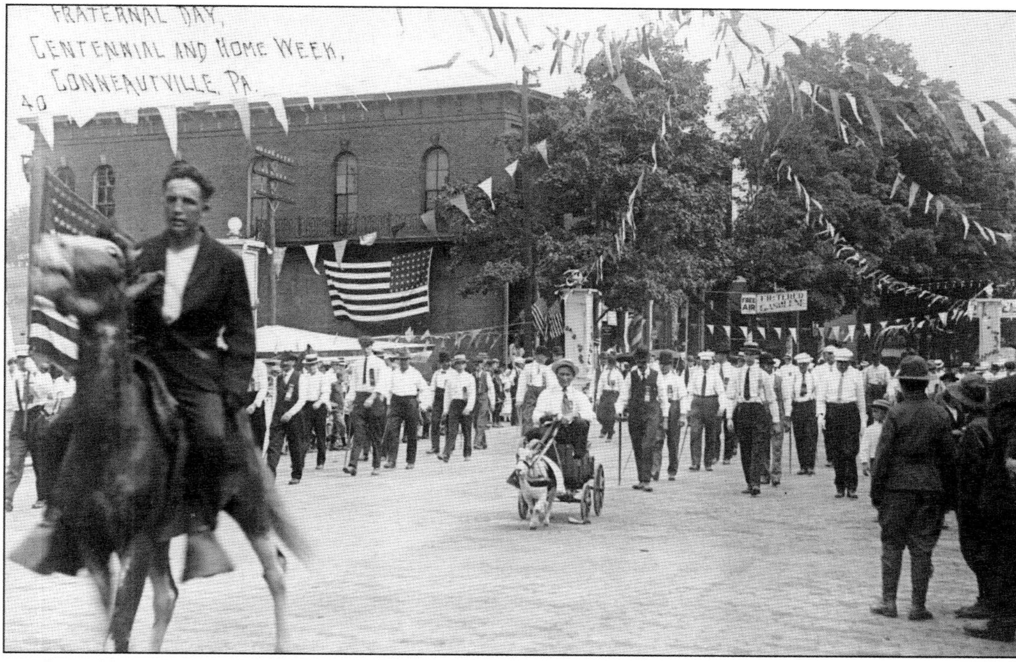

Herb Collins rides a horse in front of a goat pulling a man in a cart. Although most of the parade featured elements of town history and pride, entries like this made the atmosphere comical and exciting.

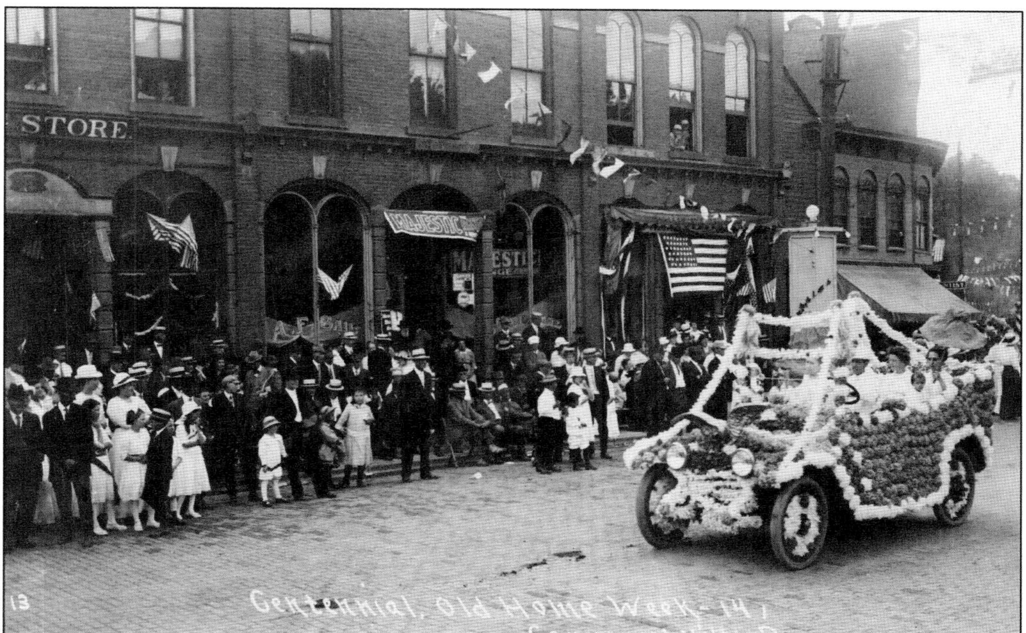

In 1914, the motor vehicle was still a curiosity to many people. Here, a Ford Model T is covered in paper and flowers as it proceeds along Main Street past the excited onlookers.

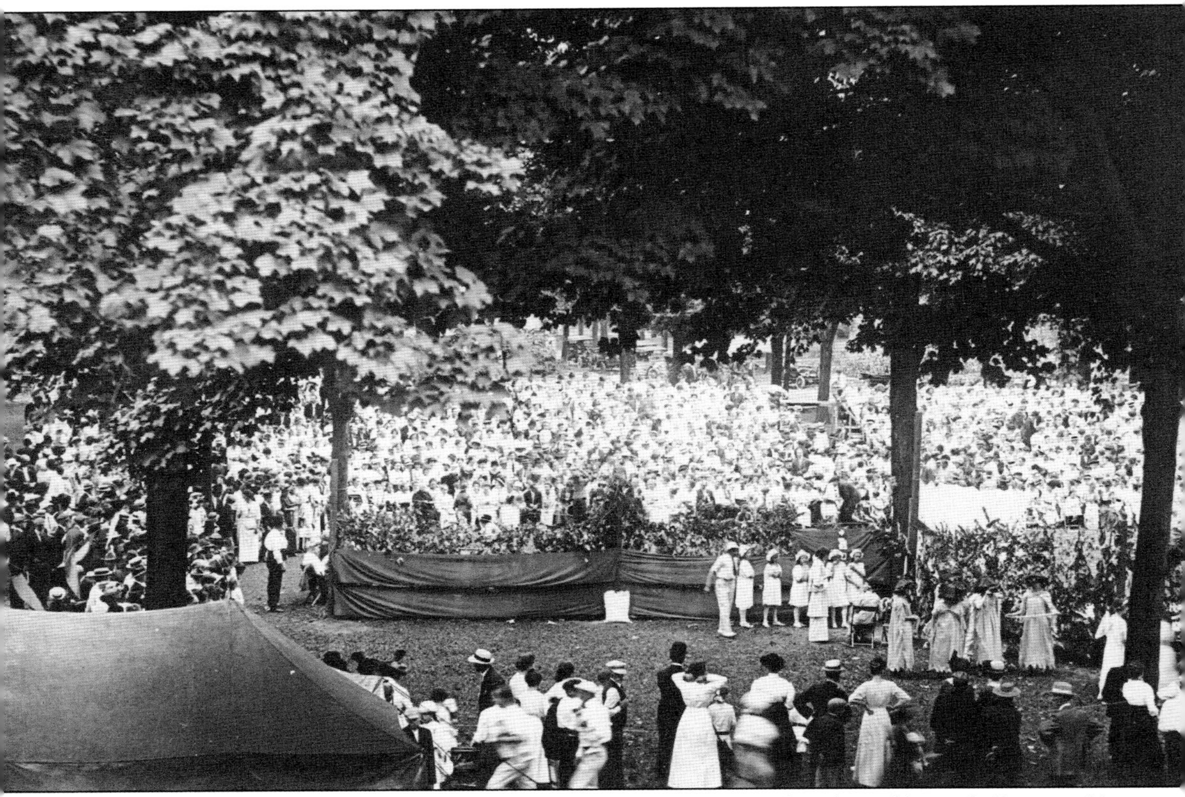

Nearly all of the festivities of the centennial celebration occurred in the public park. Designed by Alexander Power and laid out in his original plot of the borough, this park occupied the lot that is now home to the Conneaut Valley Health Center. For many years, this was a prime location to hold events because of its location near the center of town. During the centennial, bleachers were installed to seat the audience for a production of *Sleeping Beauty*. This beautiful, tree-lined space was heavily used during the summer months for gatherings, walks, and plays, and also for concerts and speeches.

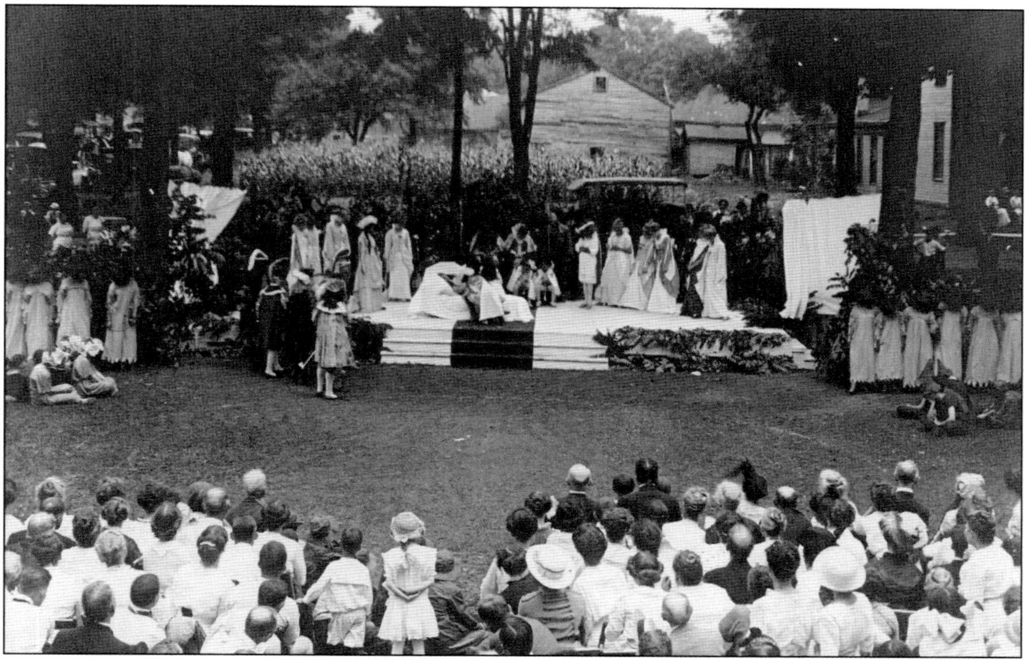

This image captures a moment during the centennial production of *Sleeping Beauty*. The large crowd may have been a reason the play was held outside and not in the Opera House.

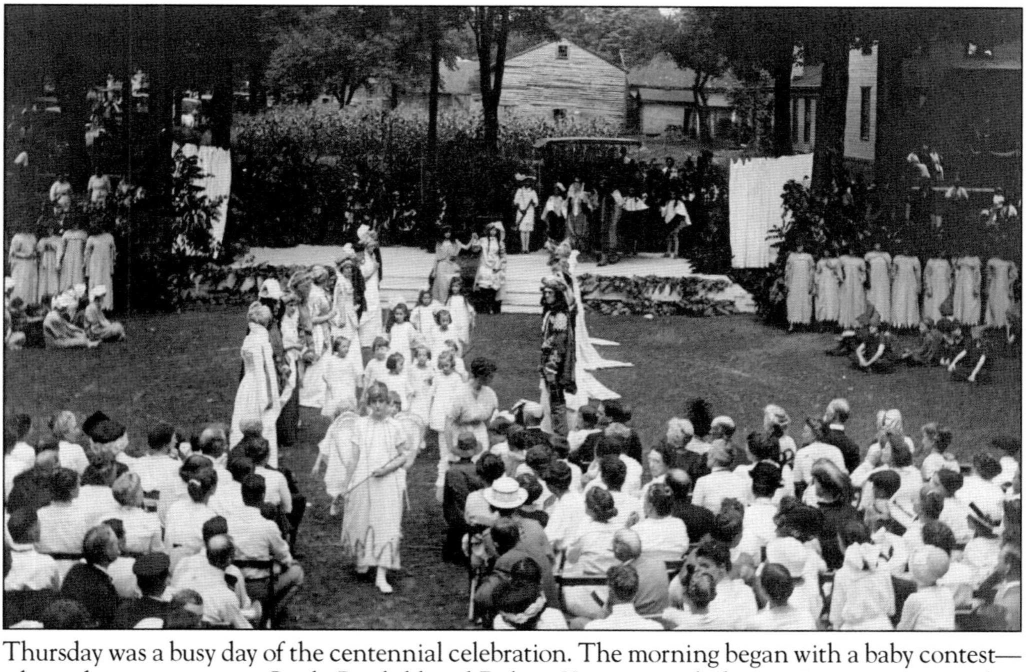

Thursday was a busy day of the centennial celebration. The morning began with a baby contest—where the winners were Sterle Penfield and Robert Knapp—and *Sleeping Beauty* was staged in the afternoon.

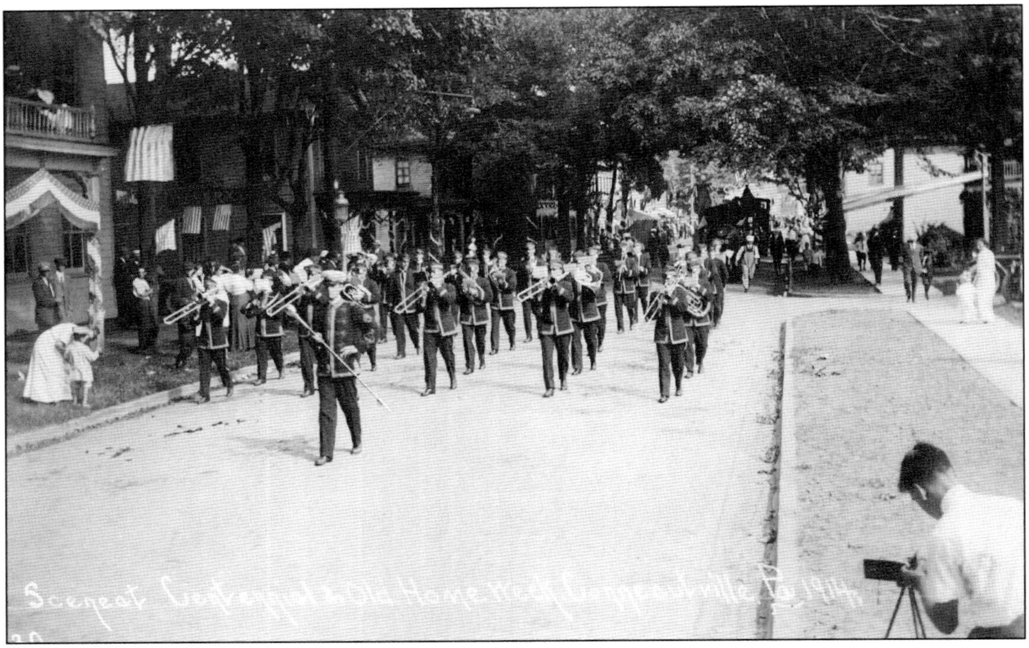

One of the many bands featured in the parade marches down Main Street. The bands were usually members of a local business or social group. Both Linesville and Springboro sent their bands to entertain the crowds. The area proved a popular spot for photographers, as evidenced in the bottom right corner of this photograph.

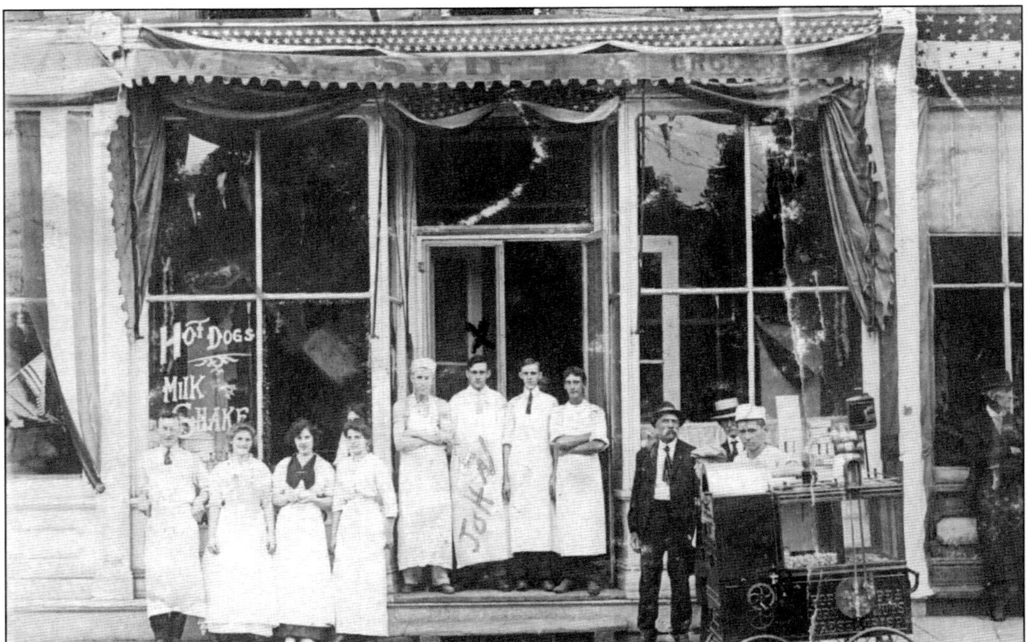

With a popcorn cart and all available employees at hand, this restaurant is ready to handle the large crowd and make the most of the centennial.

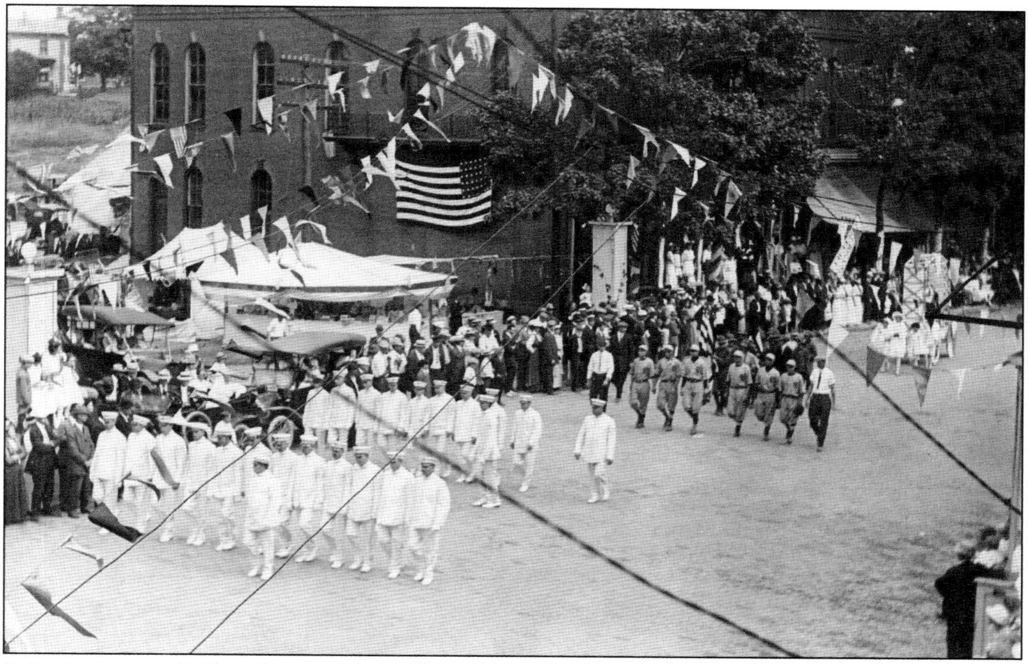

It is uncertain whether the men dressed in white are servicemen or members of a local fraternal organization. Either way, both would have surely been enjoyed along the parade route. Following them are members of Conneautville's baseball team, and behind the team are the children who performed in the Tom Thumb wedding earlier in the week.

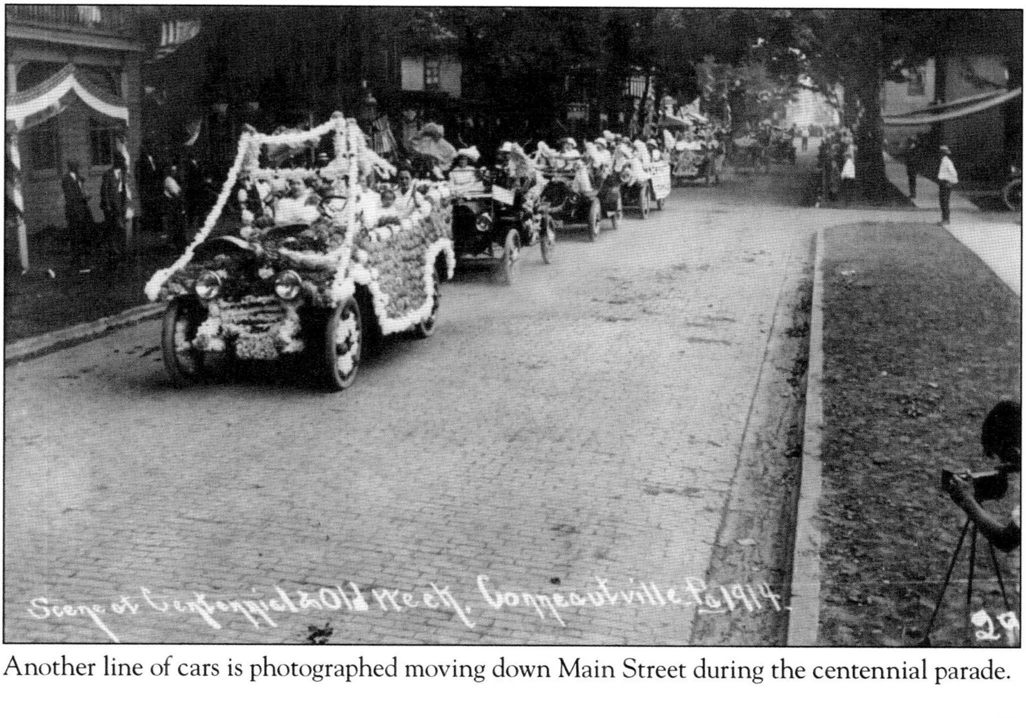

Another line of cars is photographed moving down Main Street during the centennial parade.

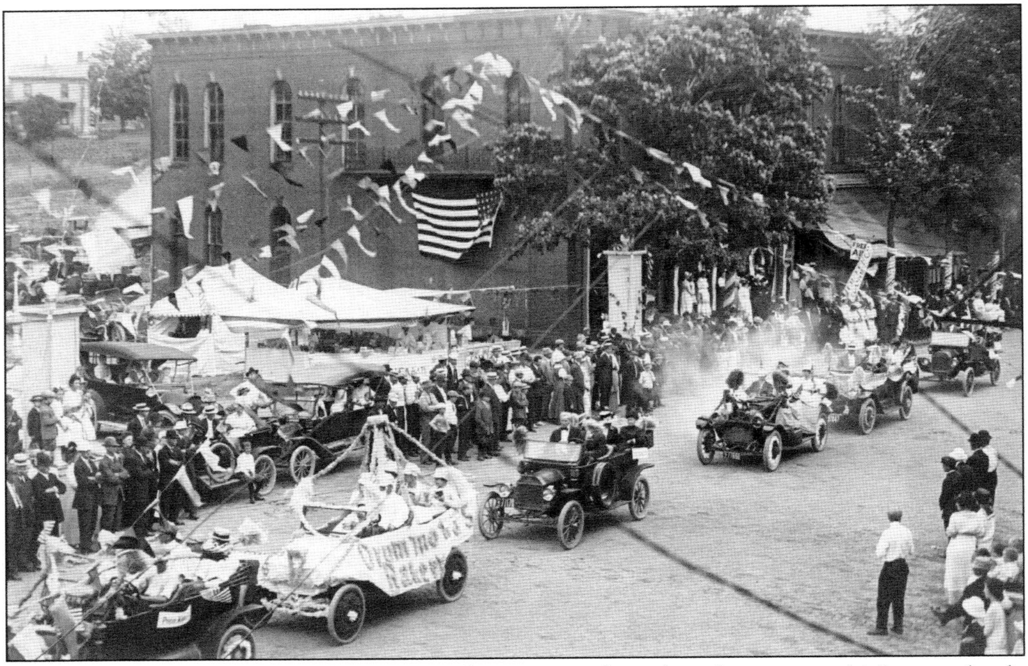

Judging from the pictures of this event, it becomes evident that the motor vehicle was clearly the most popular exhibit in the parade. Here, vehicles pass in front of the Stone Block, each one packed nearly full of people, some not decorated at all, yet all still deemed fascinating by those who came to watch.

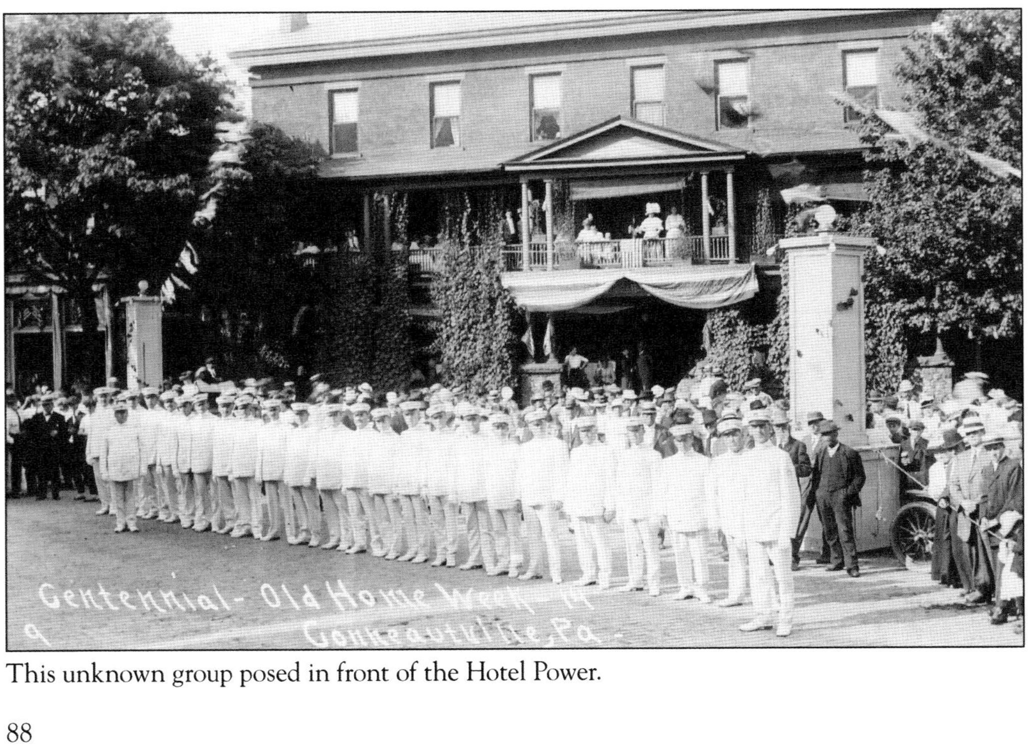

This unknown group posed in front of the Hotel Power.

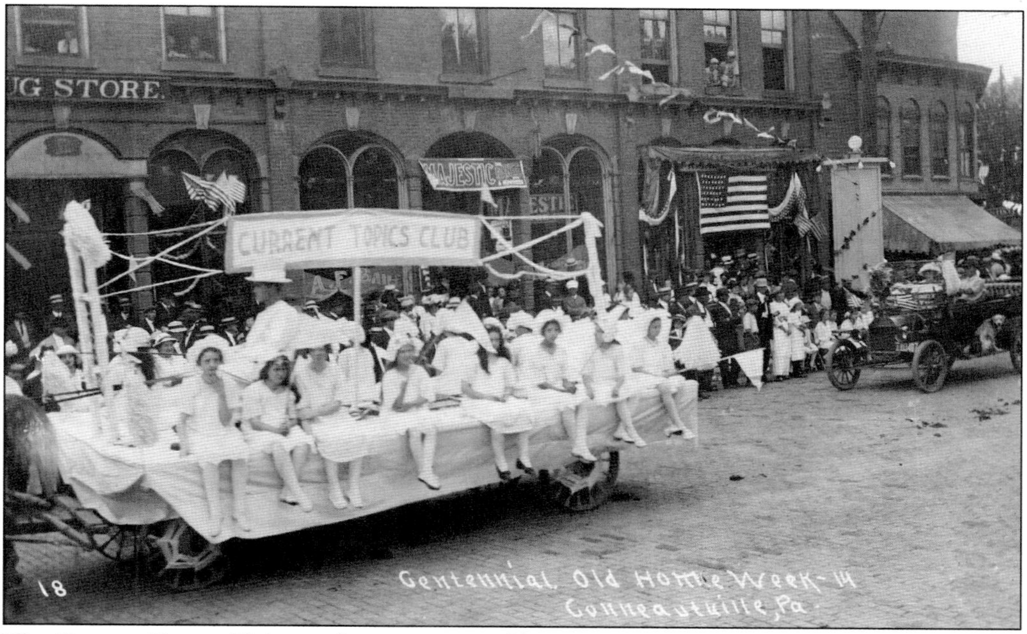

The Current Topics Club seen here is presumably moving toward their position in the parade, as they are moving against the parade route direction. In the early 20th century, Current Topics Clubs were social clubs for women that met at each other's houses and discussed matters of the day. This group took their objectives very seriously, as they conducted research and often held debates.

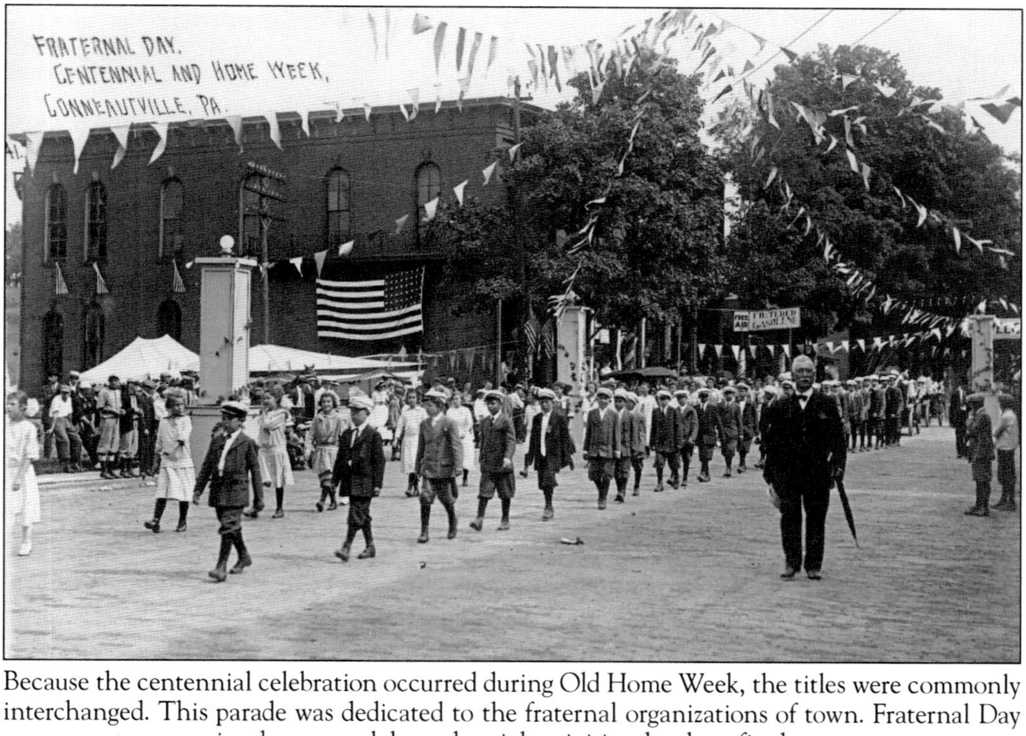

Because the centennial celebration occurred during Old Home Week, the titles were commonly interchanged. This parade was dedicated to the fraternal organizations of town. Fraternal Day was a way to recognize the many clubs and social activities that benefited town.

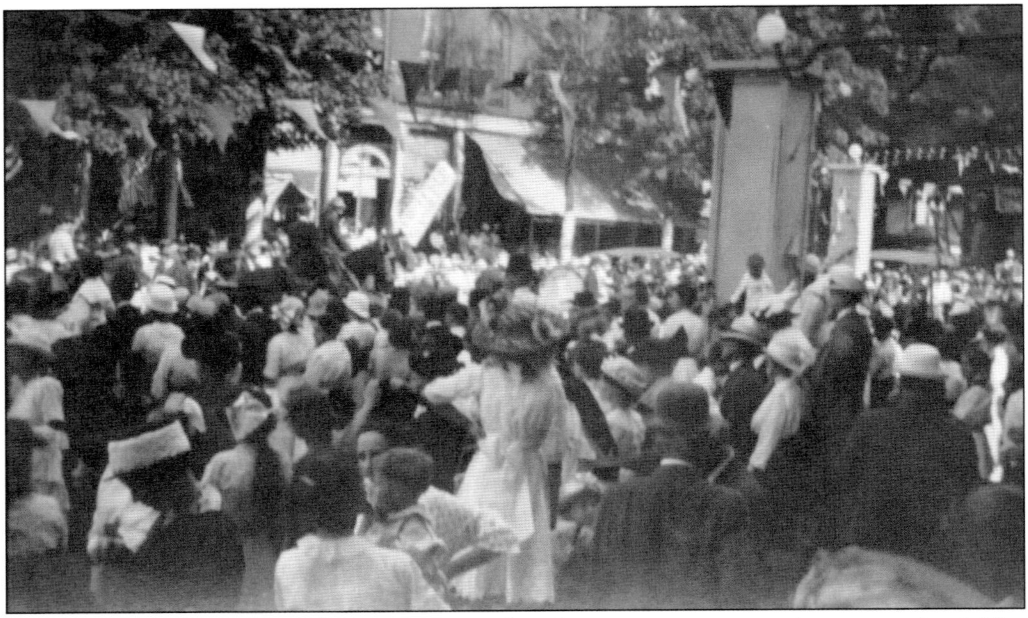

Many of the photographs of the parade were taken from a vantage point above street level. The balcony of the Hotel Power and the Pearl Street intersection were the most popular spots for photographers. In this rare image, one can see how the parade looked from the perspective of the crowd.

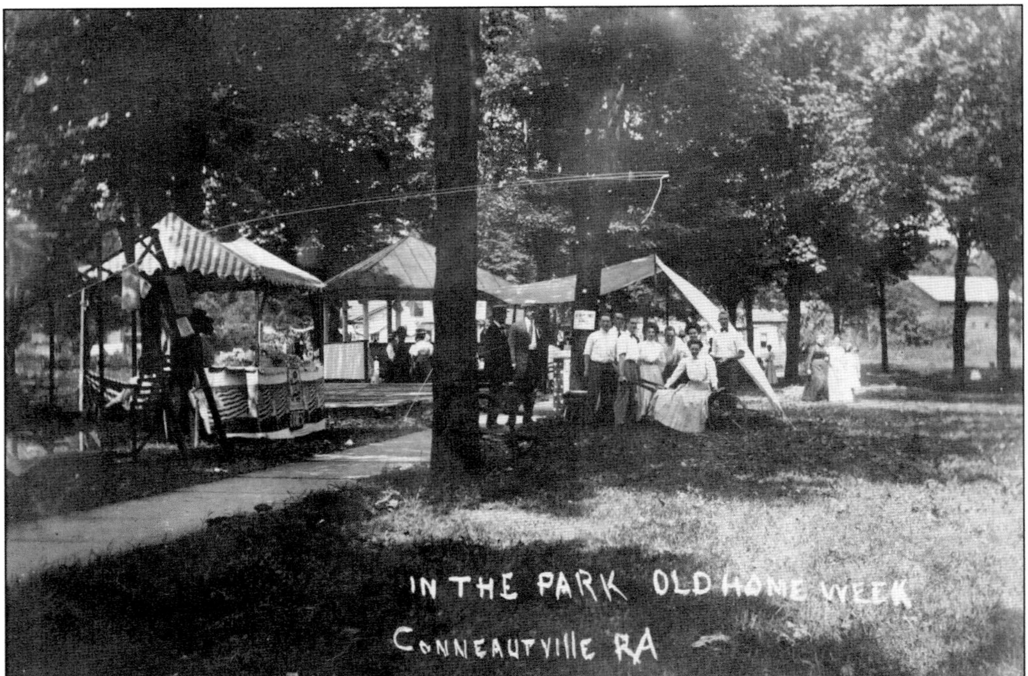

During the centennial celebration, the park was the center of activity. Unfortunately, no photographs survive of the park grounds during the festival. This image shows the park set up for Old Home Week of 1908. Situated along a plank walkway are tents with games and food. Presumably, the park would have looked like this in 1914.

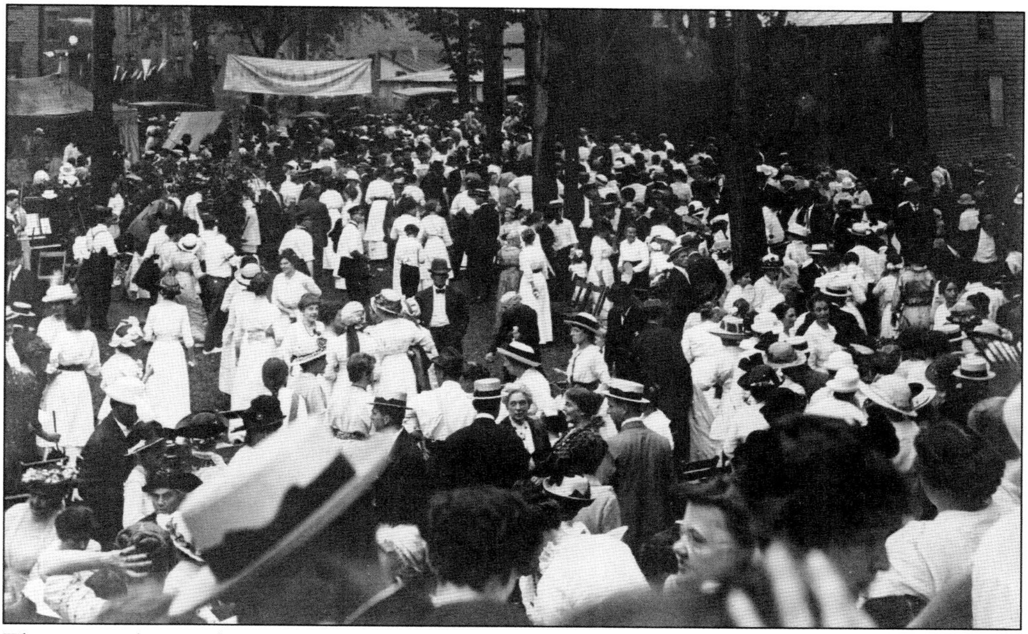

This scene during the carnival shows how numerous the crowds became during the height of the celebration. As previously mentioned, the park grounds were full of food, activities, and excitement. This photograph is an excellent reminder of how proud the people of Conneautville were to celebrate the 100th anniversary of their beloved hometown.

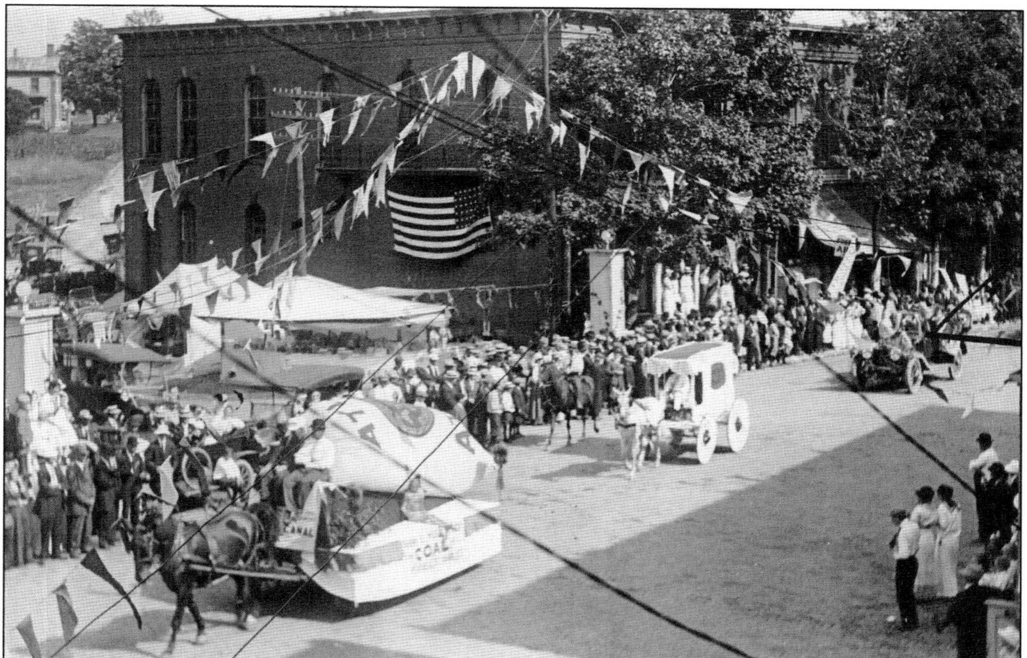

Another photograph of the parade captures more elements that made this event so memorable. The wagon at left hauls an advertisement, possibly for the Atlas Coal Company of western Pennsylvania. It appears that although the motor vehicle was popular, the horse-pulled wagon was still the most effective way to pull a float.

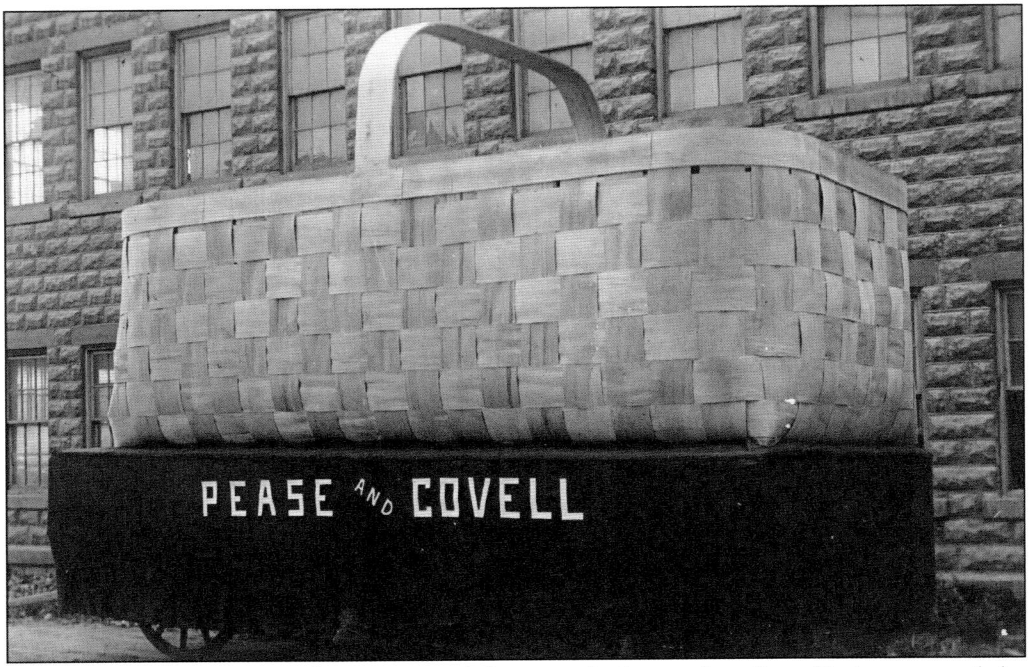

The Pease & Covell basket factory entered this giant basket as their float. Businesses used the parade not only for fun but also to advertise. A unique entry such as this would have surely amused the crowd.

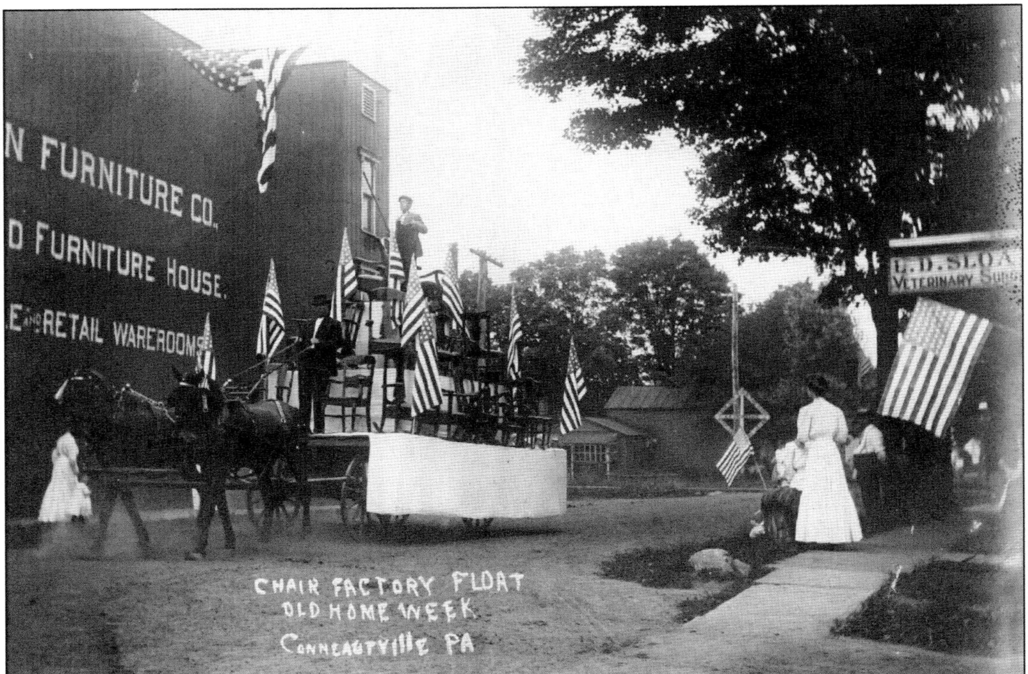

The chair factory float featured three levels of their finest handcrafted chairs. This horse-drawn float was an impressive visual representation of their expertise. The float is photographed here on Center Street behind Penn Furniture.

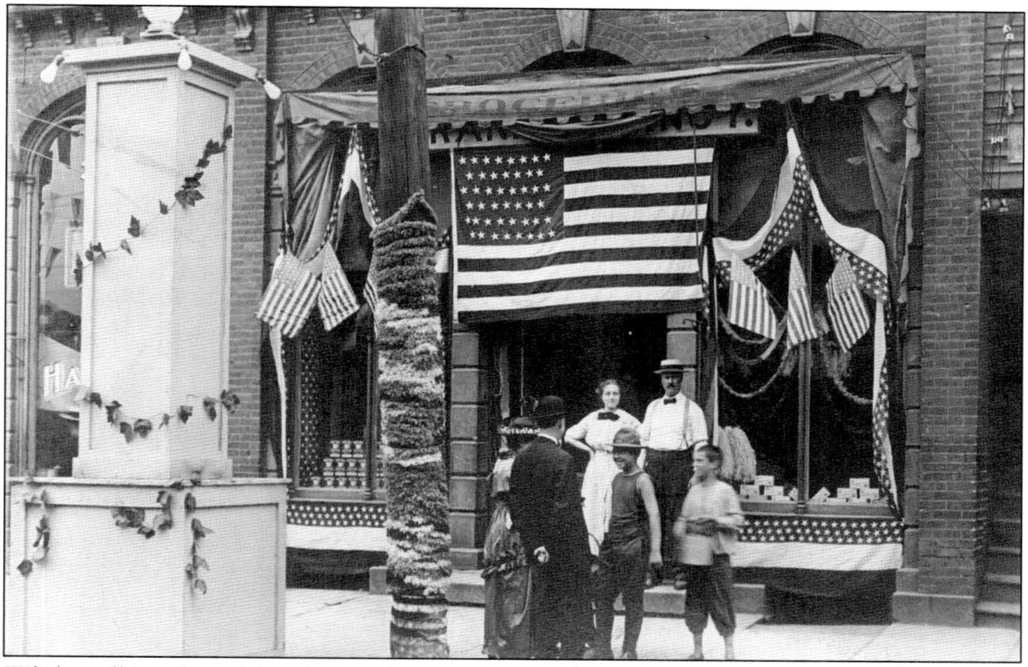

While walking down Main Street, these unidentified people stop for a conversation in front of a handsomely decorated storefront. This image visualizes the heightened level of national and local pride felt during the centennial celebration.

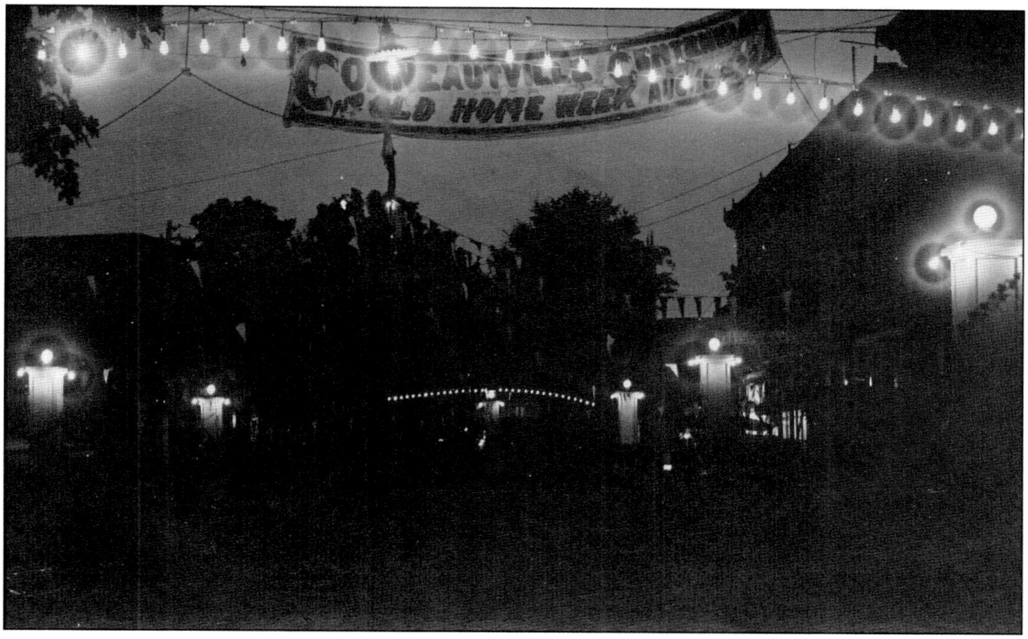

New streetlamps were installed specifically for the centennial. They are shown here illuminating Main Street.

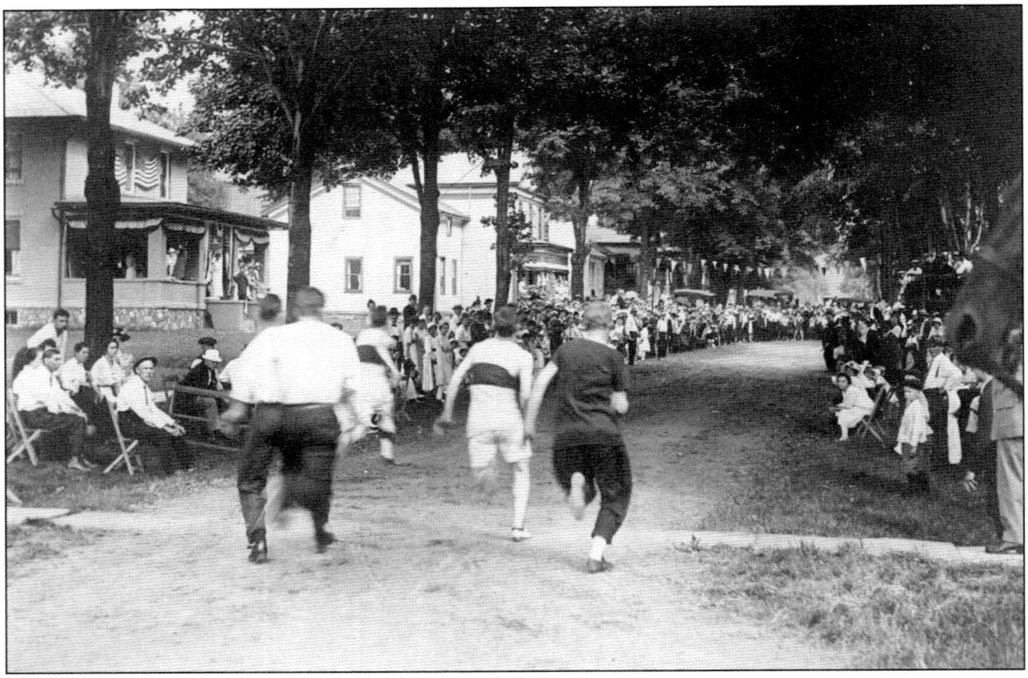

These boys participate in a race down Washington Street during the centennial week. At this time, the road was still dirt. To avoid mud, townspeople utilized crude crosswalks made of either cement or wooden planks.

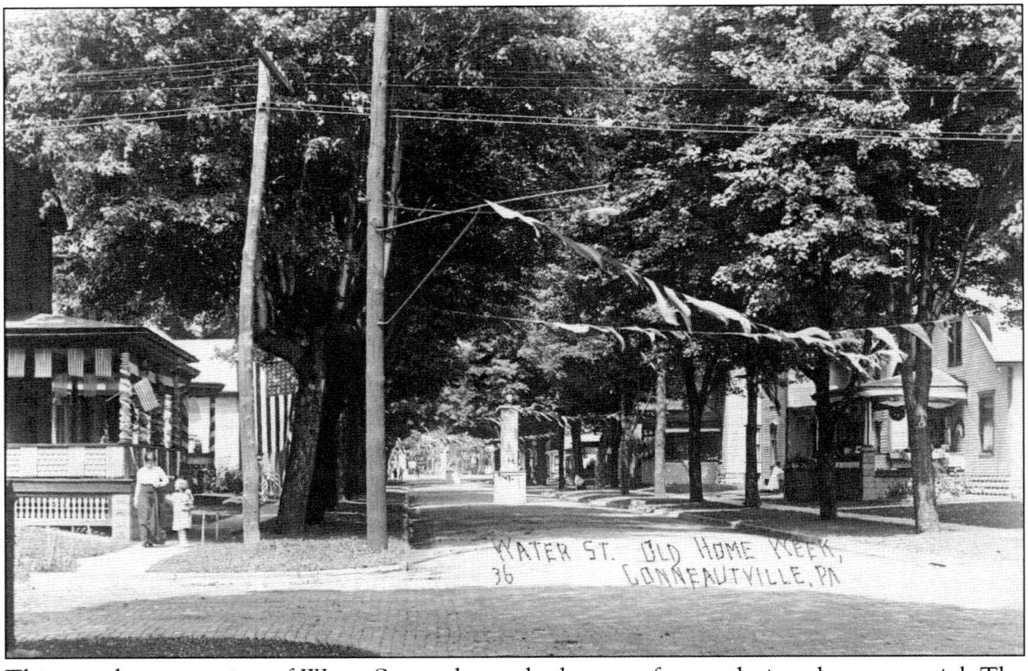

This mostly empty view of Water Street shows the beauty of town during the centennial. The entire celebration was a charming reminder of how the residents of Conneautville felt about their town and its history. It is apparent that those who took part in this festival had the pleasure of witnessing some of Conneautville's finest moments.

Five

The 20th Century

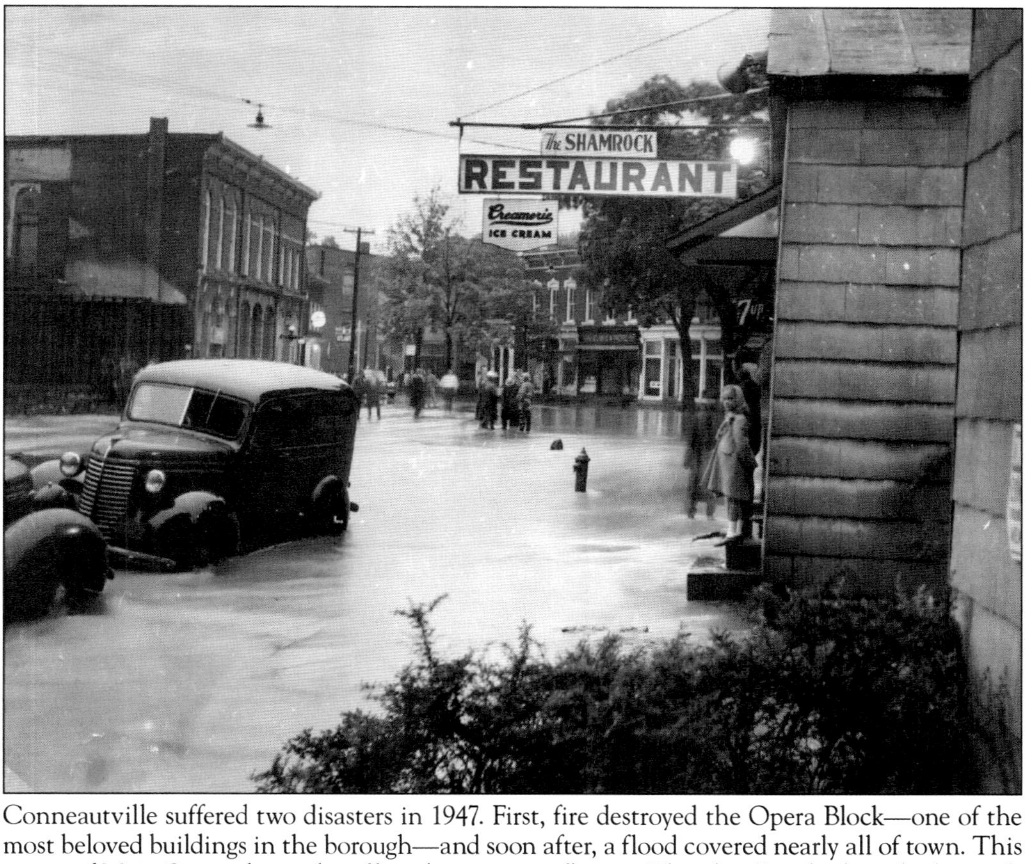

Conneautville suffered two disasters in 1947. First, fire destroyed the Opera Block—one of the most beloved buildings in the borough—and soon after, a flood covered nearly all of town. This image of Main Street shows the effect that a strong-flowing Thatcher Run had on the borough before the dam was built.

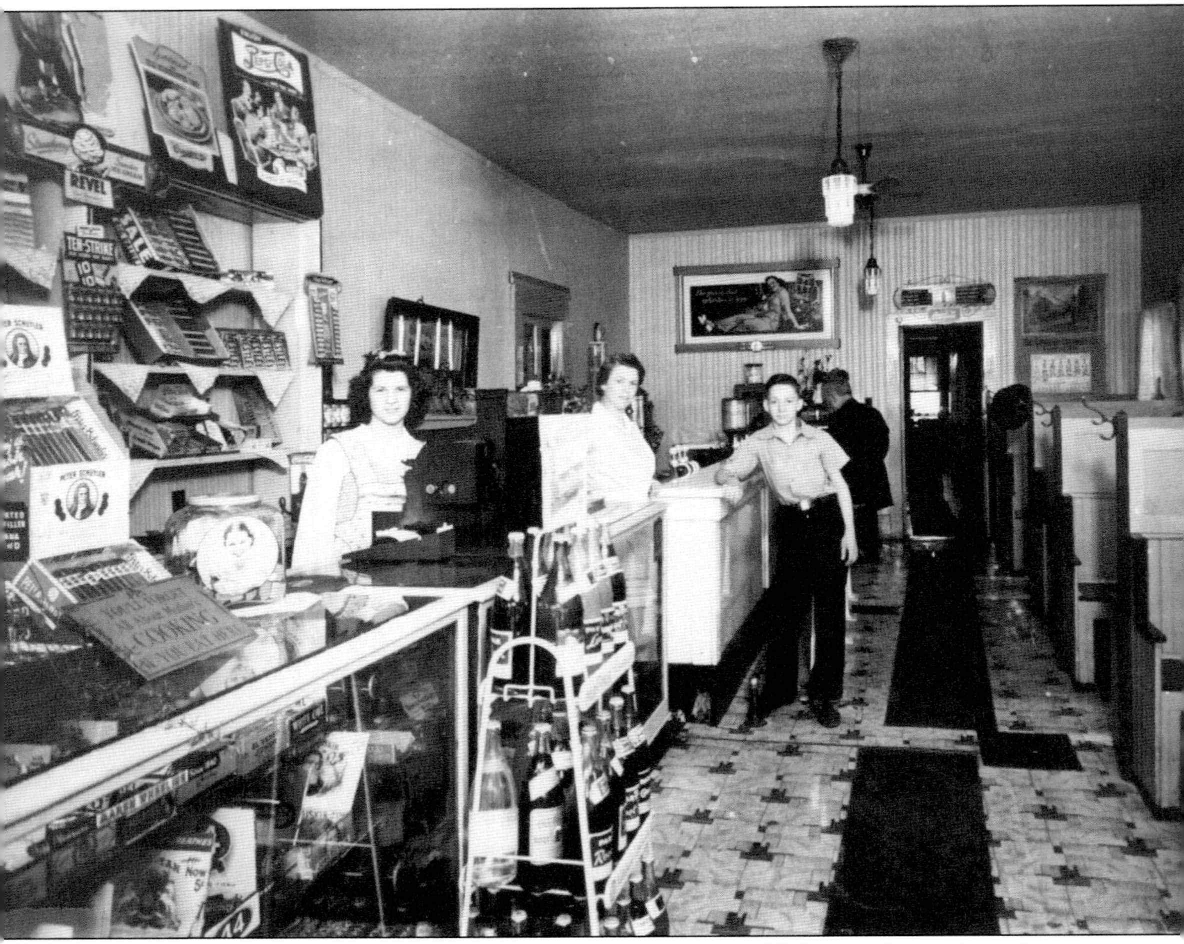

The Shamrock Restaurant was more than just an eating establishment. It was here that many high school students met with their dates and enjoyed jukebox music, hamburgers, sodas, sundaes, and homemade pies. During the 1940s and 1950s, the Shamrock was the most popular place in town. The Shamrock became the place to celebrate after sporting events and was usually filled to capacity with loyal fans. This image of the Shamrock restaurant was taken in 1941. Seen here are Esther Gibson (left), Suzy Brewer, and Jack MacMillan.

The Conneaut Creek provided one of the best natural swimming pools in the area. In addition to a rope swing, Conneautville playground visitors also enjoyed the eight-foot-deep water with the help of a diving board. An average of 50 children attended the playground daily during the summer months.

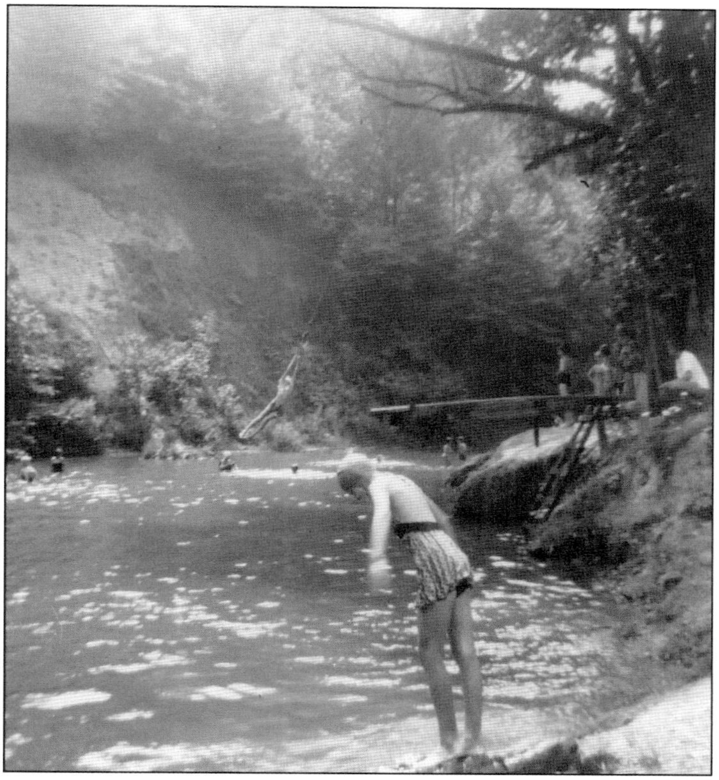

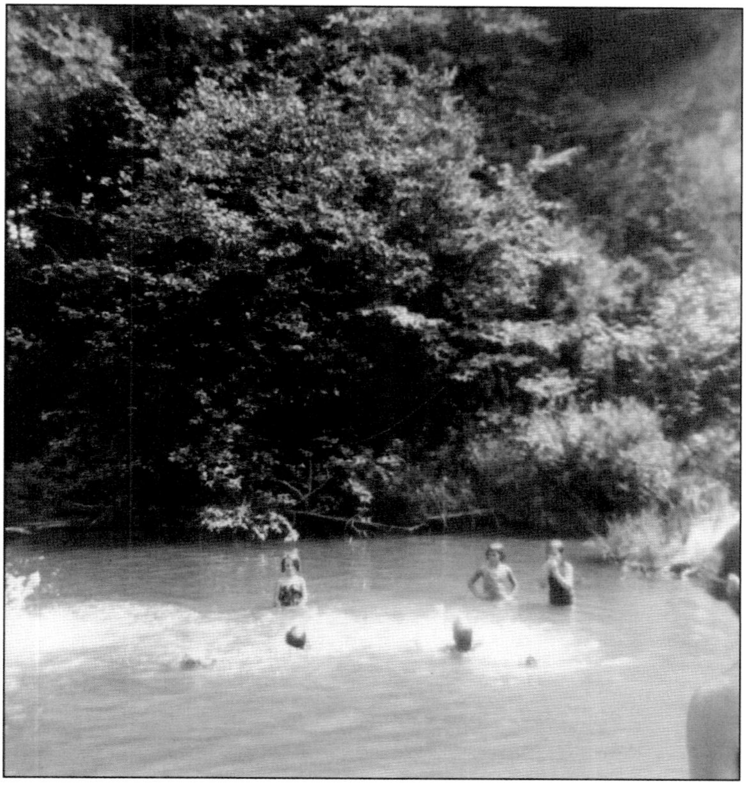

Although swimming was the major attraction at the playground, children also enjoyed basketball, tetherball, badminton, ping-pong, and crafts. One of the novelties of the playground was the small stream a vehicle had to ford just prior to the park. Occasionally, a bus would get stuck, delighting the children aboard.

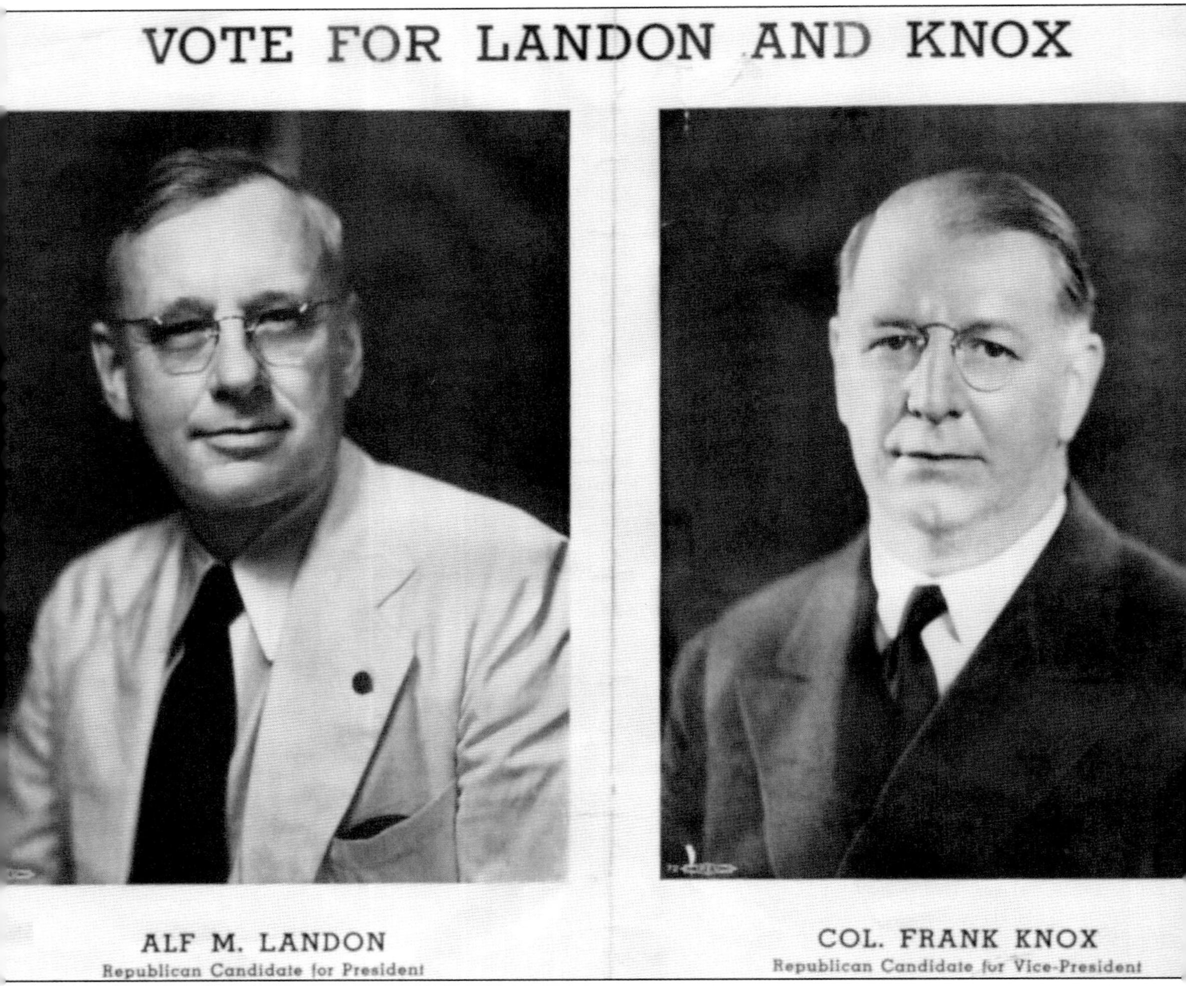

The presidential election of 1936 came to Conneautville when the Republican candidate for president of the United States, Alfred Landon, paid a visit to his boyhood home. Born in West Middlesex on September 8, 1887, Alfred soon moved with his parents to Conneautville to live with his paternal grandparents, Mary and Manuel Landon, who occupied a house on Walnut and Main Streets. After he attended his first couple years of schooling in town, the Landon family moved to Marietta, Ohio, and later to Kansas. "Alf," as he was known, would later become an independent petroleum producer in Independence, Kansas; serve in World War I; and become Kansas's 26th governor in 1932. Having gained the Republican nomination for president in the 1936 election, Landon ran with Navy secretary William Knox but was heavily defeated by Franklin D. Roosevelt.

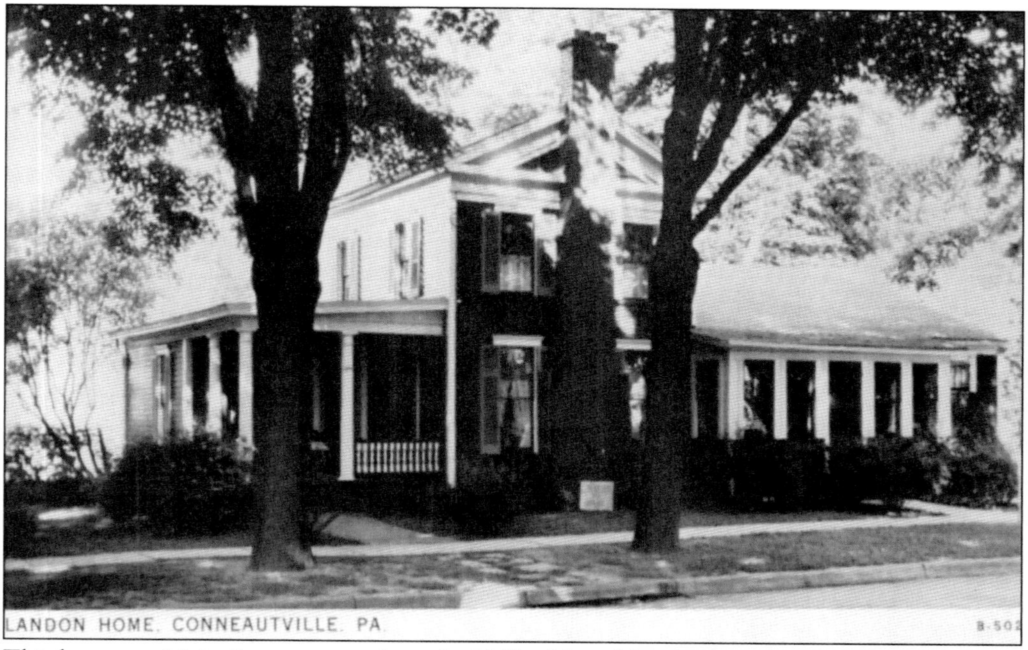

This house on Main Street, across from the Valley United Methodist Church, was home to Mr. and Mrs. Manuel Landon, grandparents of Alfred Landon. Alfred often returned to this house during his childhood to visit with them. The elder Mr. Landon died in 1894 and was interred in the family plot in the Conneautville Cemetery.

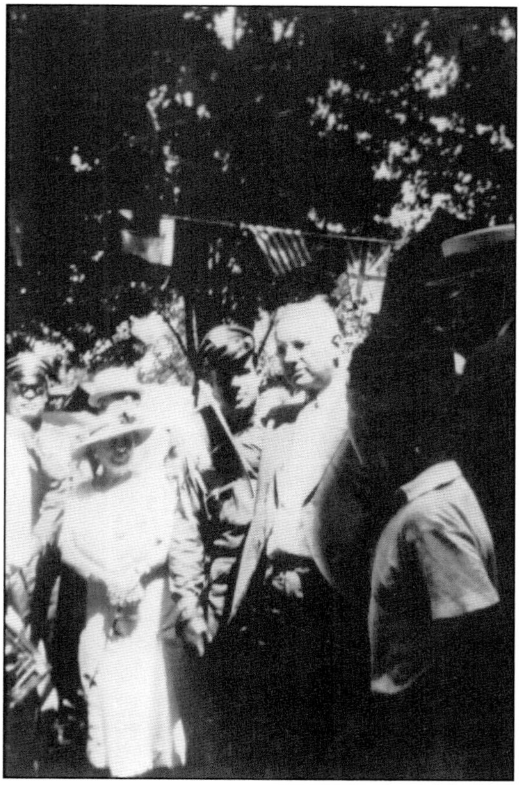

Kansas governor Alfred Landon mingles with the crowd in Conneautville as he campaigns during the 1936 presidential election.

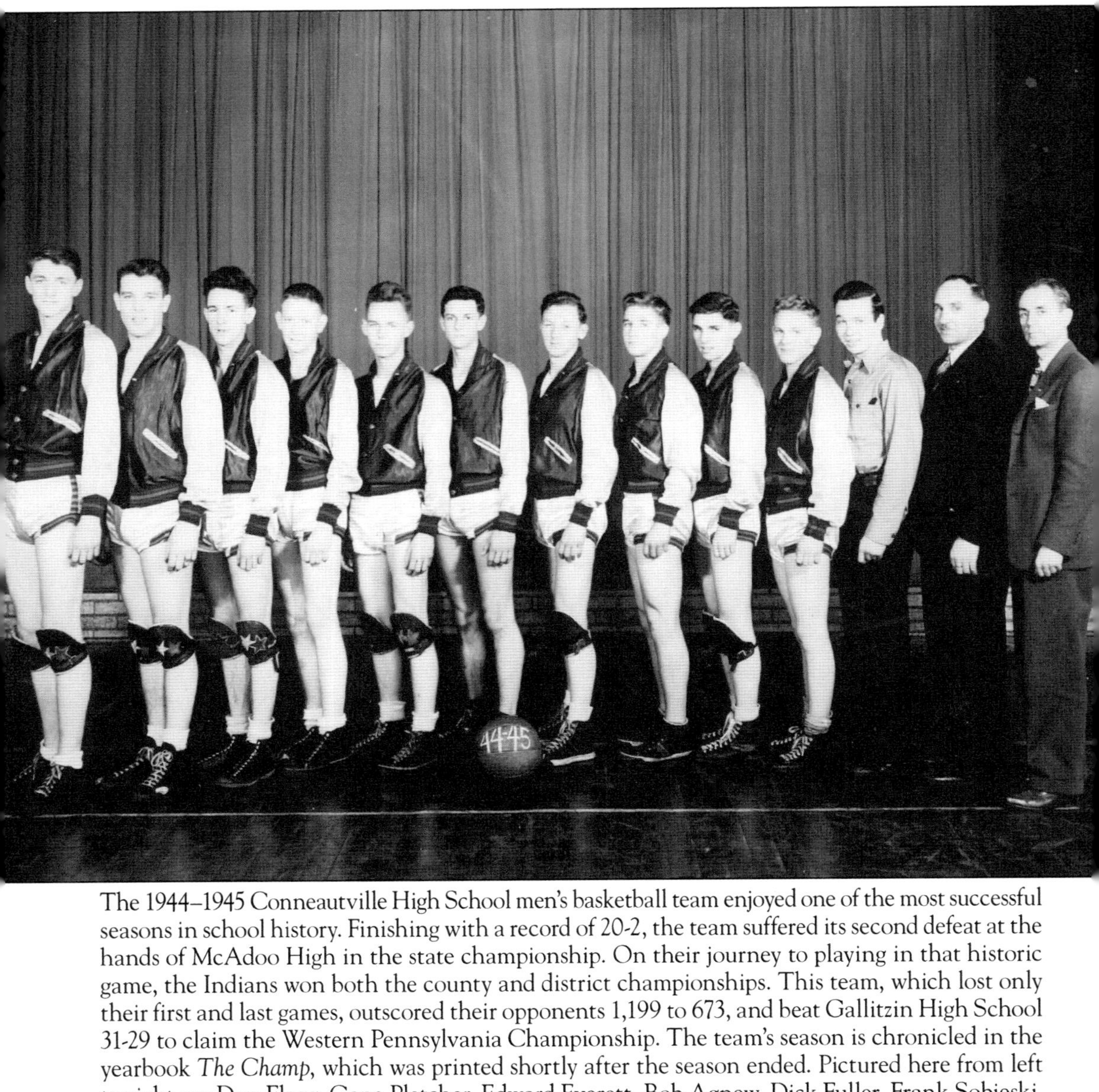

The 1944–1945 Conneautville High School men's basketball team enjoyed one of the most successful seasons in school history. Finishing with a record of 20-2, the team suffered its second defeat at the hands of McAdoo High in the state championship. On their journey to playing in that historic game, the Indians won both the county and district championships. This team, which lost only their first and last games, outscored their opponents 1,199 to 673, and beat Gallitzin High School 31-29 to claim the Western Pennsylvania Championship. The team's season is chronicled in the yearbook *The Champ*, which was printed shortly after the season ended. Pictured here from left to right are Don Flagg, Gene Pletcher, Edward Everett, Bob Agnew, Dick Fuller, Frank Sobieski, Leo Mandle, Keith Nicolls, James Baker, Charles Boyce, Albert Fields, coach Paul Gibson, and principal Chester Lingo.

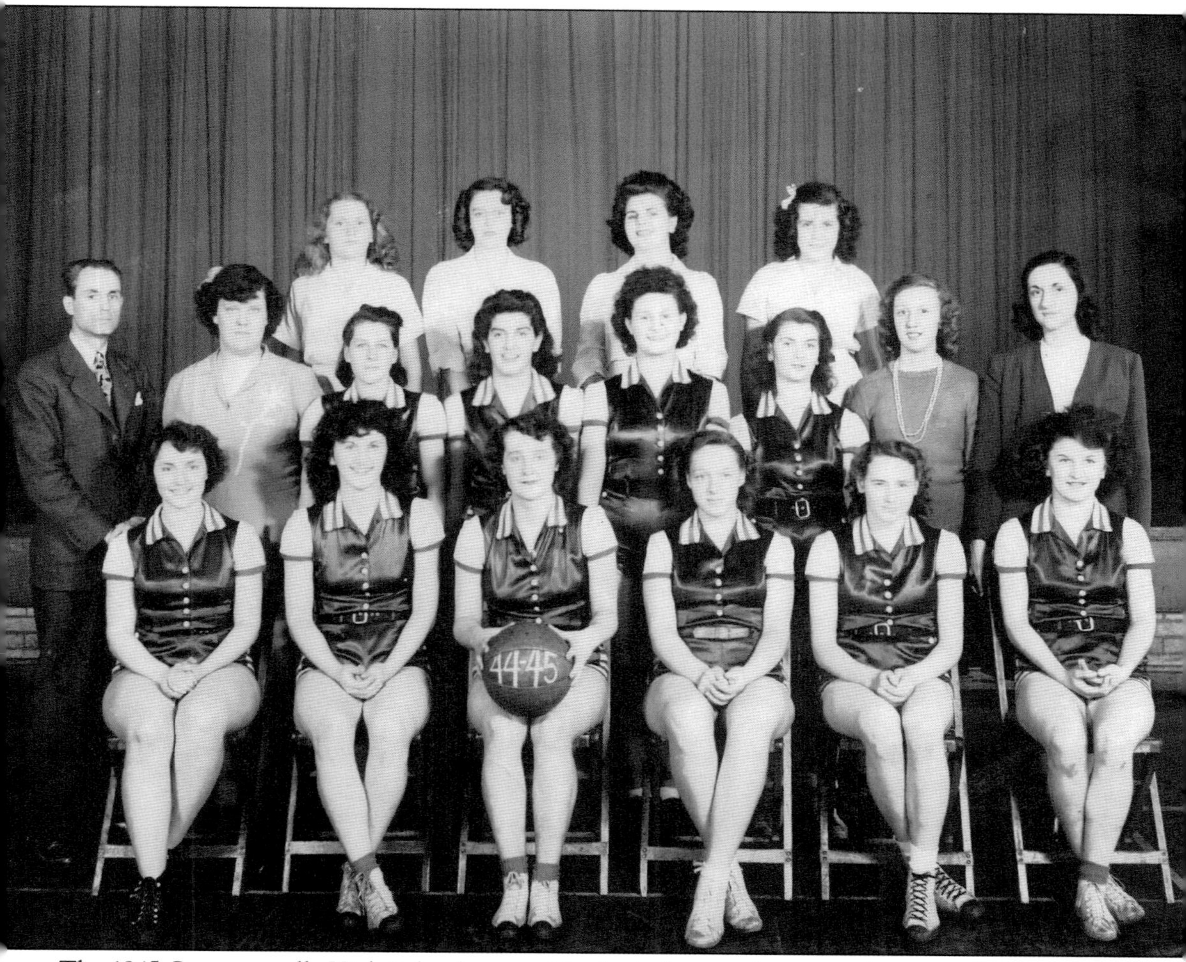

The 1945 Conneautville High School women's basketball team also enjoyed a successful season en route to capturing the county championship. Pictured here from left to right are (first row) Bea Hoover, Delores Piatek, captain Shirley Olson, Betty Adkins, Elizabeth Logan, and Jenny Piatek; (second row) principal Chester Lingo, manager Wilomenia McBride, Lucille Thomas, Lois Schaffer, Irene Gresh, Mable Fish, assistant manager Mary Doud, and Coach Alice Carman; (third row) Margaret Vendal, Ruth Faust, Julia Gresh, and Sally Gibson.

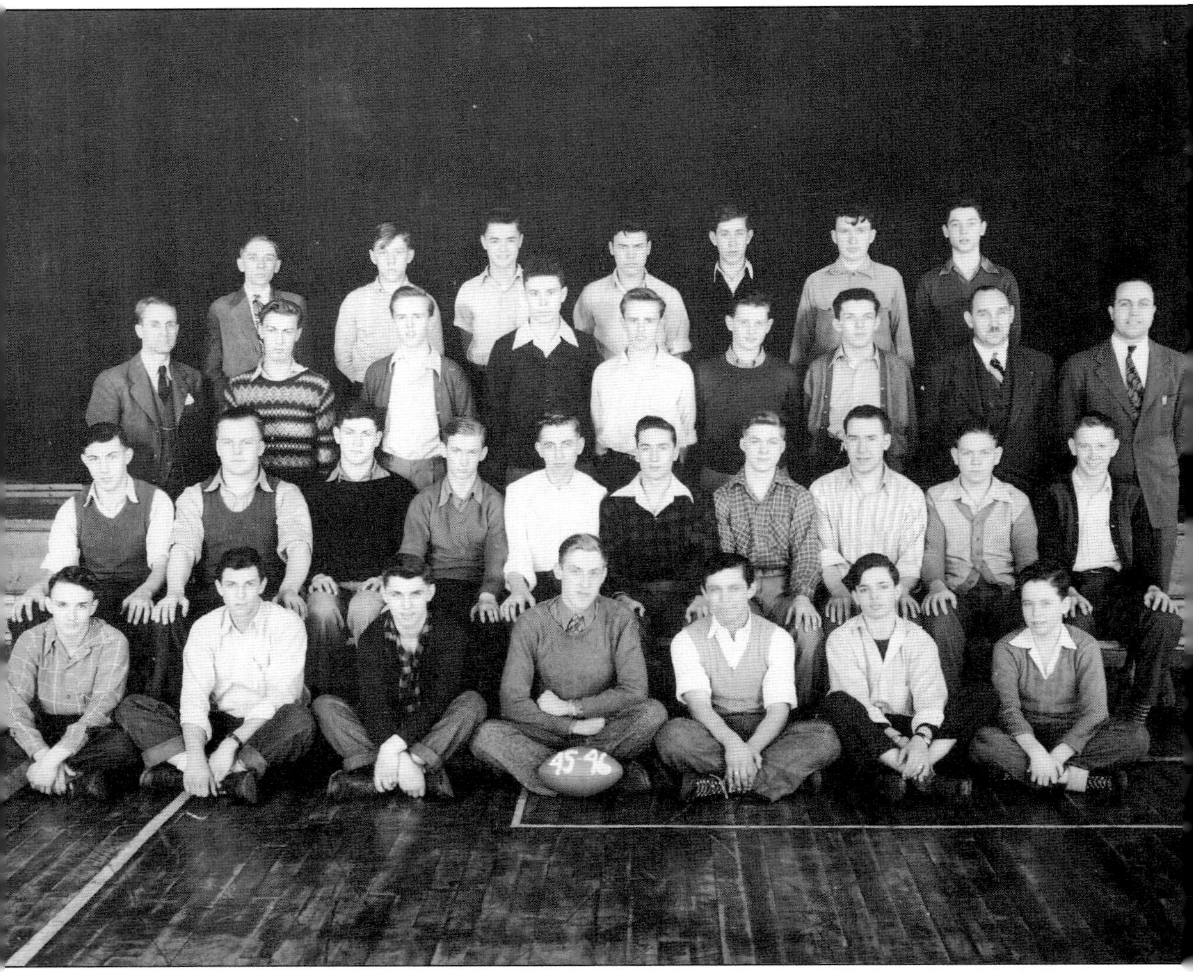

During the 1945–1946 school year, Conneautville High School fielded its first football team. Pictured here from left to right are (first row) Gerald Barnes, Frank Sobieski, James Baker, Richard Hunter, Henry Brandt, Jack Horvath, and Clyde Faust; (second row) Stanley Sowry, George Hayek, Millard Mershon, Robert Fish, Roe "Bud" Hildreth, Raymond Kazebee, Robert Wheeler, James Smith, Ted Gibson, and Bob Agnew; (third row) principal Chester Lingo, Clare Davenport, Jarold Phelps, James Cotton, Harold Phelps, Robert Hildreth, Harry Salchak, coach Paul Gibson, and assistant coach Victor Tortorelli; (fourth row) Joseph Minnick, William Minnick, Richard Baker, Blaine Thomas, George Thomas, Robert Parker, and Joseph Parlas.

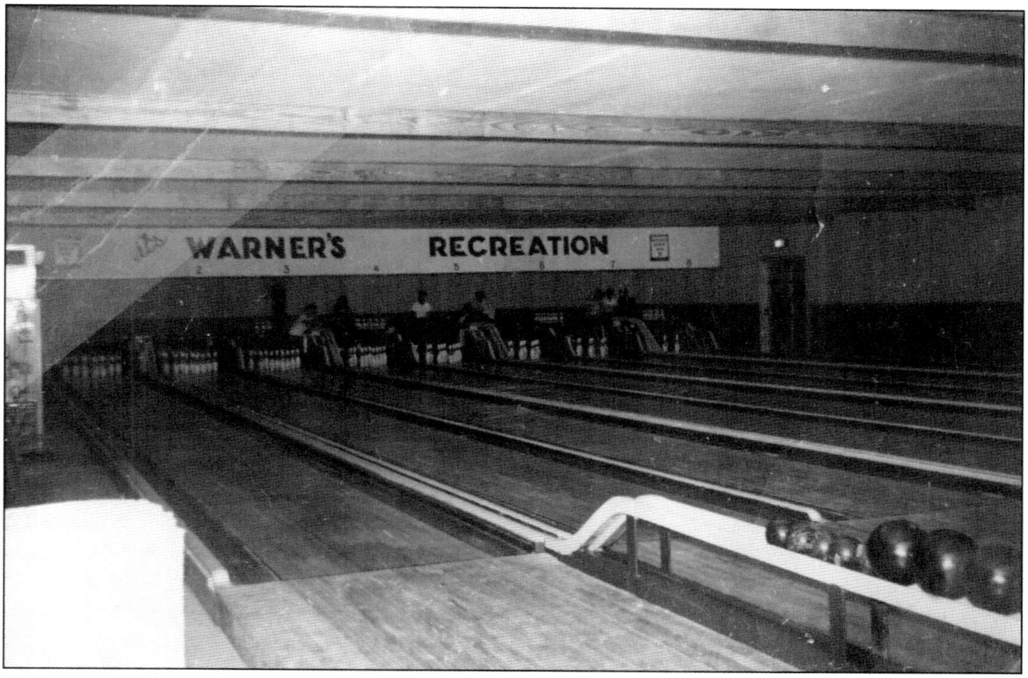

Warner's Bowling Alley offered a relaxing atmosphere and excellent lanes. It was situated along Washington Street, in the current location of the rear of the fire hall. Warner's was particularly popular among Conneautville businesspeople, who competed against one another in bowling leagues.

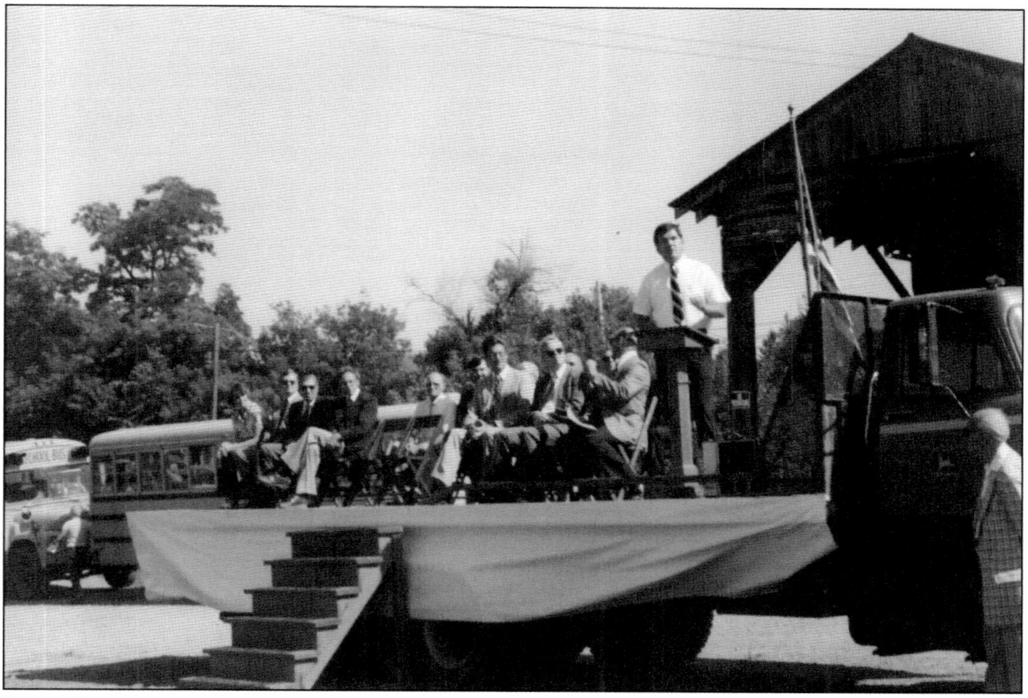

Future Pennsylvania governor and secretary of Homeland Security Tom Ridge spoke in Conneautville in 1980 at the dedication of the conduit that runs underneath town. In connection with the dam, the conduit allows water to flow smoothly away from town and into Conneaut Creek.

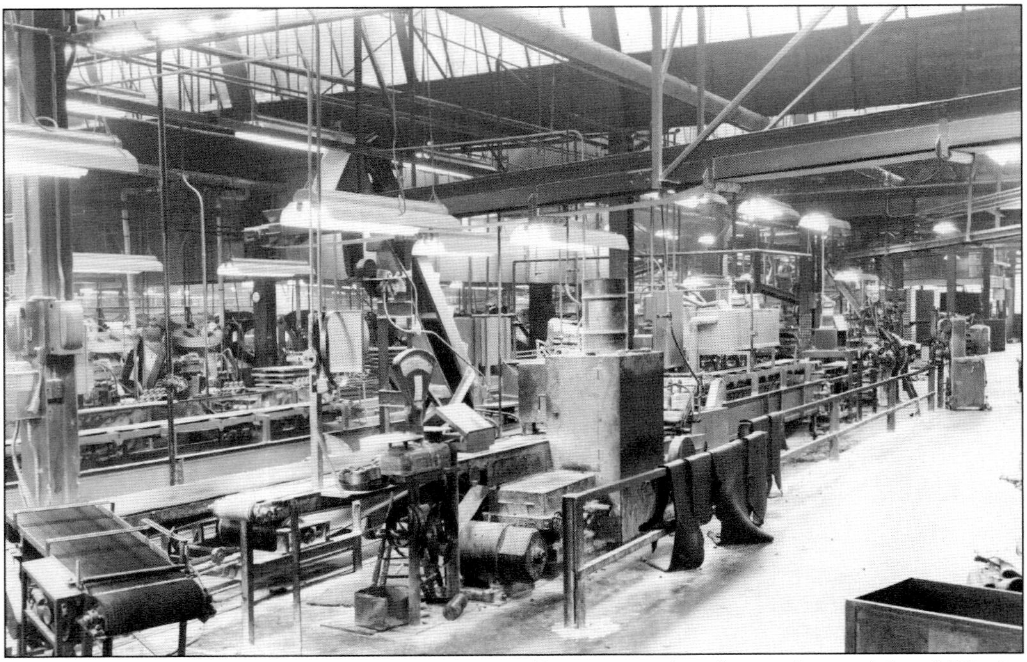

The Ohio Rubber Company came to Conneautville in 1941, after the purchase of the old Burke Electric building. At that time, the property covered 24 acres and had 97,000 square feet of floor space. Its products included tires for agriculture and industrial applications as well as flexible wire-reinforced ventilating hose. Although strongly focused on rubber products, the company also produced more than 1,000 other items. The company also operated factories in Willoughby, Ohio; and Stratford, Connecticut.

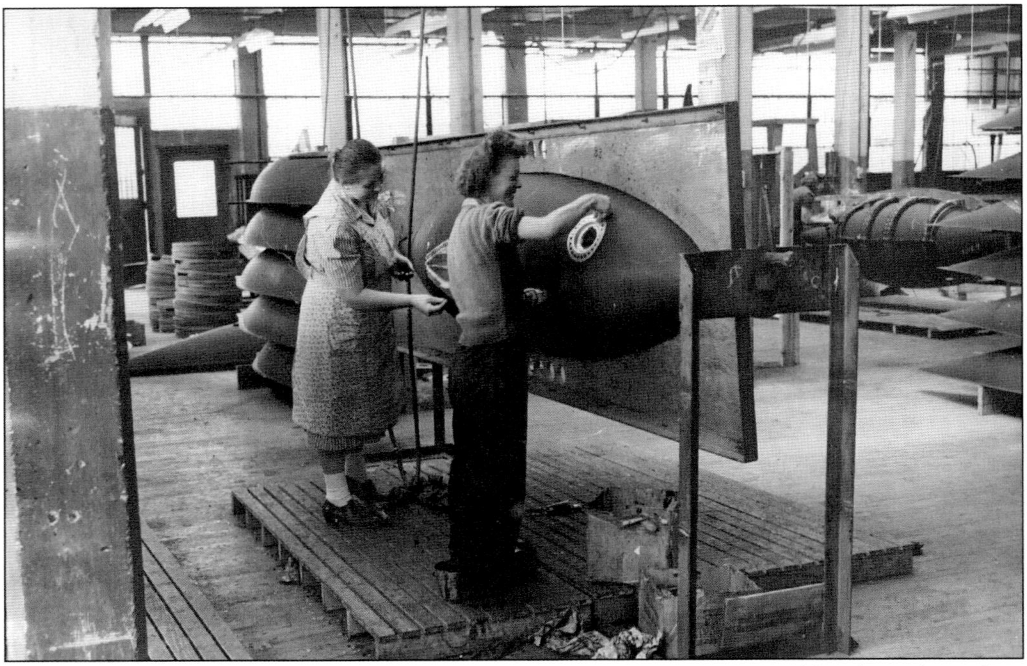

Elizabeth Katona (left) and Grace (Halbe) Swiden apply fittings to a Lockheed auxiliary drop tank. These women were photographed on September 1, 1944.

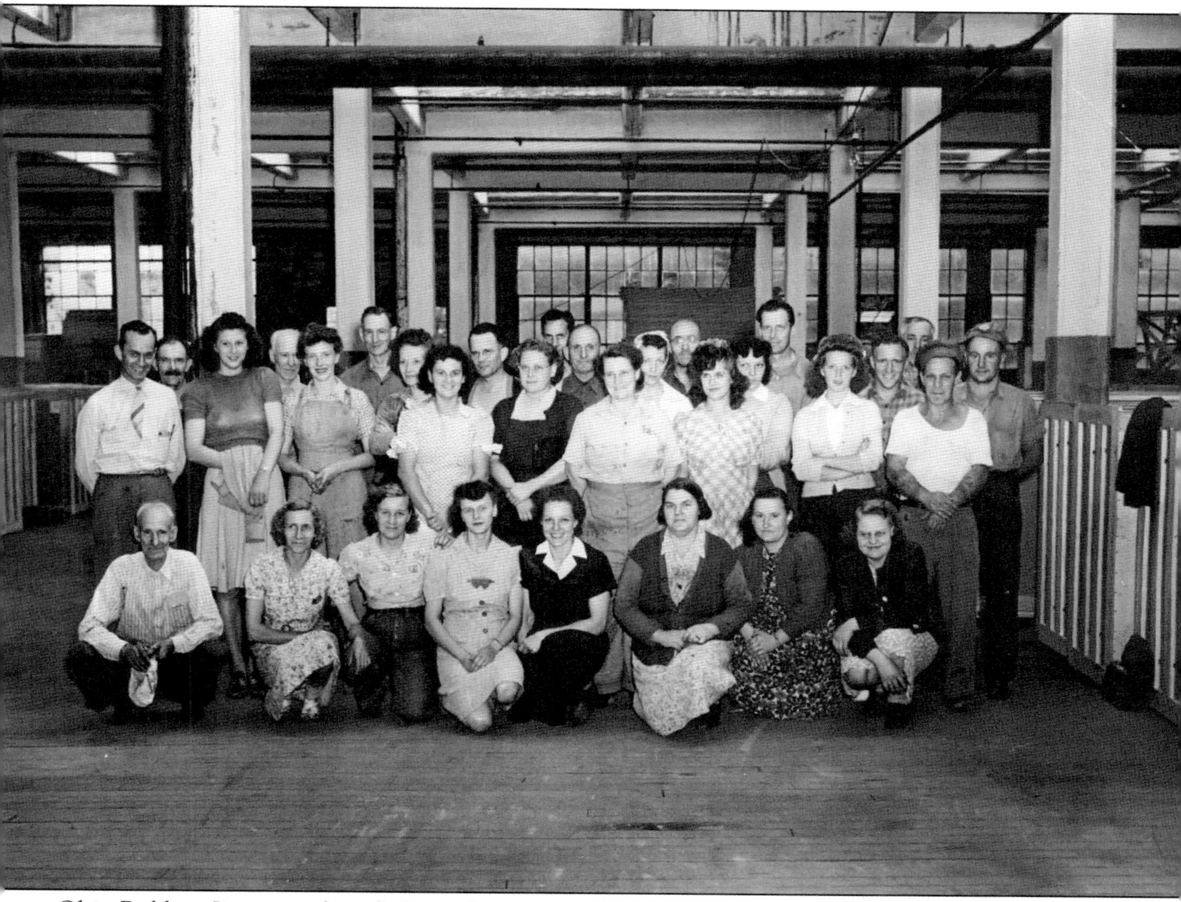

Ohio Rubber Company first shift employees pose for a picture in 1946. Pictured here from left to right are (first row) C. Carr, Mary Allen, Ethel McKissick, Laura Smith, Kate Johnston, Elda Blood, Helen Fedorcak, and Lenora Blood; (second row) Carl Baker, Pauline Kuban, Ruth Fox, Marie Braden, Sarah Kimple, Ethel Nichols, Hellen Poweska Miller, Mary Ingols, and Joe Parisi; (third row) Vensel Holets, Mott Frazier, Jas. Morris, Anne Allio, O. Dolan, Oake Wise, George Snyder, Frances Hill, Howard Judd, Jeanette Chason, Clair Walton, W. O'Neal, Tracy North, and Albert Combs.

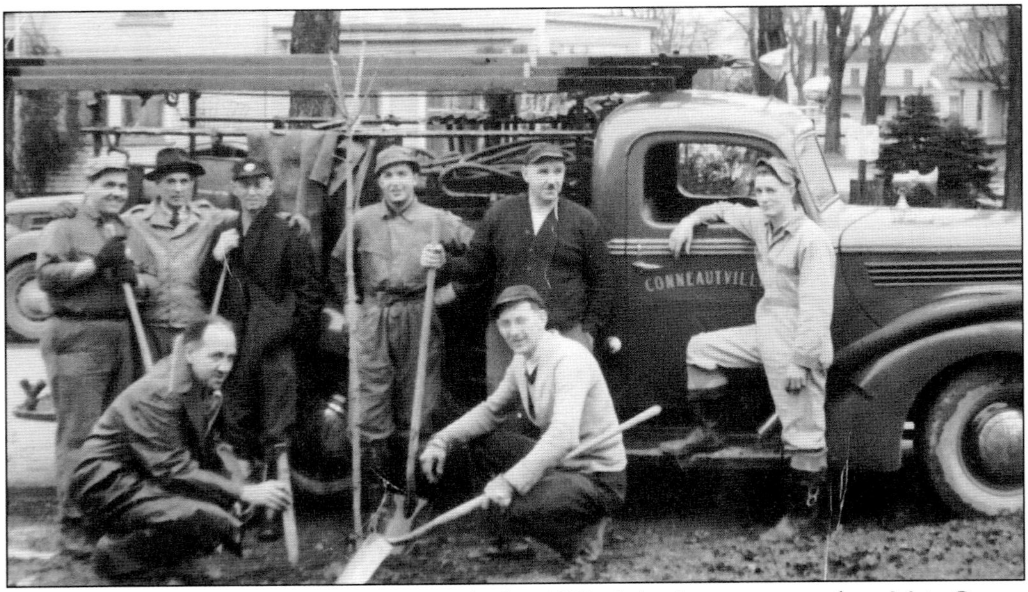

Members of the Fellows Club are photographed in 1950 while planting a tree along Main Street. From left to right they are (squatting) Carlton Irons and Howard Burkholder; (standing) Bus Adkins, Chester Lingo, Fred Barr, Charlie Swanson, Paul Gibson, and Russ Ingols.

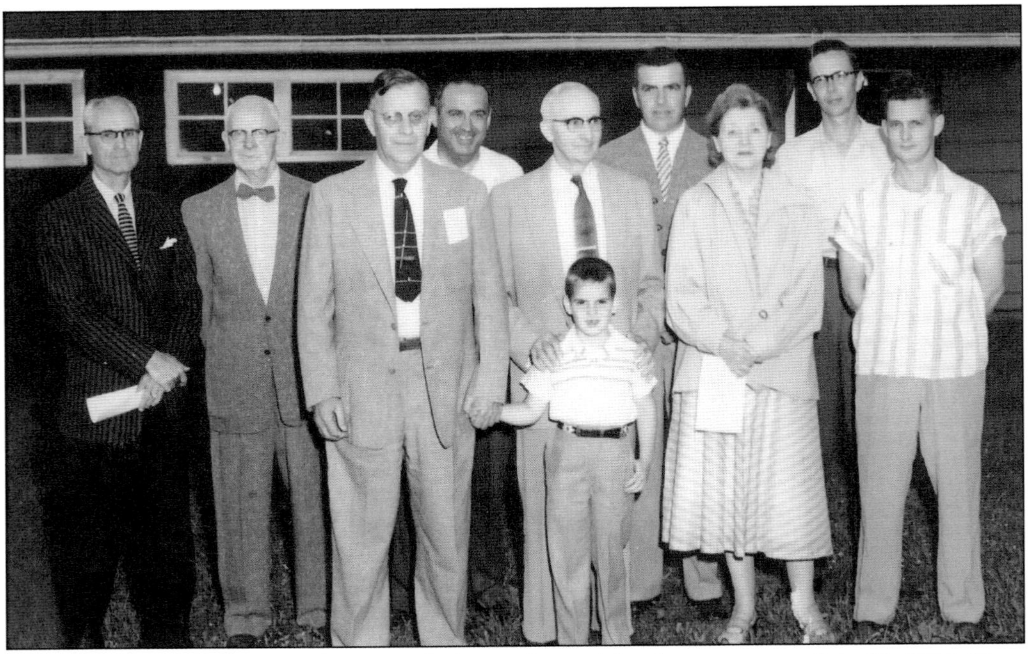

Members of the Conneautville Borough Council posed for this picture on July 18, 1956. They are, from left to right, Chester Lingo, Ormond Dean, George Williams, unidentified, Henry Shawkey, Chuck Thomas, Hilda Vher, Sterle Penfield, and Russ Ingols. The child in front is Michael McBride.

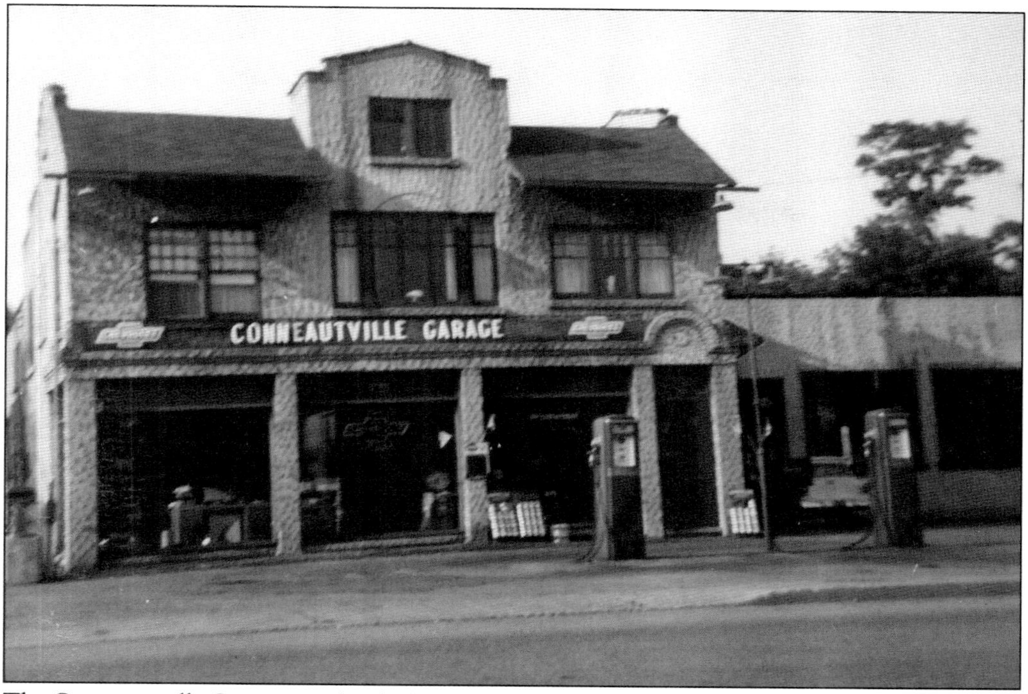

The Conneautville Garage was finished by Charlie Terril in the late 1930s and used as a Chevrolet dealership. The garage, situated on Main Street, also offered gas pumps and vehicle repair. The building is pictured here in 1959.

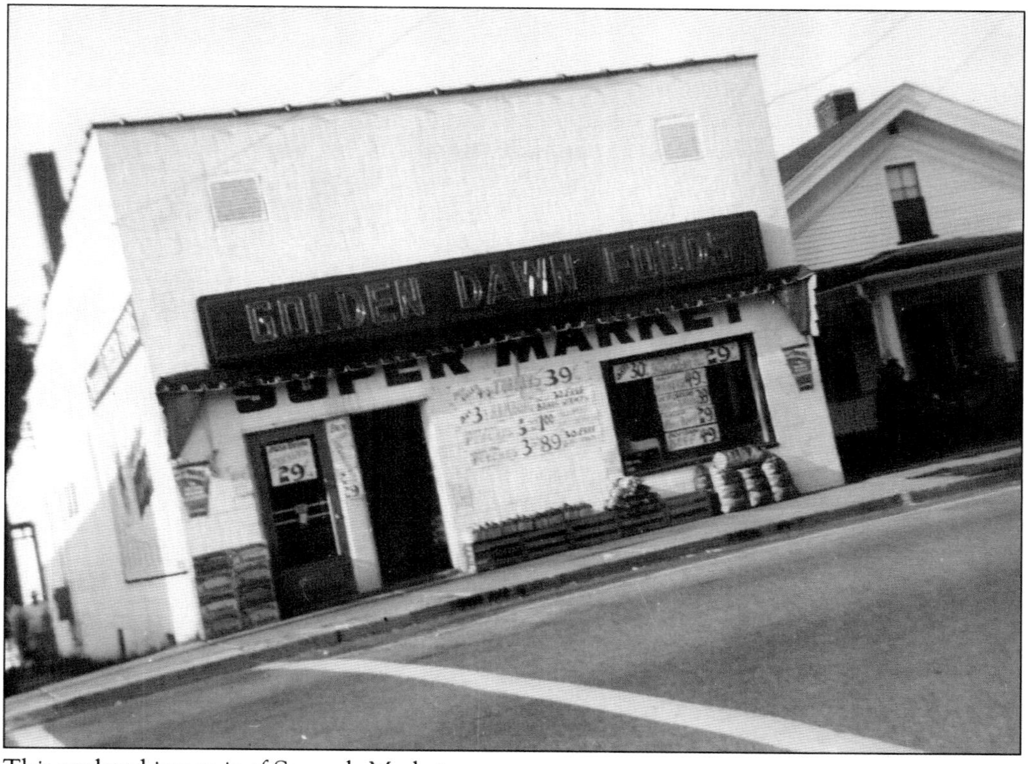

This undated image is of Samuels Market.

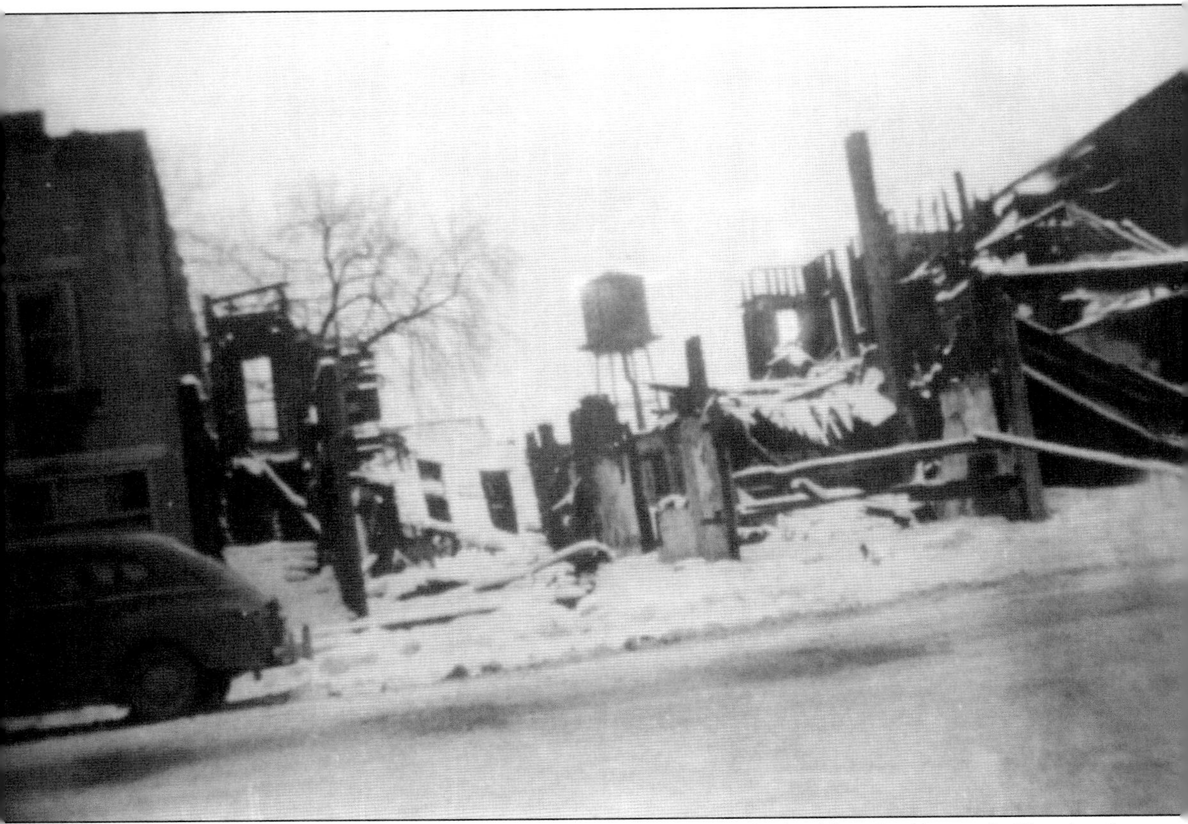

In 1947, a fire destroyed the Opera Block. Upon hearing that the building had burned, Cleveland, Ohio, resident Arch C. Klumph wrote to the *Conneautville Courier* on March 20, 1947: "I am shocked and grieved beyond measure at the news that the Opera Block is gone . . . I remember it seventy years ago, and it's loss is equal to that of a dear friend . . . I have made this statement many times, there isn't another town in the U.S.A. of one thousand population that has or ever had a theater as charming as the Opera House. There was an excellent stage; it had two beautiful private boxes with red plush and white lace. They had four full sets of scenery and a beautiful front curtain, hand painted with an English palace scene. I do hope, in some way, that another similar building can be built."

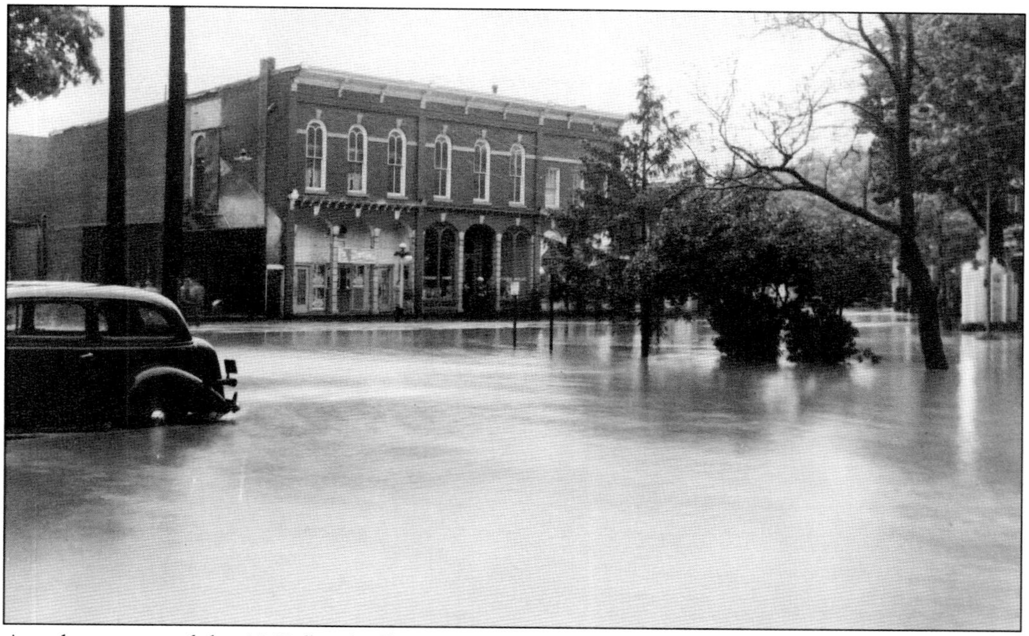

Another image of the 1947 flood offers a view of Main Street.

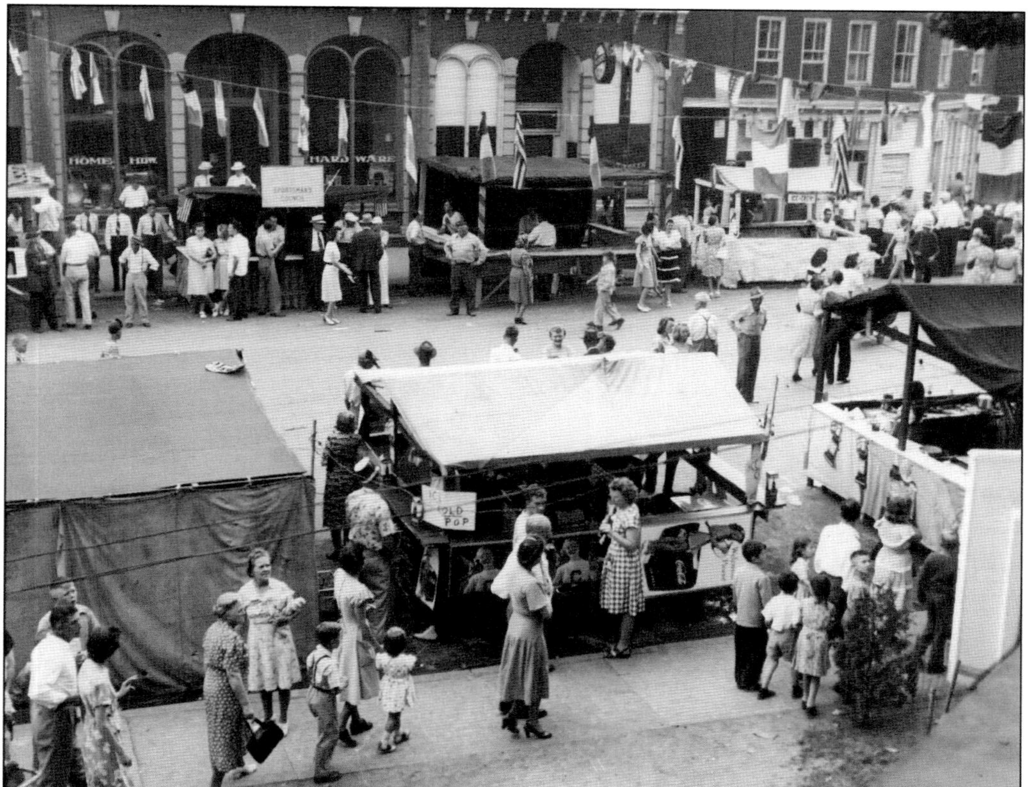

The American Legion organized a street fair during the 1950s and 1960s. Also known as "sidewalk days," the fair offered businesses an opportunity to sell merchandise along the sidewalks, where there was also food and carnival-style game booths.

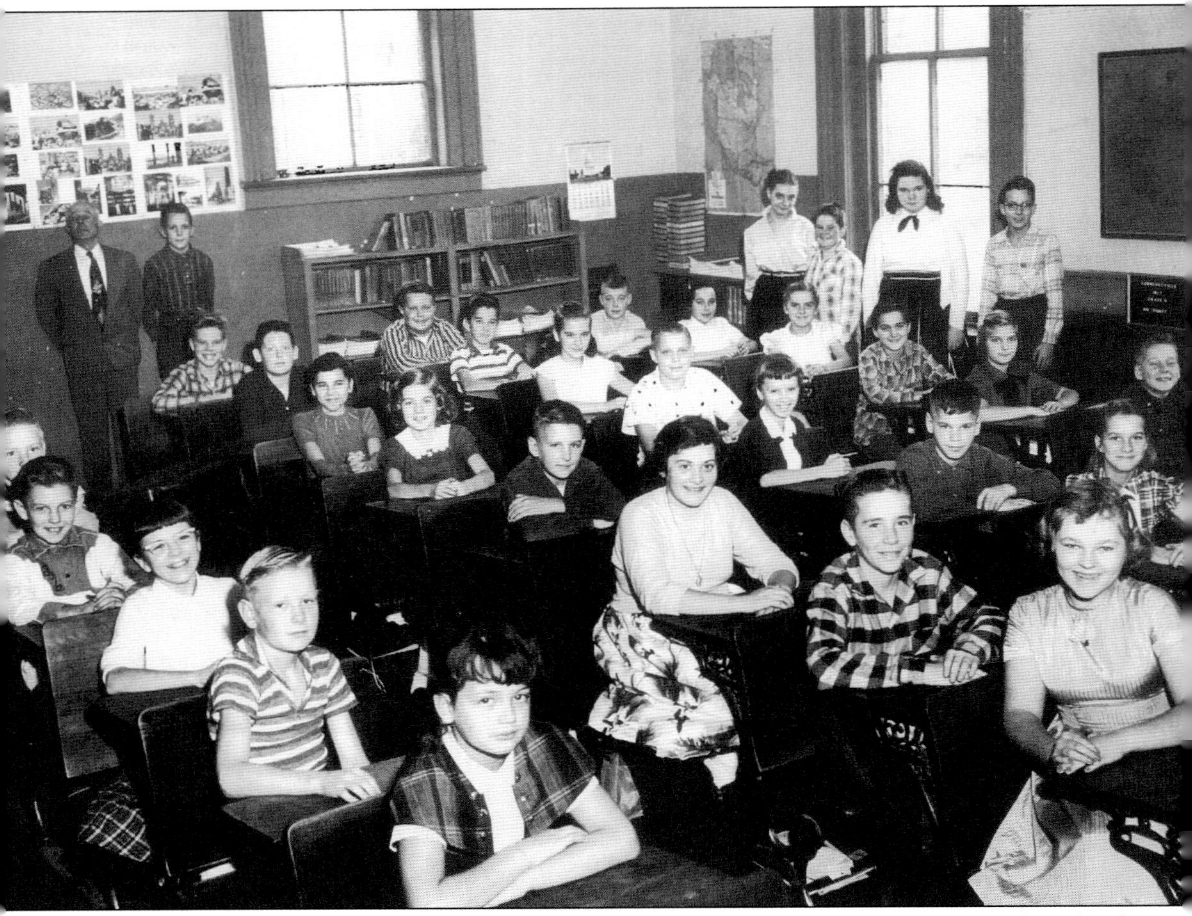

Although a new high school had been built north of town in 1955, the Conneautville School was still in use at that time. This 1960 class photograph shows Mr. Seneff's sixth grade class. Pictured here are, with rows listed from left to right and students in the rows listed from front to back, (first row) Elenore Willard, Conrad Smock, Nancy Baldridge, Thomas Peterman, and Dennis Fenton; (second row) Sandy Baker, Douglas Weibel, Joyce Bean, Tim Prince, Christine Greenfield, Jennifer Koeler, Jack Yacky, and Raymond Smith; (third row) Shirley Nicklas, Lee Barnhart, Gloria Post, Charles Kimple, Susanna Carman, Charles Swedrock, and James Heim; (fourth row) James Lehman, Bonnie Hecker, John Ransom, Joyce Berkley, Alice Cousins, and Robert Dean; (standing at far right) Barbara Foster, Gary Clark, Karen Nicklas, and Lee Thomas. Elmer Seneff is standing in the back of the room with Keith Wensel.

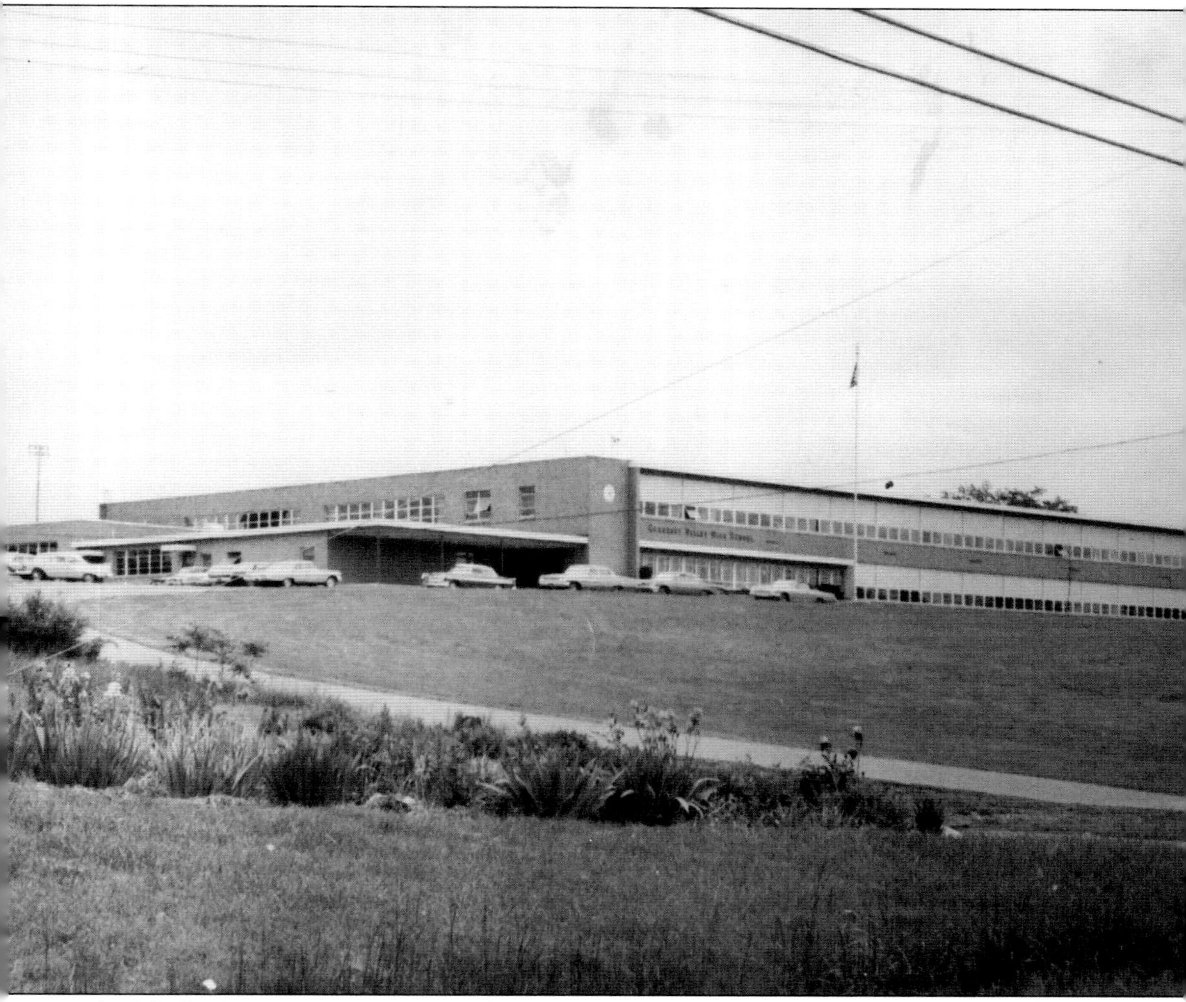

In the fall of 1954, a new junior-senior high school was opened on Route 18, roughly 1.5 miles north of the Conneautville borough, at a cost of $1,250,000. Staff consisted of a supervising principal, a principal, 28 teachers, a guidance counselor, and a nurse. The school was obtained through a joint effort of the citizens of Conneautville, Springboro, Beaver, Spring, and Summerhill Townships. The school was named Conneaut Valley High School because students attended from all over the Conneaut Creek Valley. For a time, the former school buildings of each of the above districts were used as elementary schools. In 1961, work was completed on a modern elementary building one half-mile north of the high school at a cost of $806,000. In 1962, the borough purchased the old, abandoned Conneautville High School building for use as a community center.

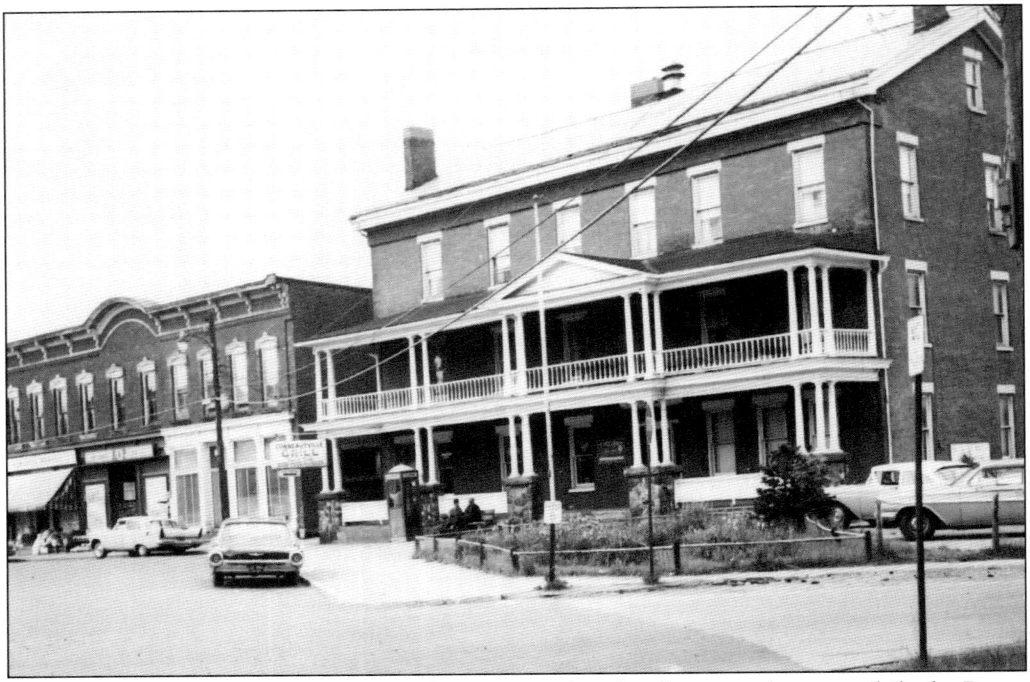

In the years after World War I, the Hotel Power was closed and remained vacant while the Power family lived in other parts of the country. In November 1935, Mrs. A.E. Robinson of Florida, the only surviving child of Horace Power, offered the hotel as a free, unencumbered gift to the Conneautville Borough. Over the next 20 years, the building was used by the Fellows Club and borough council for meetings. In 1959, Mr. and Mrs. Raymond Morris Sr. purchased the building and opened a restaurant known as the Conneautville Grill. These 1964 photographs of Main Street show the Conneautville Grill (above) and Power Block (below).

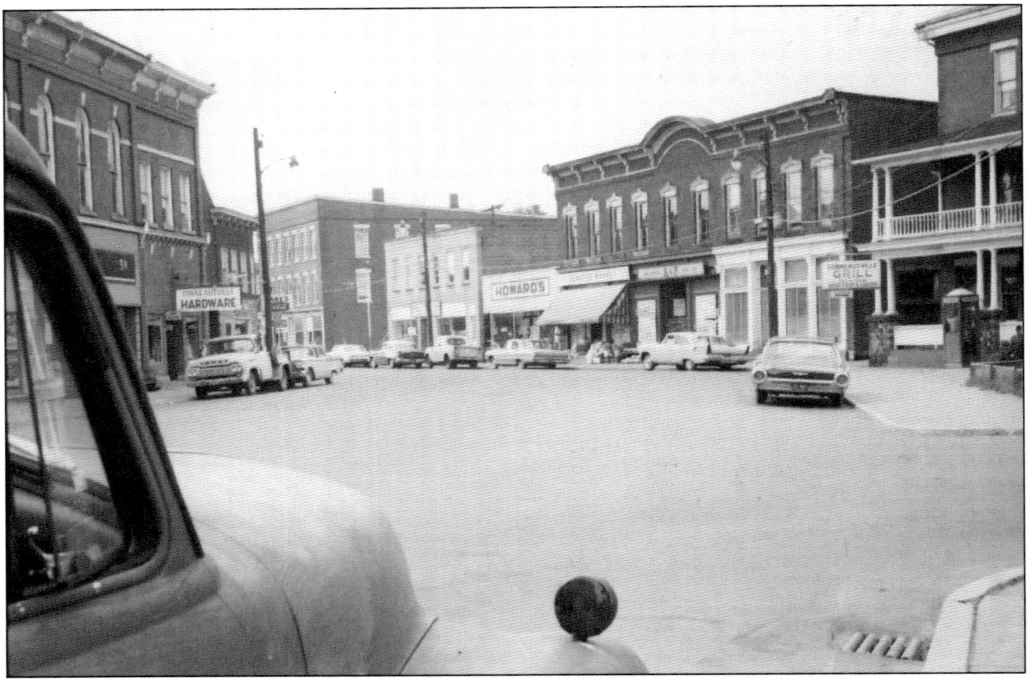

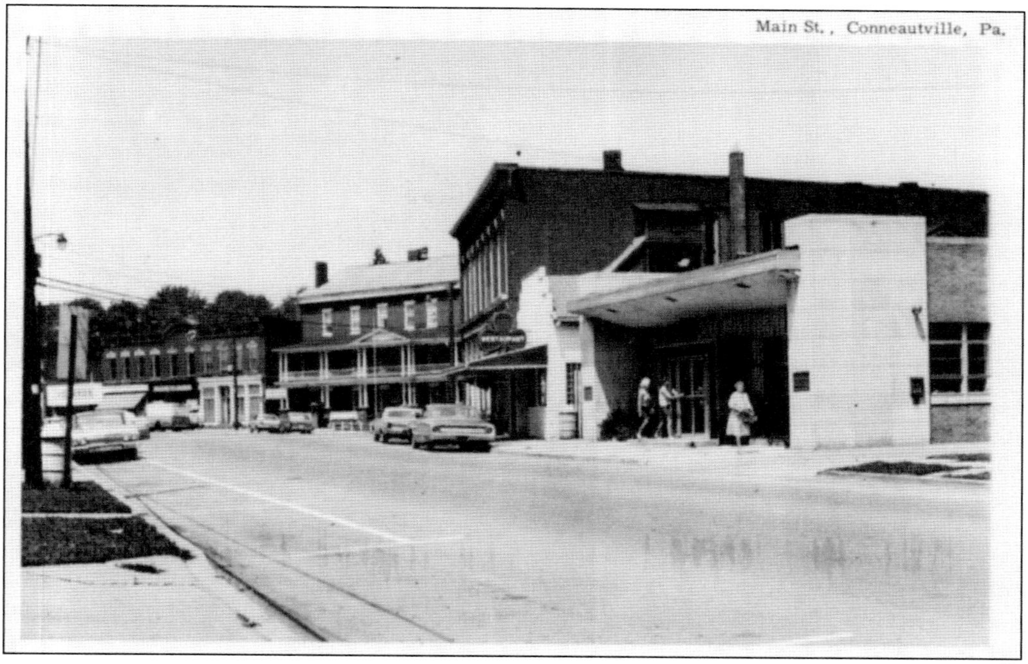

In July 1956, the Farmers National Bank moved into a newly completed building along Main Street, where it still sits today. In the above image, the bank, the Shamrock restaurant, Stone/Gleason/Van Tassel Block, Conneautville Grill, and Power Block can be seen on the right. In the image below, taken from Second Street, one can see Main Street looking south in 1964. Although these buildings have seen businesses come and go, many of them stand today as a reminder of the economic prosperity of the past.

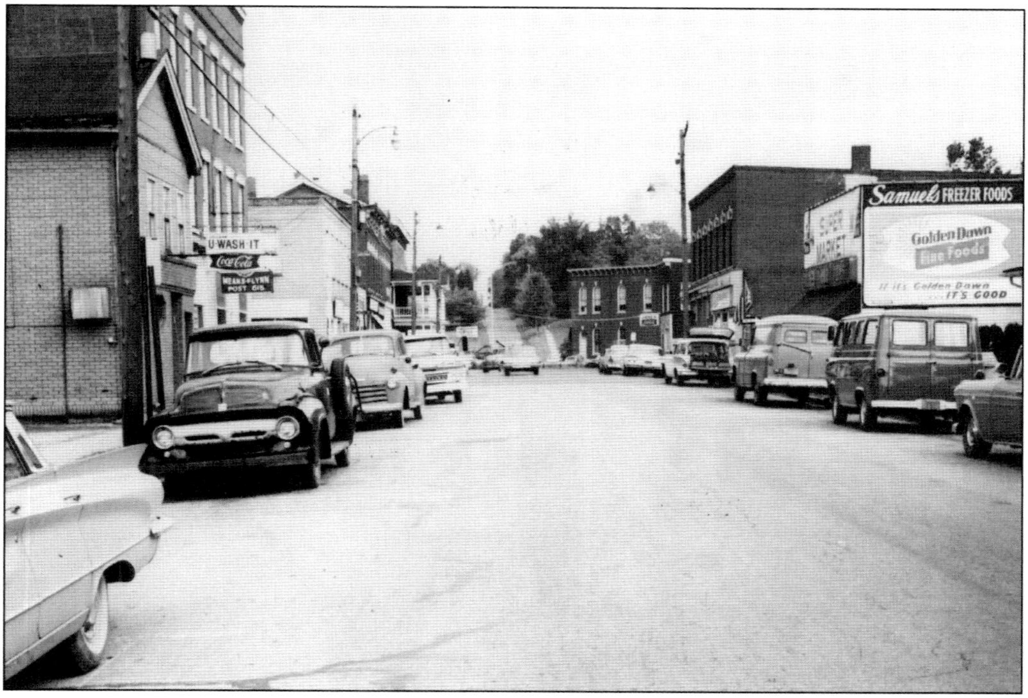

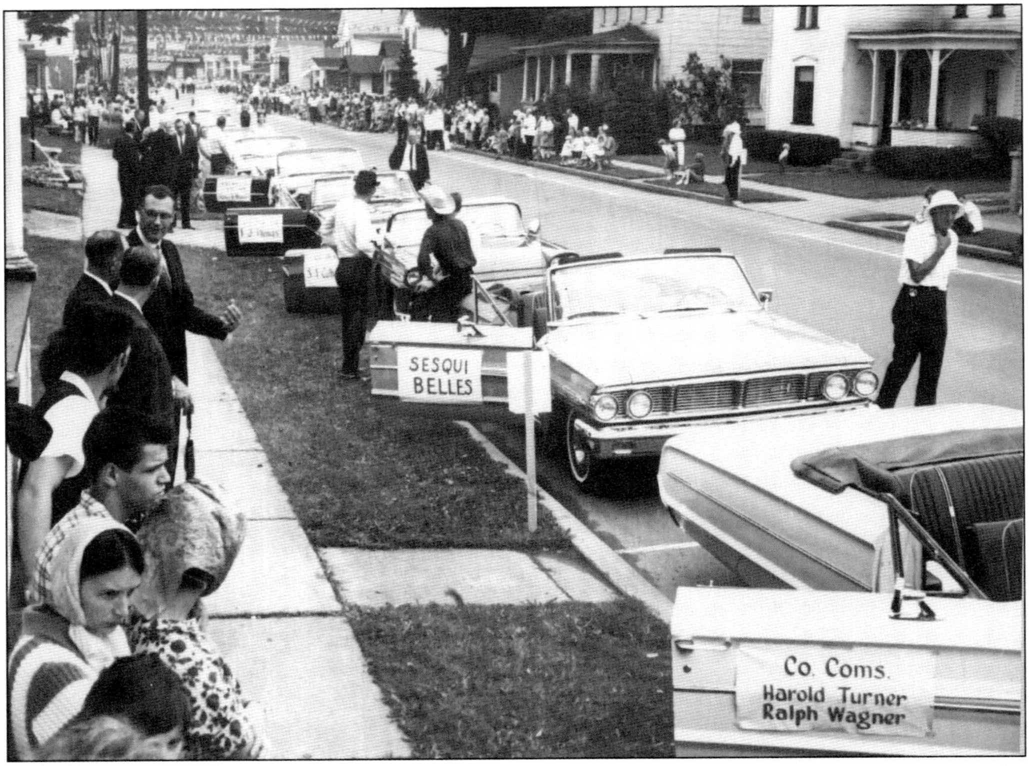

The sesquicentennial celebration of 1964 was another colorful week in the history of Conneautville. The people pictured here are waiting to fill the cars lined up for the sesquicentennial parade.

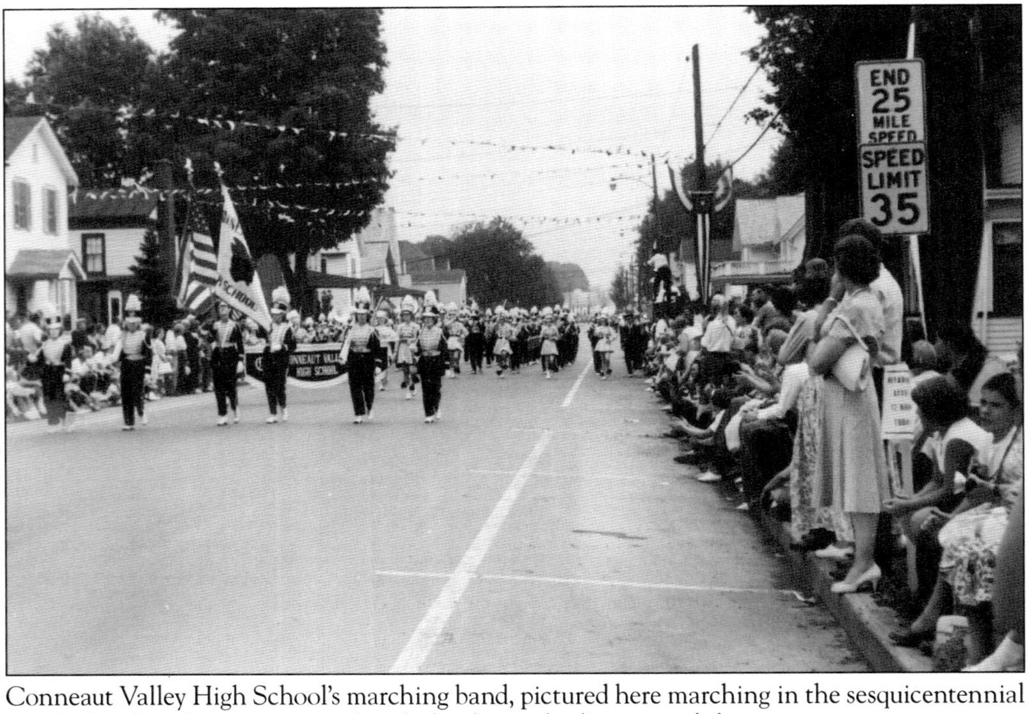

Conneaut Valley High School's marching band, pictured here marching in the sesquicentennial parade, has long been a source of pride for those who live around the area.

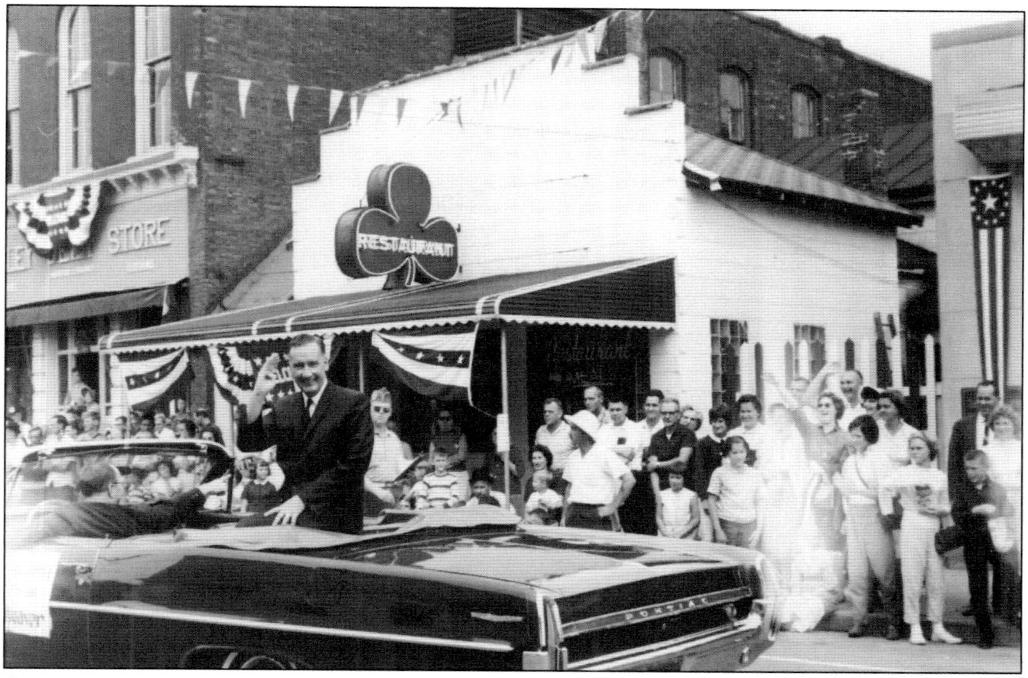

Congressman James Weaver of Pennsylvania's 24th District waves to a joyous crowd as he moves along the parade route. The Shamrock restaurant is pictured behind Congressman Weaver.

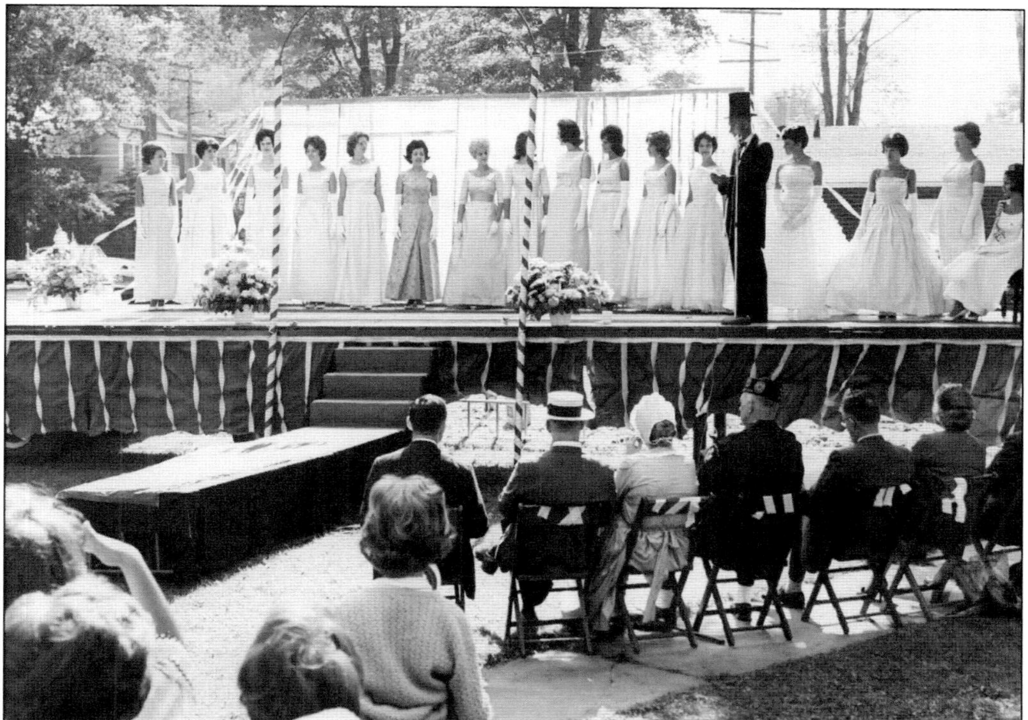

The sesquicentennial pageant was held on Monday night of the festival week and a large crowd was on hand to witness the crowning of the queen. Here, the contestants of the pageant are photographed onstage.

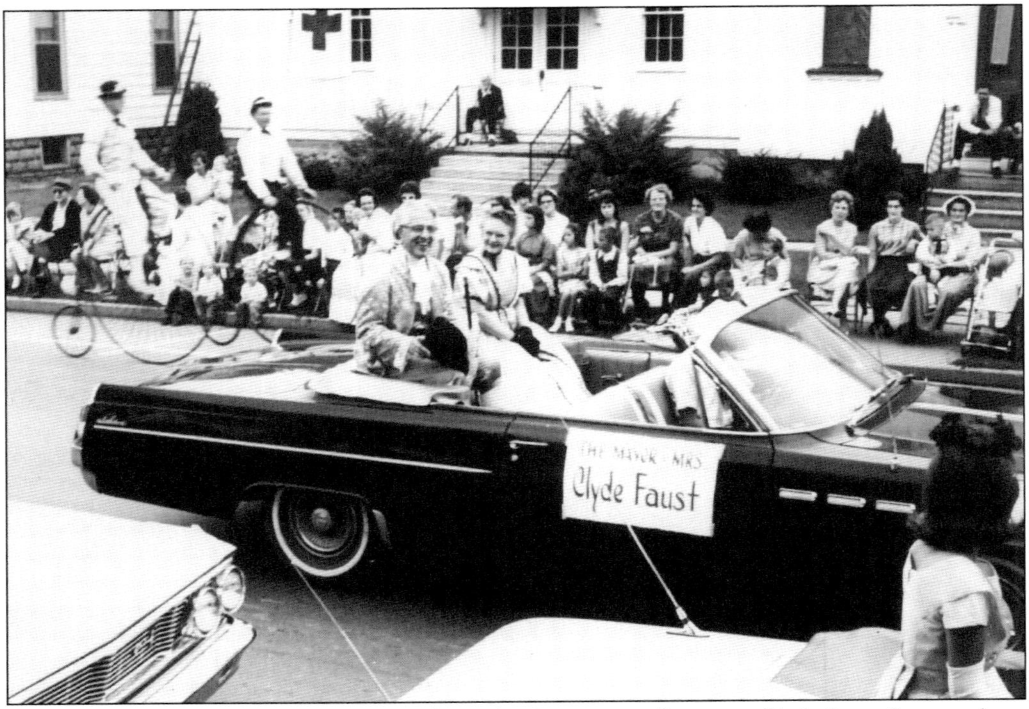

In this picture from the sesquicentennial parade, Conneautville mayor Clyde Faust Sr., seen here along with his wife, Helen, tries to bring back the spirit of the past.

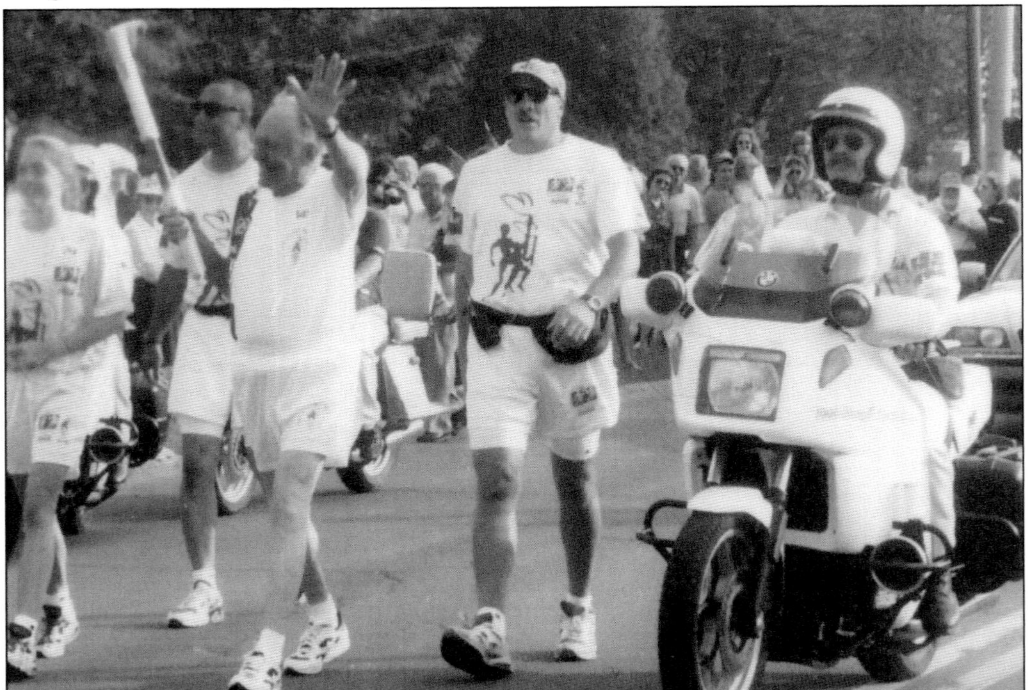

Conneautville resident Joe Mattera carried the Olympic torch as it circled the United States prior to the 1996 Summer Games in Atlanta, Georgia. Mattera is seen here waving to the crowd as he proudly walks along Route 20 near Conneaut, Ohio.

Six

SCENES AROUND THE VALLEY

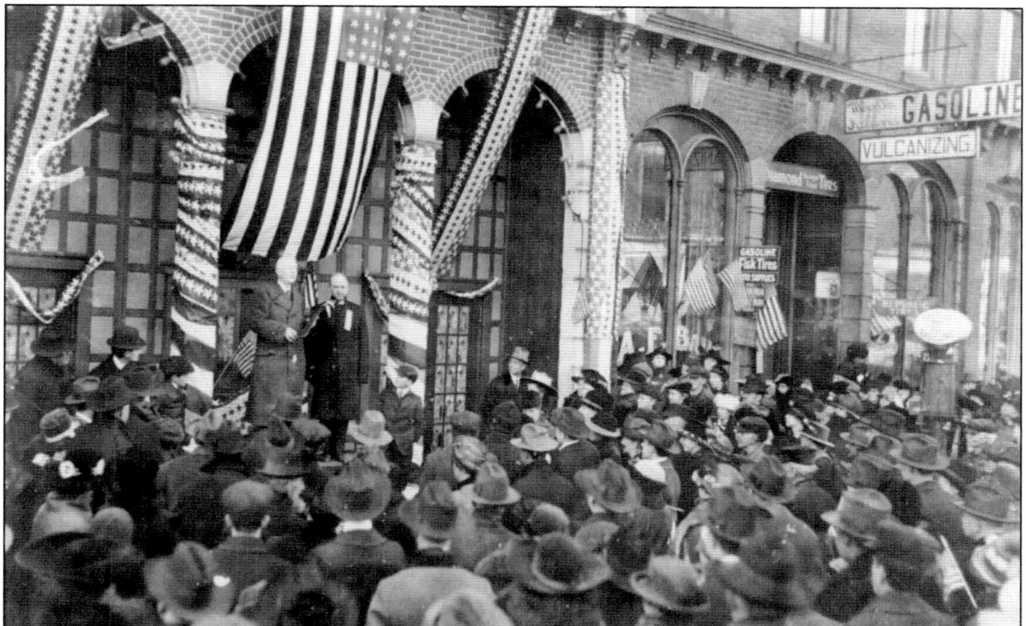

Conneautville, being the third most populous town in Crawford County by the end of the 19th century, was a crucial campaign stop for many politicians. Here, a speaker stands in front of the Enterprise Block and engages a crowd on Main Street. Although the speaker and date in this image are unknown, the strong male presence suggests that this photograph was taken sometime before the women's suffrage movement swept the country.

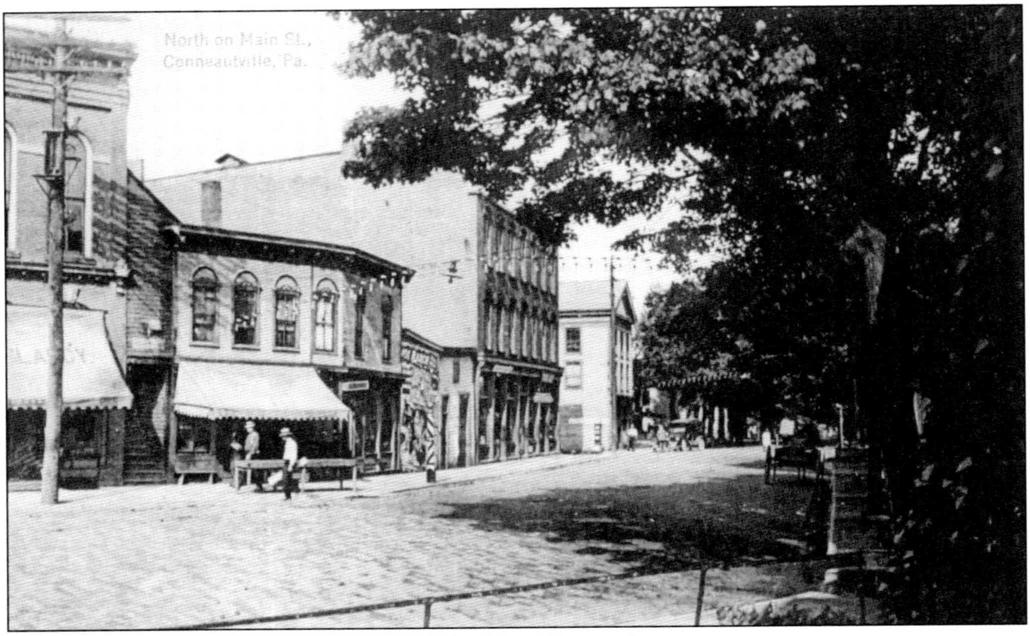

This 1910 image taken from the lawn of the Hotel Power shows a street scene.

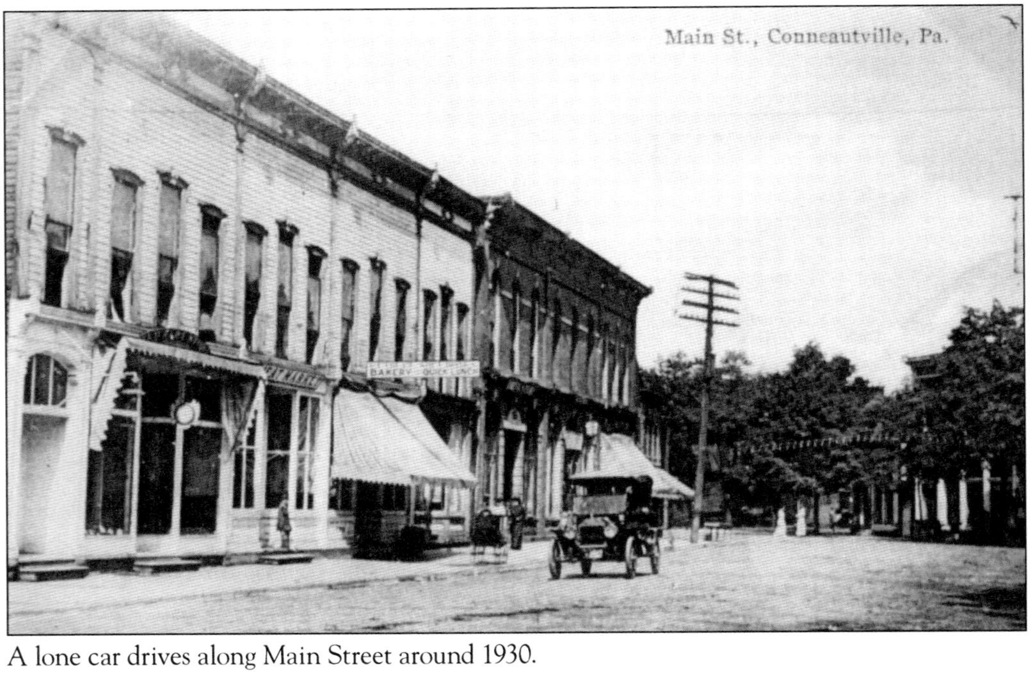

A lone car drives along Main Street around 1930.

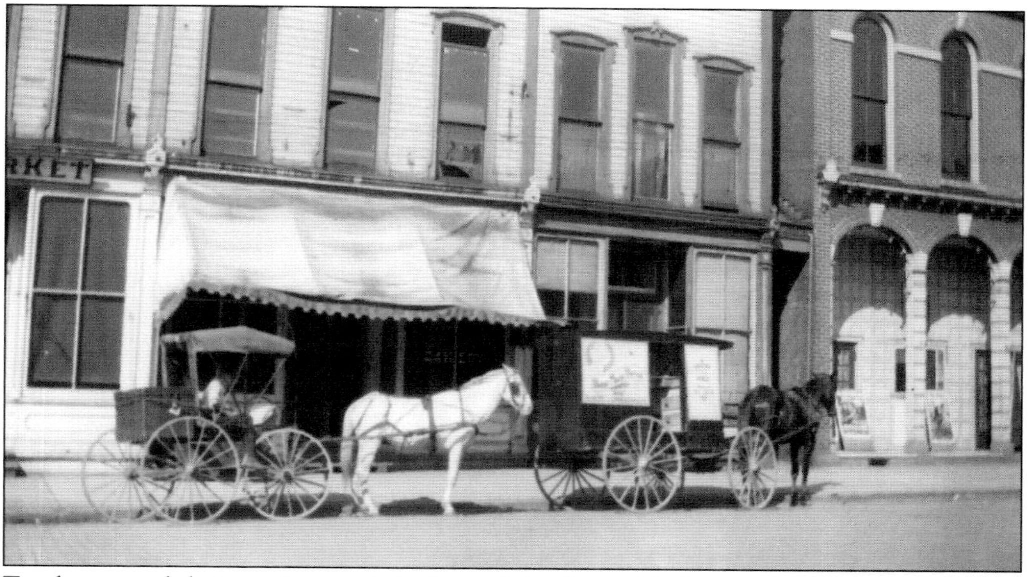

Two horses and their carriages wait in front of the Opera Block around 1920. Scenes like this would have been common while food was being loaded for delivery.

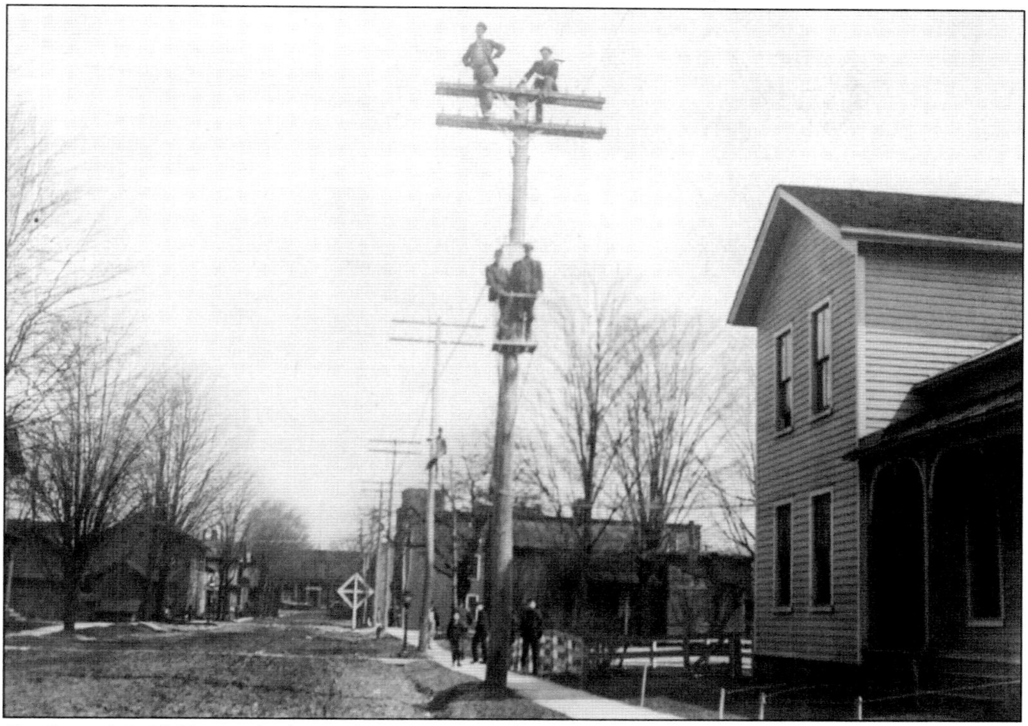

On June 16, 1882, a telephone line was completed between Meadville and Springboro (via Conneautville). In 1897, the Conneautville Telephone Company was organized and installed 60 phones at a cost of $8 for annual rental. Eva Reniff was in charge of the central office, which she ran out of her house on Water Street. By November 1897, the rapidly expanding company had installed 115 phones in the borough able to connect to Springboro and Shadeland. In July 1908, the Crawford Mutual Telephone Co. purchased the holdings of the Conneautville Telephone Co., and in 1924 they became part of the Meadville Telephone Co. system.

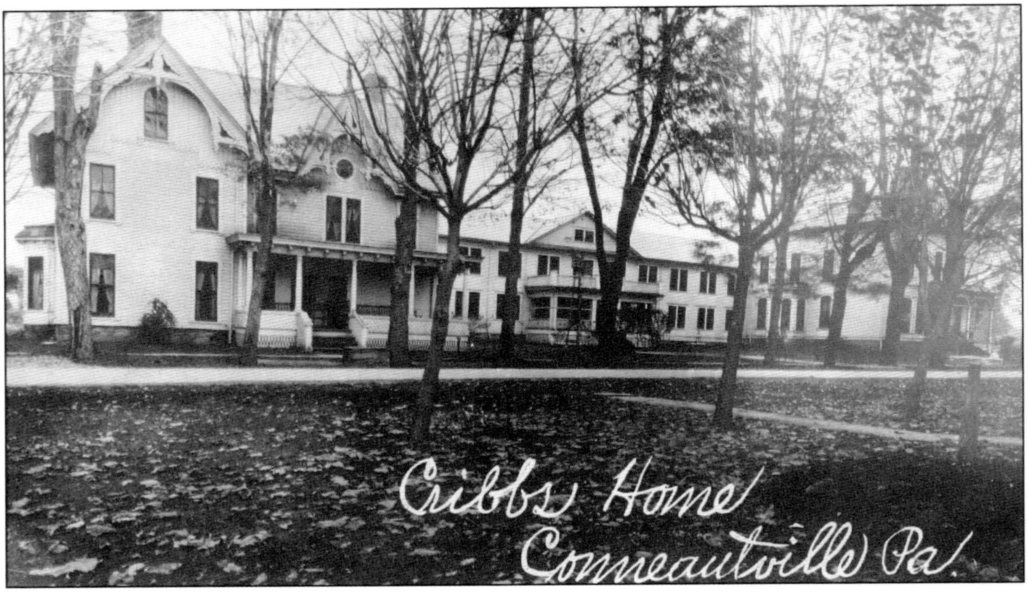

In 1918, Hyatt M. Cribbs purchased the Wormald properties, including the homes of Robert Wormald and Sarah Wormald. Cribbs presented this property to the Erie Conference of the Methodist Church on May 30, 1919, for use as a home for the aged. The home would be known as the Ida M. Cribbs Methodist Home. An addition was built to connect the two houses and the Cribbs Home opened in 1919 as a home for the elderly. In 1952, many of the residents moved to a new facility in Meadville. In 1953, Elwood Heaster purchased the property and, after much redecorating, opened another home to care for the aged.

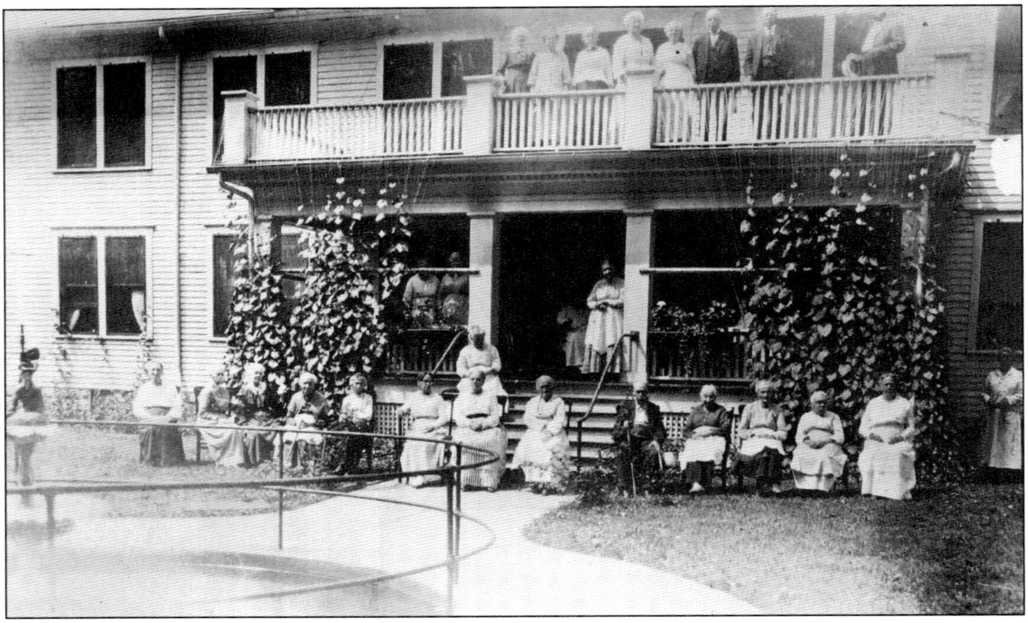

The residents of the Cribbs Home enjoy a beautiful day outside as they pose for this picture in the 1930s.

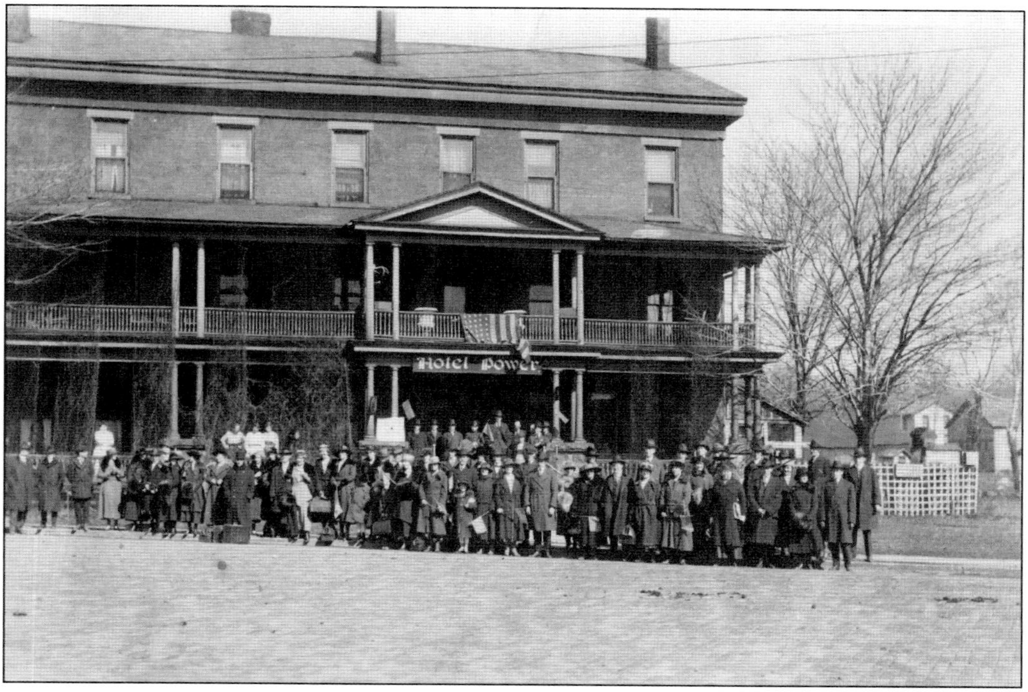

As seen in earlier chapters, the Hotel Power was one of Conneautville's most beautiful structures. Although this image has no identifying information, the crowd placement suggests that the hotel was commonly used in the background of photographs to show the beauty and prestige of the town.

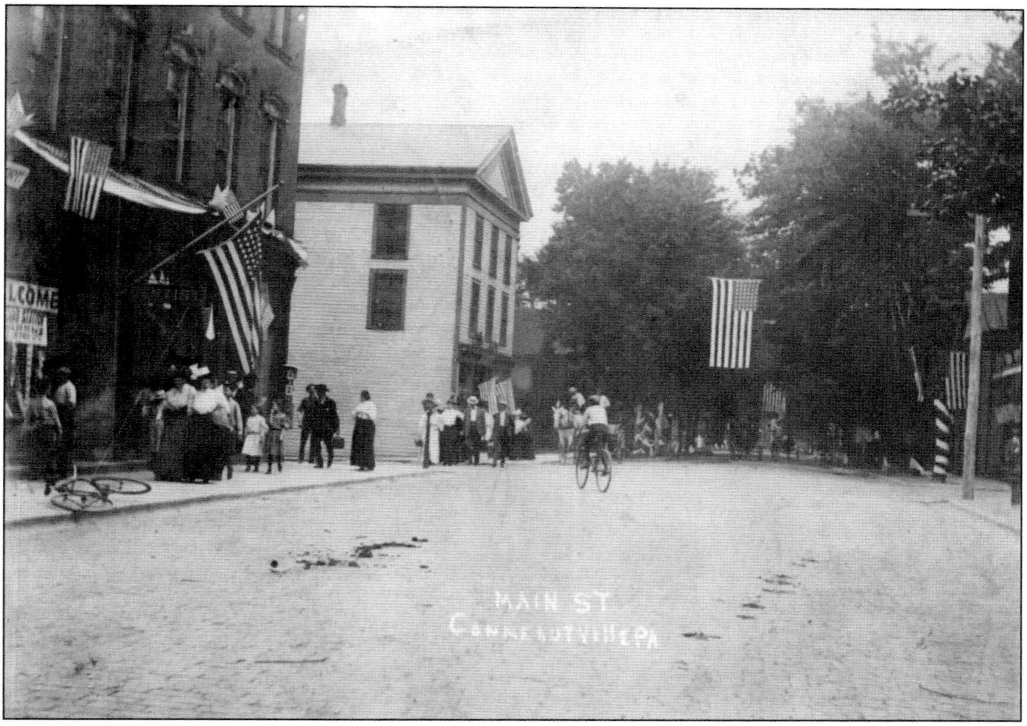

This image, dated 1906, shows a typical scene along the intersection of Main and Pearl Streets. The frame structure on the corner was home to the post office when this photograph was taken.

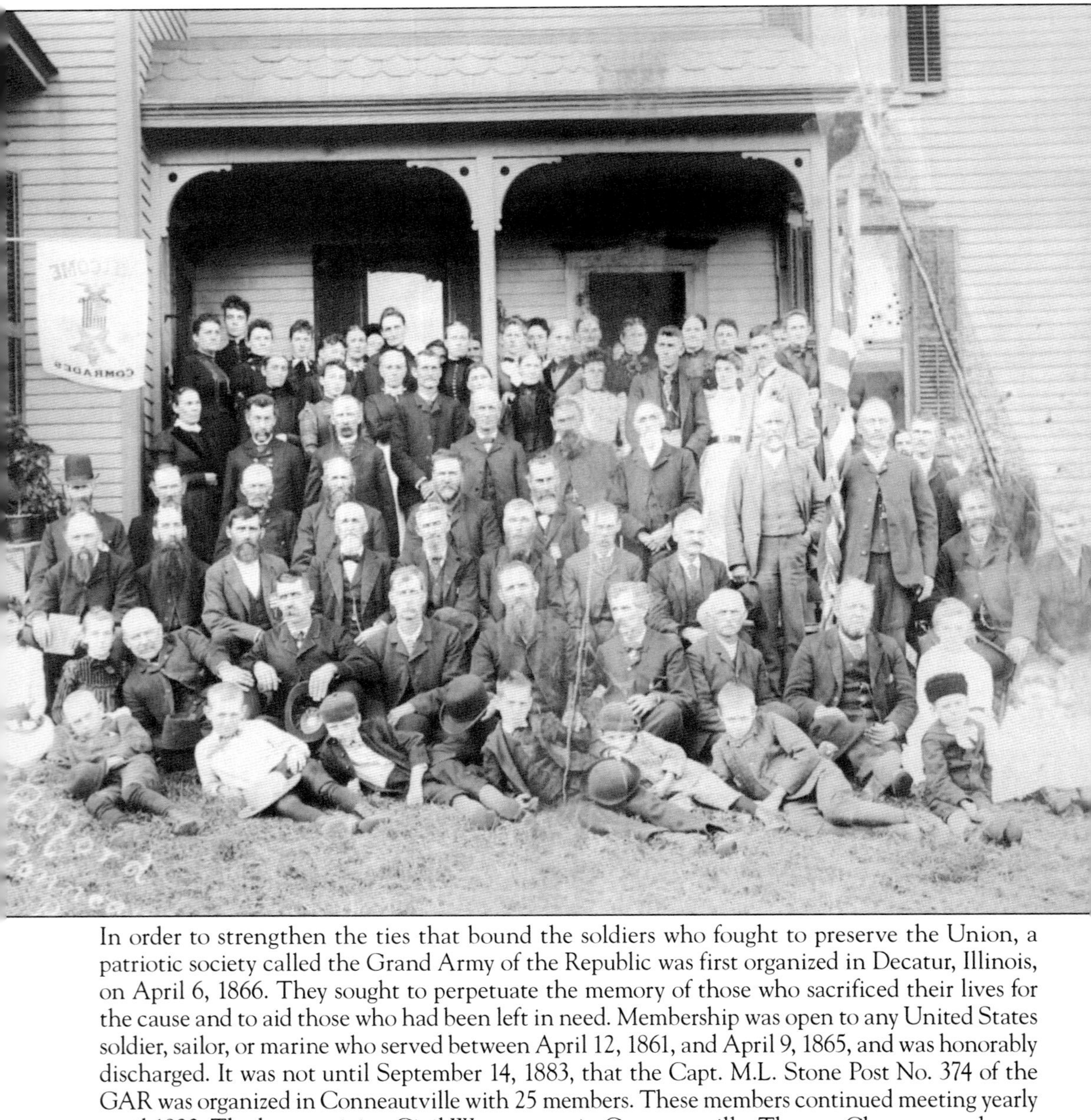

In order to strengthen the ties that bound the soldiers who fought to preserve the Union, a patriotic society called the Grand Army of the Republic was first organized in Decatur, Illinois, on April 6, 1866. They sought to perpetuate the memory of those who sacrificed their lives for the cause and to aid those who had been left in need. Membership was open to any United States soldier, sailor, or marine who served between April 12, 1861, and April 9, 1865, and was honorably discharged. It was not until September 14, 1883, that the Capt. M.L. Stone Post No. 374 of the GAR was organized in Conneautville with 25 members. These members continued meeting yearly until 1920. The last surviving Civil War veteran in Conneautville, Thomas Cleary, passed away at age 91 on December 6, 1933. The GAR of Conneautville is pictured here around 1910 during their annual reunion.

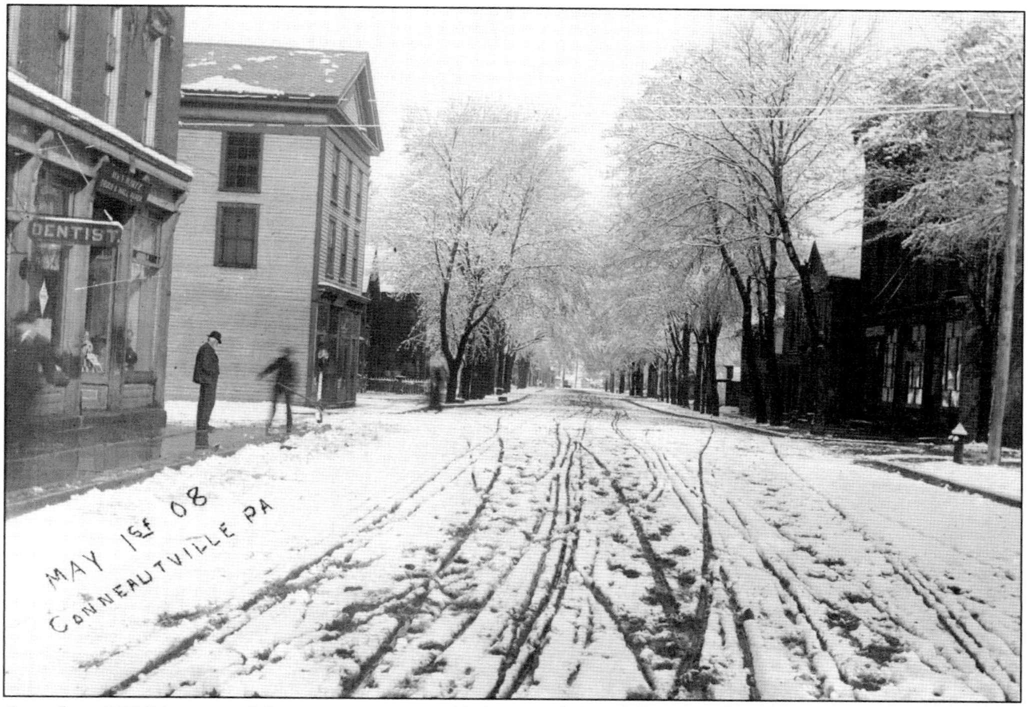

Another 1906 image of the intersection of Main and Pearl Streets shows a snow-covered road.

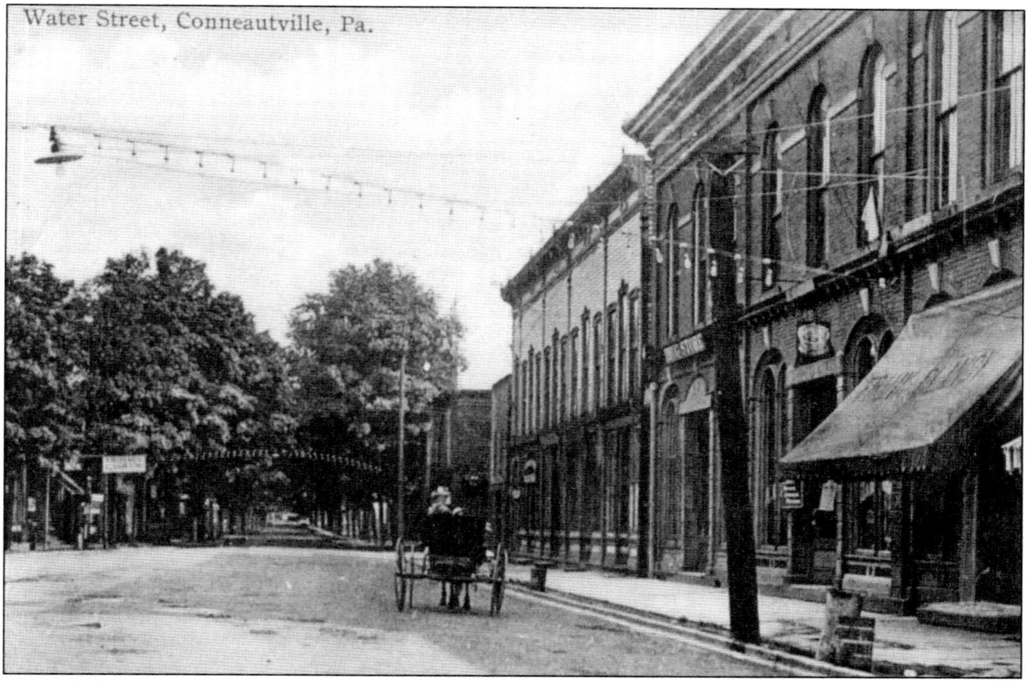

Street lighting has changed significantly in many of the images involving downtown Conneautville. In this undated photograph, the lights that spanned and illuminated the streets are clearly visible. This system was used prior to the installation of the lampposts that were erected for the centennial celebration.

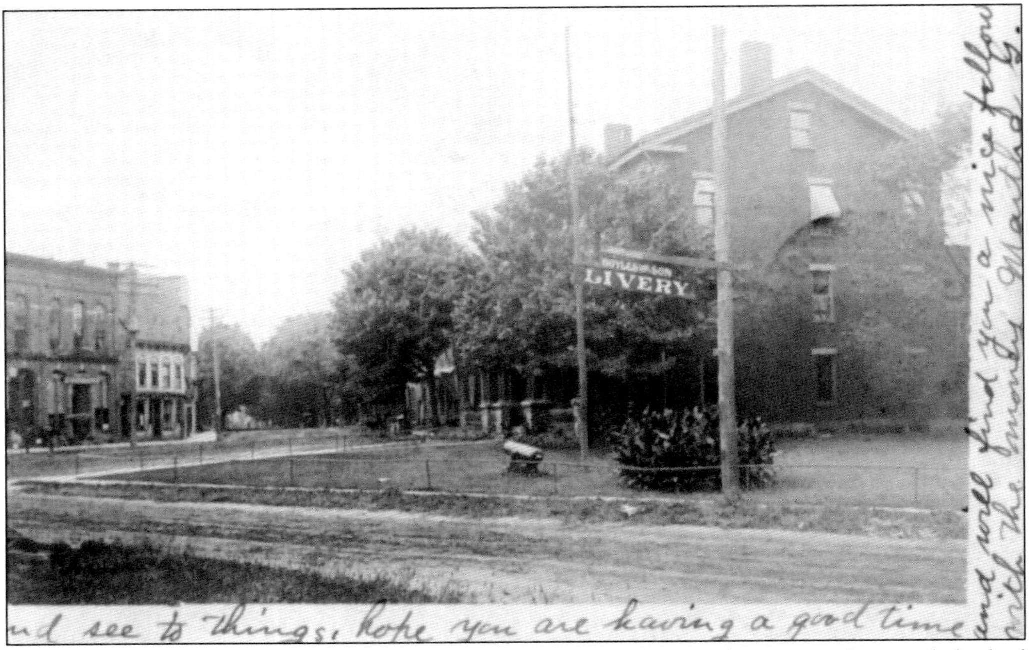

This photograph of downtown Conneautville shows how the Hotel Power and grounds looked on September 4, 1906. The Civil War cannon is also visible.

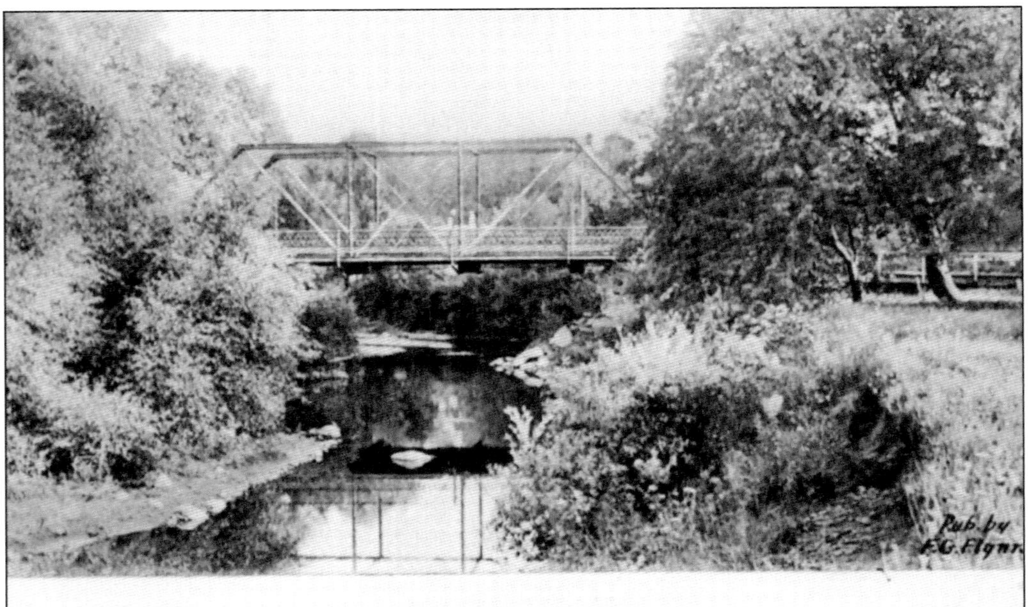

Conneaut Creek has been a significant factor in the development of Conneautville. This postcard from 1909 captures the beauty of the creek running underneath the Center Street Bridge.

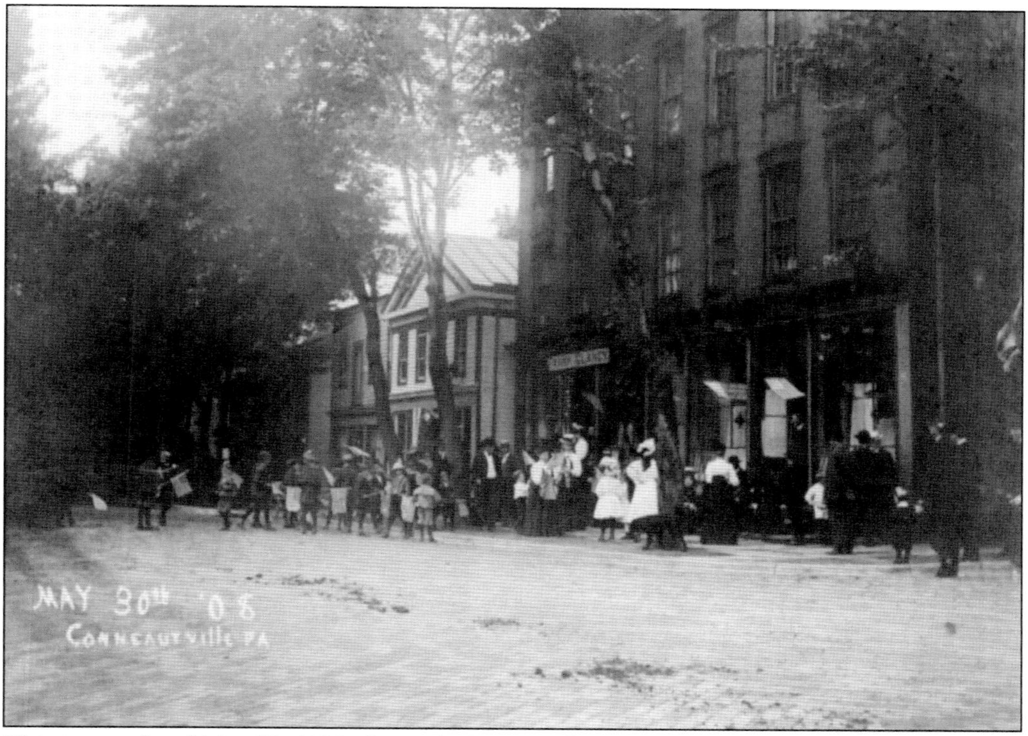

This image, dated May 30, 1908, shows the Memorial Day celebrations and patriotic displays in front of the Robinson Block.

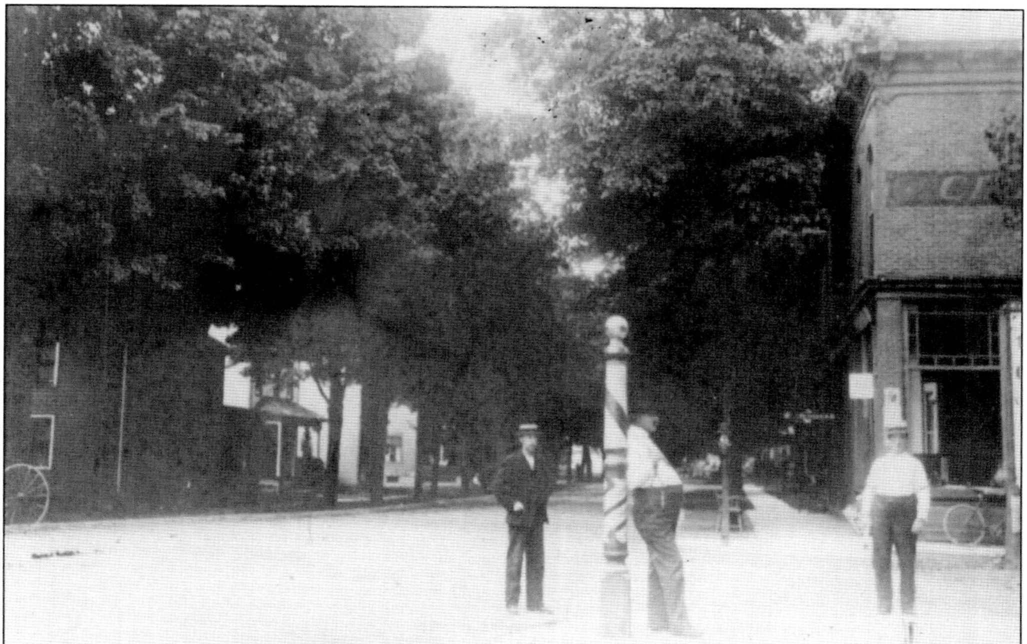

An unidentified man enjoys a rest on a barber's pole on the corner of Main and Center Streets. Dated 1909, this image also shows the brick structure that occupied the opposite corner—which at the time housed the clothing and embalming businesses of Harvey White.

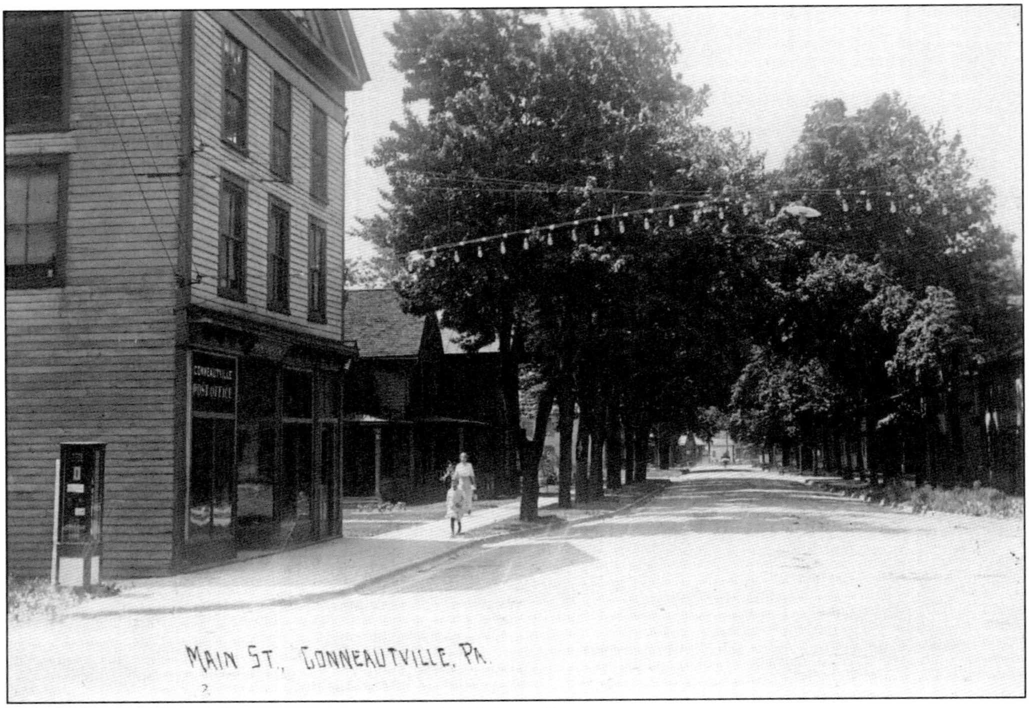

This c. 1910 image shows another beautiful Main Street scene.

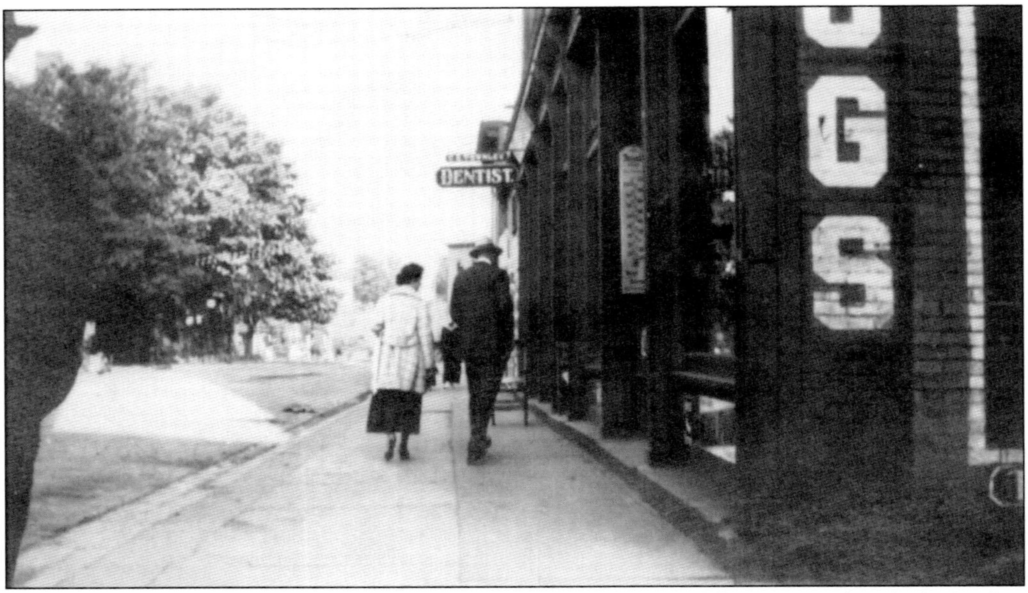

In this c. 1940 photograph, a couple is pictured walking in front of the Courtright Block. At that time, Dr. Bristol had his dentist's office on the second floor of the building.

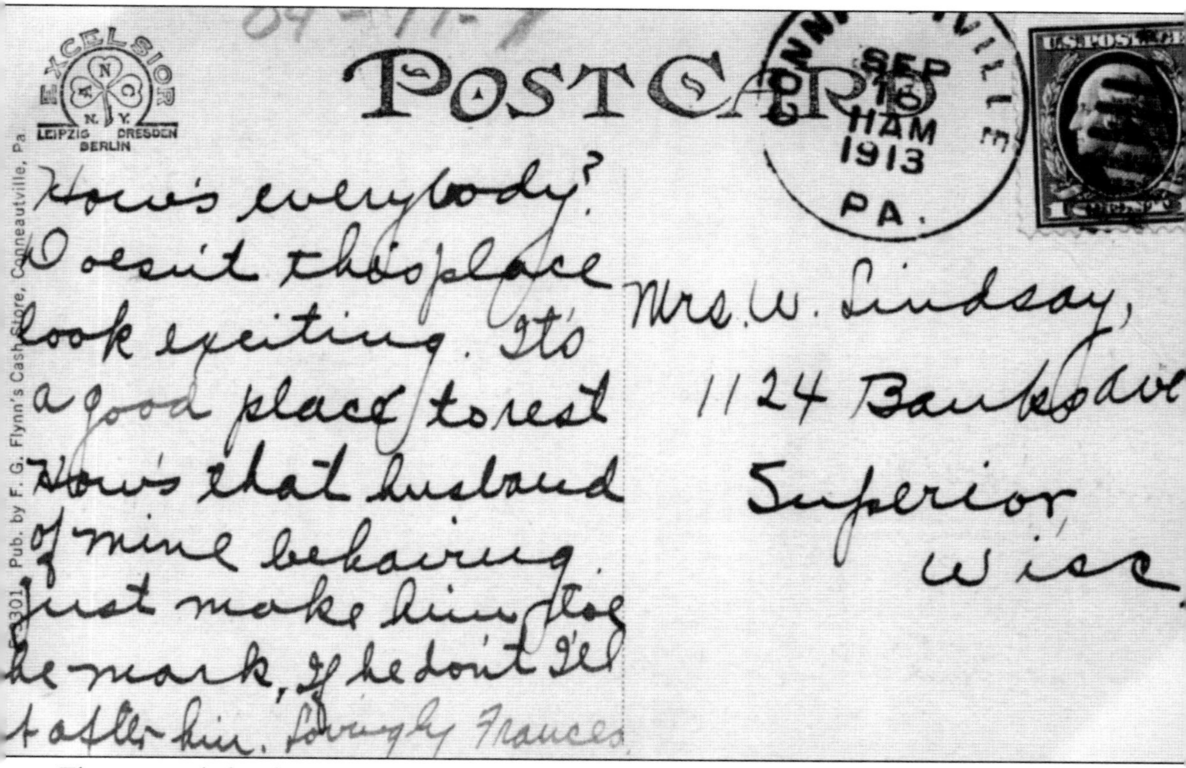

This postcard, dated 1913, offers a personal account of the life of Conneautville 100 years ago. Although time has taken many of Conneautville's most fascinating structures, the town is still organized in the same manner that Alexander Power designed in 1814.